CAR 54

Where Are You?

by Martin Grams, Jr.

Published in the USA by:
BearManor Media
P O Box 71426
Albany, Georgia 31708
www.bearmanormedia.com

ISBN 978-1-59393-723-2

Printed in the United States of America.

Book and cover design by Darlene Swanson of Van-garde Imagery, Inc.

CONTENTS

SONG LYRICS

There's a holdup in the Bronx,
Brooklyn's broken out in fights.
There's a traffic jam in Harlem that's
backed up to Jackson Heights.
There's a scout troop short a child,
Khrushchev's due at Idlewild...
CAR 54, WHERE ARE YOU?

Words: Nat Hiken
Music by: John Strauss

MEMORABLE QUOTES

"Men, I think you all better leave now.
There's nothing that can undermine the morale
of a police station, than the men seeing their Captain crying."

"You don't reason with a nut. You just do it his way."

INTRODUCTION

There are many kinds of laughter: the delight and joy of watching a child's first stumbling steps can make you laugh. A well-told joke that pokes a finger at someone's honest foibles is worth a hearty chuckle as well. There is the laughter of wordplay, of slightly smutty double meanings, and the uproarious belly-grabber as you or I relate another of the immensely stupid things we have done at one time or another.

But perhaps the oldest type of laughter is laughing at the clowns – those misshapen, clueless-beyond-all-reality dolts who simultaneously hold a mirror up to our own personal slips of foolishness and break through it into an alternate reality that defies all reason or probability ("There's no way *even* I could ever do *that!*").

Clowns have been around for thousands of years. But the rise of mass entertainment in the 19th and 20th century has stretched their art to a new level. Radio, films and TV have brought us Shakespeares of slapstick, champions of the clueless: Laurel and Hardy, the Brothers Marx, Milton Berle, the Three Stooges, each with their own special style of madcappery (and "madcap" comes from those floppy hats the original clowns used to wear.)

For two seasons on national television (and for scores or rerun seasons since), another pair of entrancing idiots captured our imagination: Toody and Muldoon, entrusted with the public safety of the largest city in the Western world, didn't do a very good job of it. And we loved them for it, as they delivered (and continue to deliver) belly laugh after belly laugh.

This book will tell the story of *Car 54, Where Are You?* (one of the best TV comedy titles ever), from its inception in the mind of producer Nat Hiken. It will document the facts and figures about those lovable, bumbling men in blue. Were you only a casual viewer? This book should fire up some hilarious memories. And if you still dress up like Gunther Toody every Halloween, you're really in for a feast.

This tome exists because of the kindness of certain individuals who took time out of their busy schedules to assist me in my labors. Their assistance varied, stretching from phone conversations, exchanges of e-mails, mailing me photocopies of newspaper clippings, recalling trivia about various episodes, reviewing whole sections of the manuscript, offering enlightening feedback, design and layout and of course, their support. In no particular order: Paul Adomites, Terry Salomonson, Ben Ohmart, Ken Stockinger, Arthur Anderson, Derek Tague, Larry Storch, Jim Widner, Roy Bright, Frank A. Absher, Jim Rosin and Darlene Swanson.

So settle back and enjoy the book. It is a tribute to a classic show, populated by classic clowns, that keeps us laughing yet today.

Martin Grams, Jr.
January 2008

Nat Hiken and the Origin of "Car 54"

N at Hiken, the comedy ace behind *Car 54, Where Are You?*, recalled, "To me the most beautiful sound is the sound of people laughing. But comedy is a terribly serious business. I never thought of doing a melodrama or adventure series."

Hiken was born with the city limits of Chicago and spent his childhood in Milwaukee. He majored in journalism at the University of Wisconsin where he was a member of the editorial board, and did a column called the "Griper's Club" for the student newspaper. After graduating in 1936 he headed west for Hollywood. After a short while he joined up with announcer Jack Lescoulie to do a morning radio show. Remembering his college column, he transformed the radio show into the daily 6-8 a.m. *Grouch Club*. The show was a success, grossing a whopping $5 a week for its author. An aspiring actor named Alan Ladd later joined them and the show grew in popularity. By 1937 the network gained control of the program, forcing Hiken to find another steady form of employment.

Two years later Hiken joined Warner Bros. Studios and it was during this time (circa 1939) that he met Fred Allen. Allen, it seems, had been a fan of the *Grouch Club* and signed Hiken as a writer for his popular radio program. Those were the golden years of radio, and his fellow writers included Roland Kibbee, Herman Wouk, and Arnold

Auerbach (author of Broadway's *Call Me Madam*). Hiken wrote and co-wrote jokes for Allen's program on and off for seven years.*

During WWII, Hiken joined the Winged Victory troupe in the Army Air Force. Hitting his full stride with the end of the war, Hiken returned to scripting radio programs. One newspaper in 1961 reported that Hiken left Fred Allen to "develop a radio show for Milton Berle, which ran for two years." While it has been proven that Hiken was writing scripts for Berle's radio program, *The Texaco Star Theater*, from September 22, 1948 through June 15, 1949, no proof has been unearthed that Hiken created the series. In addition, the show ran one season only, not two. Next, he created a radio program for Monty Woolley titled *The Magnificent Montague*, a situation comedy about a Shakespearean actor forced to make his living in radio. Hiken not only produced and directed the program, but also wrote most - if not all - of the radio scripts. The series was broadcast over NBC from Nov. 10, 1950 to Nov. 10, 1951.

Meanwhile, he started doing TV, first as producer-writer of the short-lived *The U.S. Royal Showcase*, starring Jack Carson, in 1952. While writing for *The Martha Raye Show* in 1955 and '56, Hiken created a series of comedy skits that startled show biz, using former boxing champion Rocky Graziano as the comedienne's foil.

Then Hiken conjured up a fast-talking con man/Master Sergeant named Ernie Bilko, and television history was made. Originally telecast as *You'll Never Get Rich*, the name of the series was changed to *The Phil Silvers Show* less than two months after its premiere. (When syndicated, the series was re-titled again to *Sgt. Bilko*.) The character was supposedly named after Los Angeles Angels minor-league slugging star Steve Bilko, one of Hiken's personal heroes. The weekly comedy premiered in September of 1955, and it put Nat Hiken's name in hundreds of favorable reviews in newspapers and maga-

---

* The exact dates and years when Hiken wrote for Fred Allen's show remain unknown, but the earliest year known is 1942 and the latest is 1948.

zines. In 1956, *Time* magazine voted Hiken "the funniest writer in television."

"Nat was the best," recalled Aaron Ruben, a script writer for *The Phil Silvers Show*. "When he was working for Fred Allen, there was a guy named Doc Rockwell, who would come in with off-the-wall ideas. Once, he came in with a notion that the city is getting so over-populated, you can't just keep building skyscrapers up, up, up. 'You have to start building down.' So we wrote this stuff and gave it to Nat, and he put in an incredible joke. Why didn't it occur to us? Because we didn't have Nat's mind. He said, 'Ground scrapers, you see, you're building the building into the ground, and then if some-body dies, you just throw him out the window.'"

"Nat's point of view pervaded on *Bilko*," script writer Coleman Jacoby recalled, "which was very realistic and very satirical of human nature." *

"Only in television is there this compulsion to tell the truth as a public service," Hiken wrote for a column in the *New York Herald Tri-bune* (July 20, 1960). "The public, during the quiz show scandals, have already demonstrated how they feel about this service rendered them. As one, they rose with a roar of outraged anger. Not against the quiz fixers, but against those who had to go and tell them about it."

"Almost all comedy," Hiken remarked, "can be reduced to two classic situations. In one, which we call farce comedy, normal peo-ple are shown in unusual situations. In the other, which is character comedy, abnormal people are shown in normal situations . . . In all comedy, the audience is the straight man. You can see the principle at work in its simplest form in burlesque comedy where the straight man often doesn't even look at the comic. He looks at the audience, with which he identifies himself. He'll say to the comic, while looking

---

* Quotes by Ruben and Jacoby reprinted with permission from *The Box: An Oral History of Television, 1920-1961* by Jeff Kiseloff, from Penguin Books USA, Inc.

out front, 'Do you mean to stand there and tell an intelligent audience like this that . . .?' You know the pitch."

The Phil Silvers Show lasted four years and would probably have continued if Silvers had not off-handedly told a reporter for a southern newspaper that he was tired of doing the show. Silvers' remark got national attention, even reaching the normally closed minds of sponsors, who figured that maybe viewers felt the same way Silvers did. They dumped the program.

The final broadcast aired in September of 1959. Before long, Hiken was pitching series ideas to the major networks and studios. His name and the *Bilko* success carried plenty of weight. One proposal, a comedy about two patrolmen in the New York police department, would only last two seasons, but garnered the same amount of critical acclaim that the *Bilko* series accomplished during its four seasons.

The Snow Whites

When exactly Hiken created the series has not been established, but the earliest-known time frame was during the autumn months of 1960, when Hiken visited a New York precinct house. He was amazed that policemen sounded just like any other group doing a job. "I'd never seen a policeman on TV talk or act like these guys. I began to think about the possibilities, particularly for humor," Hiken recalled. He began researching *Car 54* by sitting around the New York precinct squad room for several weeks, listening to the banter and gossip among the men. "I spent hours there watching what went on. It was a neighborhood atmosphere. Many of those persons brought in were repeaters who were greeted by their first names. I never once saw a cop grab anybody by the collar, which is what television normally shows them doing. I found it a very warm, friendly atmosphere," he said. "They never mentioned any 'grim, humorless' aspects of their jobs."

After summarizing the idea of a pair of Mutt and Jeff cops in two

paragraphs, Hiken submitted an expanded outline (8 pages) entitled "The Snow Whites" to Procter & Gamble in mid-summer 1960.
The company and its ad men liked the offbeat notion. Encouraged,
Hiken prepared an expanded outline for Pete Katz, Program Production Manager of Eupolis Productions, Inc. in late October, 1960. A
number of correspondences and meetings began taking place between Howard Epstein, President of Eupolis Productions, Inc. and
Richard Zimbert of the Leo Burnett Company, Inc., an agency representing Procter & Gamble Productions, Inc.

On Nov. 18, 1960, Pete Katz wrote to Nat Hiken: "Your plans and
story outlines for 'The Snow Whites' sound delightful and extremely
interesting." Hiken agreed to certain terms related to the production
end of the series. Most of the terms were standard, but one stipulation was that the pilot was to be finished by the end of January.

Since the premise had been documented in detail and accepted
by Eupolis, Hiken composed a story outline for the pilot, as well as a
finished script, and delivered it to Pete Katz by December 7. During
the week of December 12, Hiken presented the script and a general
show presentation to the networks, in hopes that one would accept
the proposal. Eupolis could have had anyone on their payroll do
the job, but with the Phil Silvers *Bilko* show under his belt, Hiken
took the chore, under the assumption that this credit would lend
credence to the proposed series. NBC showed the most interest, and
verbally expressed a desire to view the finished product.

On November 21, a commitment letter was drafted by Leo Bur-
nett Company, Inc., the advertising agency representing Procter &
Gamble Prod., Inc., referring to the series as "The Snow Whites."
The agreement between P&G and Eupolis clearly stated that Procter
& Gamble would finance the entire pilot, for no more than $75,000.

P&G had the option, after viewing the pilot, not to pick up the
series. If that option were chosen, P&G had the right to recoup the
financing expenditure from any subsequent licensing of the pilot -
either alone, or as part of a series. If the pilot was licensed alone,

Procter & Gamble would receive 50 percent of that license fee and 50 percent of any subsequent fees thereafter until the investment was repaid. If the pilot was licensed to others as part of a series deal, Procter & Gamble's entire investment would be returned to them, amortized on a per show basis over the first year's commitment.

After delivery of the pilot, P&G had 45 days to choose whether or not they would agree to pick up the series for a fall 1961 start, based on a commitment of 26 new episodes (one of which could be the pilot), and pocket five percent of the proceeds. The commitment between P&G and Eupolis dated November 21 also granted the sponsor the option to add new episodes to the fall lineup, up to 32 episodes maximum.

The cost factor involved for the series would be $55,000 per episode (maximum) and the price could be increased to cover Eupolis' actual out-of-pocket increased costs arising out of contract escalators and/or union increases. If the series was going to be carried in Canada, Procter & Gamble insisted that any sponsors who were considered to be "competition" to the Corporation *not* sponsor the Canadian airings.

Eupolis had creative control over the series, coupled with a duty to listen to any views P&G may have regarding the content in the scripts. (During the entire two years of production, *Car 54* never received suggestions for improvement or change to any of the scripts before they were filmed.)

Procter and Gamble did retain the right to use the title of the show, and any of the elements of the shows, names and characterizations of performers, as well as articles and items of personal property referred to in the show for use in connection with packages, premiums, contacts and advertising.

On Nov. 22, 1960, it was agreed by all parties (Howard Epstein of Eupolis and Richard Zimbert of the Leo Burnett Company) that Nat Hiken would be assigned as the head writer and supervisor for the entire production. This was made formal under contract that same day and signed by Hiken.

The announcement went public when *Variety* reported in their January 11, 1961 issue: "Nat Hiken has sold a series of comedy half-hours to Procter & Gamble for next season. Sponsor and producer are now whopping around for a network berth of the show, called *Snow Whites*. All three webs - ABC-TV, CBS-TV and NBC-TV - have been pitched by the bankroller. It's understood that for the moment, NBC-TV has the inside track on placement of *Whites*." *

Production for the pilot began Jan, 16, 1961, and lasted six days, completing January 23. Filming on the first day took place on location outside Vin-Syd Mold Shoes, Inc., located at 1191 Jerome Avenue, in the Bronx. The owner and operator of the company agreed to allow the production company to film the exterior of his premises (the street scene in which you see Toody and Muldoon calling the patrolmen over to inspect the shoes in the window display) under the condition that the name of his store remain intact and on camera, for publicity purposes. Robert Sylvester of the *New York Daily News* wrote in his Feb. 18, 1961, column of "Dream Street," that "Nat Hiken shot the first of his new TV series at a place called Vin-Syd Mold Shoes in the Bronx. Must have gotten a lot of feet of film . . ."

In mid-February, the pilot film entitled "The Snow Whites" was previewed to all three networks, four agencies, and three Divisions of Procter & Gamble. But the pilot had competition. Apparently there were other pilots commissioned by P&G and all were previewed as fairly as "The Snow Whites." According to an inter-office memo directed toward Bill McIlvain of the Leo Burnett Company, the pilot was generally favored when compared to the other pilots. "I can tell you that I don't think many would survive such an ordeal," the memo stated.

---

* The October 1962 issue of *Pageant* reported that CBS and ABC had their chances to land the show, but claimed they couldn't find the right time slot.

Where is "Car 54"?

The National Broadcasting Company agreed to broadcast the series, and air the series following the popular *Disneyland* program, but a major suggestion was made, which proved to be a valid point: not to use the "Snow Whites" title. "Nobody who saw the film knew what it meant," the same memo explained. "While we know we can explain it, we don't think that kind of title is much of an asset in this competitive scene. Following *Disneyland*, we face the ridiculous possibility of attracting people to a wonderful cartoon which they might be disappointed not to see. We plan important publicity for the show before, during and after its debut in the fall. It will be a burden to have to explain the title in publicity."

Just a month before, Howard Epstein approached the law offices of Johnson & Tannenbaum, located at 1619 Broadway, New York, N.Y., to inquire whether or not it would be practical to keep the "Snow Whites" title or create a new one. "We wish to advise you that this title, SNOW WHITE or SNOW WHITE AND THE SEVEN DWARFS, is in the public mind," explained Samuel W. Tannenbaum, "associated with the fairy tale by the Grimm Brothers, Jacob, who died in 1863, and Wilhelm Carl who died in 1859. The tales of the Grimm Brothers are in the public domain throughout the world. The title is practically wholly associated with the Grimm Brothers fairy tale, adaptations, dramatizations and picturizations thereof."

This five-page letter addressed to Epstein, dated January 24, 1961, broke down every known book, periodical, dramatic presentation, motion picture, radio and television presentation and notice in both newspapers and trade papers in the United States and abroad. While most of the 32 entries and numerous trade paper excerpts were related to dramatic stage adaptations and copyrighted motion pictures, one entry revealed a "possible" conflict with Walt Disney and Eupolis Productions.

Almost a year before, in March of 1960, Chanford Productions had found itself to be the meat in the sandwich when it announced plans for an upcoming Frank Tashlin comedy, *Snow White and the Three Stooges*, registered with the MPAA. Chanford received protests from both ends - Columbia Pictures filed protest on the strength of their "Three Stooges" properties, and Walt Disney had come up with an MPAA protest, with their *Snow White and the Seven Dwarfs*.

On June 29, 1960, 20th Century Fox and Chanford won the title arbitration involving the Stooges movie, still planned as an exploitation feature to be made by Frank Tashlin, under the argument that the 'Three Stooges' portion of the title prevented any confusion with the Disney film. Walt Disney, however, still regarded the title as conflicting with its *Snow White and the Seven Dwarfs* release.

The matter gained momentum when, on November 15, Chanford Productions began preparing *Snow White and the Three Stooges*, in association with 20th Century Fox, and laid groundwork for a sequel to the fairytale. Vice President of Chandford, Charles Wick, registered ten "Snow White" titles with the MPAA. "*Snow White and the Three Stooges* is being blueprinted as a classic fairytale," Wick explained to the press, "noting further that the Stooges will play 'lovable oafs' who act as they would have in the period depicted."

The Nov. 23, 1960 issue of *Variety* reported in their usual slang: "While Chanford Productions veepee Charles Wick anticipated no title conflict problem caused by his registration of ten *Snow White* titles for a projected sequel to his *Snow White and the Three Stooges*, the problem has arisen. Walt Disney strenuously objects to the registrations and has filed protest with MPAA's Title Registration Bureau."

According to the March 1, 1961 issue of *Variety*, the time slot for the comedy series was discussed in great detail between Procter & Gamble and NBC. The network apparently provoked intra-product fussing and feuding. Procter & Gamble made an all-out pitch for a Wednesday evening time slot in which to install the new Nat Hiken comedy series. But when Lever Bros., which had been sponsoring *The Price is Right* in that period, tentatively agreed to move to Monday to accommodate, along with it went the proviso that no rival product - meaning P&G - would get the same time slot even if it were a different day of the week. Since the NBC-Lever Brothers deal was $25,000,000 in NBC billings, the Nat Hiken series was given a Sunday evening time slot that kept P&G content.

The same issue of *Variety* reported that (including the cost of productions of "The Snow Whites"), the total bill of sale to NBC for sponsorship would be $4,275,000. This was economical considering the cost factor for other series - Disney sponsors would be paying about $12,000,000 per annum, and Chevy was paying $21,000,000 for *Bonanza*. *

The March 26, 1961 issue of *The New York Times* featured a column by Val Adams, reporting: "The National Broadcasting Company plans a daring step next fall. It will televise a police show without crime. This is even more daring than a newspaper drama in which no one yells, 'Stop the press!' . . . The title for Mr. Hiken's show has not yet been decided. Initially, he had planned to call it 'Snow Whites' (because of the white tops of New York police radio cars), but this has been abandoned. One reason is that Walt Disney will have a Sunday night show on NBC next season and the public might confuse 'The Snow Whites' with Mr. Disney. The dropping of the title of 'The Snow Whites' may have been quite a blow for Mr. Hiken's sponsor - the Procter & Gamble Company, soap manufacturer."

While the question of what to call the series continued, Nat Hiken spent the months of February through June preparing for filming - the first episode set to go before the cameras in July. While the cast for the series was put into place for the pilot, weeks would pass before the actors could commit to a weekly filming schedule. Fred Gwynne, for example, was currently appearing on Broadway in

---

* This budgetary figure is equally impressive when you consider that in 1955, CBS invested a cool $1,000,000 in Nat Hiken's judgment for *The Phil Silvers Show*, and that budget was for the first 16 episodes produced!

Irma la Douce. But by March 26, a New York newspaper was already reporting Joe E. Ross and Fred Gwynne were signed to play the leads (they had signed back in January), and Nathaniel Frey was the only name mentioned in the same article, for playing a supporting role.

Harold Reidman, a retired New York detective who maintained direct contact with old buddies still on the force, was hired as a technical advisor for *Car 54*. "The hardest part of a policeman's job," he explains, "is to overcome the onus of meeting the public only in unpleasant situations, like giving out tickets. As they see it, Toody and Muldoon help to overcome this impression with kindness and understanding, and they feel that, by being depicted on the screen as likable human beings, Toody and Muldoon are putting over the message that other cops are 'nice guys' too."

Years before his involvement with *Car 54*, in 1942, Reidman was involved in a controversial incident involving Wallace Armstrong, a 30-year-old mentally unstable man who was armed with a knife. Conflicting reports about the details prevent the true facts of the case to be revealed, but the result was that Reidman shot and killed Armstrong in what Reidman claimed was self-defense, when Armstrong attacked a police officer with a knife. When news of his death circulated, an angry crowd surrounded the Harlem Hospital, and pushed into the lobby shouting abuse at Reidman. Fearing a possible riot, the NYPD dispatched 46 officers and mounted units to disperse the volatile gathering.

THE CAST

Fred Gwynne

Fred Gwynne's acting journey wound through Groton, Harvard, classic drama and Broadway. The son of a stockbroker, Gwynne was born in New York City on July 10, 1926. He studied portrait-painting before enlisting in the Navy in World War II, during which he served as a radio operator in a submarine-chasing vessel. After the war, he attended the New York Phoenix School of Design, then went to Harvard. There, he drew cartoons for *The Lampoon* and became its president. He also acted in the Hasty Pudding Club. Upon graduation, he joined the Brattle Theater Repertory Company in Cambridge, Mass.

He made his Broadway debut as a gangster named "the Stinker" in *Mrs. McThing*, with Helen Hayes in 1952. After successful roles in *The Frogs of Spring* and *Love's Labour's Lost* on Broadway, he began working as a copywriter for the J. Walter Thompson advertising agency where he stayed on for five years. A talented artist, he illustrated several books including *The Battle of the Frogs and the Mice: An Homeric Tale* by George Martin. It was published in February of 1962 by Dodd, Mead & Co.

Gwynne was writing copy for Ford Motors while he was under employment with the advertising agency, where he devised the slogan, "the world's most beautifully proportioned car." "I was sort of a Walter Mitty over there," he said modestly. While he was working for the ad agency, he was still making appearances on stage and at the same time was appearing on television programs in small, supporting roles. He got the co-starring role on *Car 54* through a number of determinations. He had written an idea for a television show. Since he had played the role of Private Honergan in two episodes of the Phil Silvers' *Bilko* programs ("The Eating Contest" initial telecast Nov. 15, 1955, and "It's for the Birds" from Sept. 25, 1956), he took his idea to Nat Hiken, the producer.

"This is Fred Gwynne," he began.

"*Who?*" asked Hiken.

Finally, the producer remembered having met Gwynne, but he was too busy to see the actor face to face. For seven weeks, Gwynne kept calling and finally Hiken said to meet him in Lindy's bar for lunch. Gwynne showed Hiken the idea. Hiken thought it was good for a Sid Caesar sketch, but, in passing, mentioned he was working on another show.

Three weeks later, Hiken called Gwynne and asked him to come in and test for the role of Officer Muldoon. "I'm sure that if I hadn't met him that day for lunch," recalled Gwynne, "he would never have thought of me for the part."

Fred Gwynne agreed to play the co-starring role of Patrolman Francis Muldoon for $650 per episode, per five-day workweek. He signed a contract on Jan. 3, 1961. The contract provided the stipulation that if the series would be renewed for a second season, he would be paid $800 per week under the same terms.*

While he was portraying a cop for the first season's worth of filming, he was playing the part of a French gangster in *Irma la Douce* by night.

---

* All salary contracts signed with the stars commenced on June 25, 1962.

"The day we started work on *Car 54, Where Are You?*, Fred Gwynne and I were shown to our dressing room," recalled Joe E. Ross. "It was a huge gray room with nothing but a table, a mirror, a daybed and a sofa. Fred volunteered to take the daybed as his headquarters, since he hates pillows. I was glad to get the sofa. I love pillows!"

Fred Gwynne was a sensitive, solemn, reflective kind of guy who became sick watching himself on television. During the two seasons *Car 54* was produced, he commuted to and from his home in Westchester. He claimed his wife, Jean, would grade his performances. "I keep telling him that it's a good thing he doesn't ask his youngsters, Keiron and Gaynor, to do it," explained Joe E. Ross. "Just the other day, Fred was grinning ear to ear, something unusual for such a sourpuss. He went up to Nat Hiken and said: 'My wife fell off the couch watching last night's show.'

Hiken looked at him coldly and without cracking a smile, said: 'You mean she doesn't do it for *all* of our shows?'"

Every Friday, after filming was completed for the week's efforts, he dashed out straight to the suburbs to mow the lawn or spend time with his children.

"Joe E. has gotten it into his head that I'm really a stand-up comic," Fred Gwynne complained. "He is determined to lure me onto a night club floor. Every time I start telling him about which Shakespearean roles I think he could do best, he begins telling me how I'll love playing Vegas. I admit it sounds tempting. It's the one form of acting that I've never tried."

For the observant fans, Gwynne can be seen in a bit part in *On the Waterfront* (1954), his film debut. Three years before the premiere of *Car 54*, Gwynne's first book, *Best in Show*, was published. From Shakespearean productions and Broadway musicals, challenging dramas and lowbrow television comedy, Gwynne was an experienced actor who fit the 6 foot, 5 inch part of Francis Muldoon.

Joe E. Ross

The comic actor known for his trademark "Ooh, ooh," sound was born Joseph Rozawikz in New York City on March 15, 1914. Joe E. Ross (his professional name) reportedly weighed 149 pounds and stood 5 feet, 11 inches tall when he starred on *Car 54, Where Are You?* His parents were deceased before he began his television career, but his wife, Loretta, enjoyed watching *Car 54* and offering her opinion of his screen work.

Before working on television, Joe E. Ross had served in the U.S. Navy, and had received a medal for his service in the Pacific. After the war, Ross began a 20-year career in burlesque and as a nightclub comic. Before that, during Prohibition days he worked as a singing waiter in a Manhattan speakeasy frequented by some of the town's less reputable citizens. "I used to sing heartbreaking songs to the hoodlums," he recalled. "They'd cry in their beer. With a voice like mine, I guess I was lucky they didn't shoot me."

Ross loved doing stand-up comedy before a live audience, and went back to it every chance he could. After putting in a tough five-day week on *Car 54*, he would spend his Friday and Saturday evenings at a nightclub job, just to keep his hand in. He appeared in the 1955 burlesque film, *Teaserama*, with co-stars Bettie Page and Tempest Storm.

Ross received his chance to do television courtesy of Nat Hiken, who spotted him in a Miami night spot, and knew right away he had the perfect man to play Ritzik in *Bilko*.

Early on during filming of *The Phil Silvers Show*, Joe E. Ross fought to keep his burlesque training from projecting. "My lines come out and I shout them to the audience," recalled Joe E. Ross to columnist Erskine Johnson. "I'm still thinking I'm working in night clubs and burlesque. Phil blows. I'm driving him crazy, see, and he says to me: 'Joe, you gotta learn how to listen. You gotta learn how to react. You stand there and shout your lines to the audience. You're punching. And then you stand there and you don't even move a muscle when I tell you my grandmother is dying.' My answer to Phil was 'I don't move a muscle because I've read the script. I know your grandmother is dying, but I'm not an actor.'"

Silvers suggested that Ross go to the movies and start studying how actors act and react. That was when Ross caught a showing of MGM's *Gaslight* (1944) with Ingrid Bergman and Charles Boyer. "Man, she could listen good. Also react good," recalled Ross. "So I went from one Ingrid Bergman movie to another and I watched her. All of a sudden I caught on and I'm listening to Phil and I'm reacting and he says to me, 'Congratulations, Joe. You're acting now. Who taught you?' I told him Ingrid Bergman - and he thinks I'm a little nutty." Television (and Ingrid Bergman) could say they rehabilitated Gunther Toody and Joe E. Ross.

Gunther Toody's trademark "ooh, ooh" sound originated from the character of Ritzik. Ross did it quite unconsciously, on the *Bilko* show. It was not in the script. He had just been told that Bing Crosby was coming to the Army camp where the scene was laid. "Ooh, ooh - Bing Crosby! He's great and I can't wait to see him," Ross blurted. He later apologized to Nat Hiken, the producer. But Nat was intrigued. He told the actor to "ooh, ooh" whenever he had the urge. For *Car 54*, Joe E. Ross did it all the time for the show, and it was even written into the scripts. But the trademark was a "natural" for Ross, who admitted in an interview that he said it when he was away from the studio, too. "I find myself doing Toody on the street. I think like Toody. Make a face like Toody. One of these days I'll find myself putting tickets on windshields," he joked.

"Fred and I had not only never worked together before *Car 54*," Ross admitted, "we never even met until the day we started shooting the pilot. Fred had done a few *Bilkos*, too, but we had never been in the same episodes." *

---

* The surreal comic strip *Zippy the Pinhead* once had a panel by artist Bill Griffith, referring to the *Car 54* series and the Joe E. Ross "ooh, ooh" trademark. There was a sign reading, "Joe E. Ross Fan Club" and the members in attendance were chanting, "Ooh, ooh!"

Joe E. Ross agreed to play the co-starring role of Patrolman Gun-ther Toody for $1,500 per episode, per five-day workweek. He signed a contract on Jan. 6, 1961, three days after Fred Gwynne signed on. The contract provided the stipulation that if the series would be re-newed for a second season, he would continue to be paid $1,500 per week under the same terms.*

Joe E. Ross was a bachelor during the two years he was in *Car 54*. He lived in an apartment in midtown Manhattan. "To me, the week-end means I can stay up late with the other comics who hang around Lindy's or catch the new acts in clubs around town," Ross explained.

"We seldom see each other after the show," Gwynne explained. "I live in Westchester, and he has an apartment in mid-Manhattan. He's always complaining about having to get up at 6 a.m. for work. When he worked in nightclubs, he slept until three in the afternoon. I know that on the Saturdays Joe has off, he'll travel to an upstate resort to do a night club act. He claims it keeps him from getting stale. He really misses the reaction of a live audience while doing the TV series. Joe has had several offers to do serious dramatic roles, but has turned them down. 'It's a waste of time. I never played straight before,' he keeps telling me."

Paul Reed

Paul Reed was born to Russian immigrant parents in Highland Falls, New York on June 16, 1909. Born Sidney Kahn, he changed his name first to Paul Roberts and later to Paul Reed. His early days as a New Yorker in search of ways to survive brought him to vaudeville theaters where, during intermission, he dealt in chewing gum bought by the pack and sold by the stick. Soon finding the performers to be a bet-

---

* For fans of the program wondering what a supporting player received for their minimal efforts (actors who did not have a repeated role on the series), they were paid between $90 and $180 for their appearance, depending on whether they were needed for one or two days of filming.

ter clientele than the audience, Reed established his place of business at the stage door. On one occasion, a performer grabbed and hauled him out onto the stage where, in the glow of the limelight, Paul had his first encounter with the allure of show business.

Paul Reed was a veteran hand at television comedy, having appeared in practically every show Sid Caesar did after leaving *Your Show of Shows* in 1954. Reed played all sorts of parts - Sid's father, brother, and lawyer; his friend and foe. And in the Caesar spoofs of Japanese movies, Reed was both narrator and actor. Reed played the role of Sidney Kruger in one episode of *The Phil Silvers Show*, "Bilko's Vampire," initially telecast on Oct. 1, 1958.

Reed started on the stage 25 years before *Car 54*, and on radio years before that as a radio singer. "[*Car 54*] reminds me of the old Mack Sennett Keystone Cop stuff, only in modern dress," Reed told a reporter. "Although it might sound like the show holds policemen up to ridicule, it doesn't come out that way." Reed played the role of a police officer previously in the mid-to-late forties when he accepted the role of Lt. Brannigan on the stage production of *Guys and Dolls*. He played the role of a corrupt policeman in the movie, *The Phoenix City Story* (1955) and as a plainclothes man in *Sweet Smell of Success* (1957).

Paul Reed was filmed for the pilot, and then waited a few months to learn if the series was to be picked up and filmed, or dropped. In the meantime, he was offered a role in *How to Succeed in Business Without Really Trying* on Broadway. "One thing in this business," he explained, "you never turn anything down. Take the first thing that comes along." According to the contract at the time he was filmed for the pilot, he initially agreed to play the role of Captain Block for $700 per episode, per five-day workweek. The talent contract provided the stipulation that if the series would be renewed for a second season, he would be paid $900 per week under the same terms. This offer, however, had a stipulation: Since Reed was presently seen on stage in *How to Succeed in Business Without Really Trying*, and was already receiving a paycheck, a counter-offer was made. He would receive $700 for each episode in which he performed, but if he continued in *How to Succeed* on stage, he would receive $500 for each episode and if they required his services for four or more days, $650 for each episode. Reed chose the latter of the options, performing in front of the camera during the day, and in front of an audience by night. He signed a contract on Feb. 23, 1962.

During filming of the first season's episodes, Reed had to work out an arrangement with the producer. "They agreed to shoot around me," he explained. His scenes were shot so that he had Wednesdays off so he could do two performances on Broadway.

Al Lewis

Born Albert (or Alexander) Meister in New York City on April 30, 1923, Al Lewis spent some of his youth in Brooklyn. It was there that the six-foot-one-inch teen began his lifelong love affair with basketball. Supposedly he became a vaudeville and circus performer, appeared in Olsen and Johnson's *Hellzapoppin'*, the Broadway hit of 1938, became a union organizer in the South, worked as a radio actor, and worked on a doctorate in child psychology, which he was said to have earned at Columbia University in 1941 or 1949. (After decades of interviews, Al Lewis challenged the concept of chronology, and many of these claims remain in question.) His career, however, didn't take off until the advent of television.

A supporting player in big-screen movies can go through life without anyone except his creditors noticing him. Television, however, can make any actor a celebrity. Al Lewis, best remembered for his role as Grandpa in *The Munsters*, got his big television break not on that spooky comedy, but on *Car 54*. Lewis made his first appearance as Officer Schnauser in the episode entitled "Put It in the Bank" (production #13), thus becoming a regular to the *Car 54* series, in mid-season. "I was originally hired for a one-shot on the program," recalled Lewis. "I played the harassed construction man in the show with Molly Picon. Remember it? I want her to move out so we can knock down the building and she refuses to budge." The episode was "I Won't Go" and Lewis played the role of Mr. Spencer. "Then they used me in the program about stealing cars. I guess they liked me because, before you know it, I'm out of the comic villain class and on the force."

"I do a lot of work for the Police Athletic League," Lewis told a reporter for the *Richmond Times*. "Last week I did a show in Central Park with another actor who has a part in a Broadway show. I bet him five bucks that five times as many people would recognize me. It was no contest. I was mobbed and no one noticed my co-star, Robert Morse [the star of Broadway's *How to Succeed in Business Without Really Trying*]. I think at that moment somebody could have signed Bobby for a TV series."

In true New York fashion, Al Lewis worked in the Bronx, lived in Manhattan, but was born and bred in Brooklyn. He attended Thomas Jefferson High School and then found himself engaged in a series of widely diversified professions . . . most of them in Brooklyn. At one time or another Lewis was a salesman, a waiter, a hot dog vendor (at Ebbets Field where the Brooklyn Dodgers played), a seaman, a poolroom owner, and a store detective—or so he said.

It was in 1949 that he seriously turned to show business. A friend suggested that he join Paul Mann's Actor's Workshop. There, with classmates Sidney Poitier, Pat Benoit, Vic Morrow and others, Lewis began to develop his comic style. It wasn't long before he began to find work on television. As he put it, "I was seen if not heard on practically every live show from New York." Viewers probably recognized Lewis from his work on *The U.S. Steel Hour*, *Armstrong Circle Theatre*, *Decoy*, *The Big Story*, *Deadline*, *Studio One* and various specials, including featured roles in *A Tale of Two Cities* and *The Moon and Sixpence*.

Al Lewis made his Broadway debut in the 1958 production of *The Night Circus*. Columnist Robert Coleman of the *New York Mirror* commented: "Al Lewis stands out as a wolfish and amiable tavernkeeper." Later he appeared in *One More River* on Broadway, the City Center production of *Street Scene*, and in a stock presentation of *Girl Crazy*. Anyone assuming Lewis' first turn as a policeman was on *Car 54* needs to check again; he had played an ex-cop (one of four different parts) in the Circle in the Square's highly successful revival of Eugene O'Neil's *The Iceman Cometh*.

In fact, the ex-schoolteacher had been stealing scenes on Broadway from Phil Silvers in a dismal musical entitled *Do Re Mi*. The show was a complete bore until Al came on stage as "The Shtarker," a professional killer who carried an attaché case and had set rates for all sorts of exterminating jobs. Every night for the entire Broadway run, Al Lewis came on stage unrecognized and left to scene-stealing applause. All during the first season of *Car 54*, Lewis was doubling as a gangster by night and a Bronx cop by day.

When *Do Re Mi* went out on a brief tour, Lewis went with it, and only then did he discover the joys of being a television cop. While in Detroit, a local police precinct got wind of his arrival and invited him to inspect its station house. Soon news of Schnauser's presence reached other precincts, and before he knew it, Lewis was besieged with invitations to inspect local police precincts.

A compromise had to be arranged, and one sunny afternoon, Lewis found himself on the steps of City Hall literally reviewing the troops. Lewis walked down the rows of 400 representatives of the Detroit force, shaking hands and signing autographs. "It was a genuine thrill," he commented. "Now I know how Queen Elizabeth feels."

Having played two supporting roles on *Car 54*, Lewis was paid $225 for each episode. When approached about playing a regular supporting role of Patrolman Leo Schnauser for $550 per episode, per five-day workweek, he signed a contract on Feb. 19, 1962. The contract provided the stipulation that if the series would be renewed for a second season, he would be paid $750 per week under the same terms.

Al Lewis' character, "Schnauzer" was printed on his locker, but was spelled "Schnauser" during the closing credits and on the score-board in the Bar Mitzvah episode. A *TV Guide* article entitled "A Volcano Called Schnauzer" spelled his name with the letter z. Two television scripts had his name spelled with a z while the others had his name spelled with the letter s. The closing credits always spelled it "Schnauser." The educated answer to the question fans have asked about: his name was actually spelled both ways, but the majority of the times spelled "Schnauser" with an s, not a z.

Beatrice Pons

As she did in a number of episodes, Lucille Toody flung open the window of her apartment and, in a wailing screech, informed one and all of her marital distress: "Listen, America! My husband is a nut!" In what *TV Guide* labeled a "superlatively loud-mouthed moment," actress Beatrice Pons made her bid for television immortality. Years before, Audrey Meadows proved to television audiences that the New York housewife can have the final say regarding her husband's schemes in *The Honeymooners*. Lucille Ball proved that the housewife doesn't have to become the head of the house to generate laughs. But shortly after Beatrice Pons out-staged her husband in the demeanor that became an almost regular staple for the series, Lucille's witticism was publicly labeled "brilliant" by no less an authority on the female nag than Gertrude Berg of *The Goldbergs* fame.

This yelling-out-of-the-window routine may have become a staple for the *Car 54* episodes, but Nat Hiken explored this comedic scene years before. In a short skit for a comedy variety program with Bert Lahr and Nancy Walker, Bert was insanely jealous over his homely wife. He saw her as a beauty. He shouted out the window to his neighbors, "Eat your heart out."

By the end of the second season of *Car 54*, Beatrice Pons had statistically spent almost one-fifth of her 25-year-long career in curlers and bathrobes. She previously played the evil-tempered wife of actor Joe E. Ross - in his role as Sgt. Rupert Ritzik, one of Bilko's sidekicks on *The Phil Silvers Show*.

"She is a godsend to a comedy director," commented Nat Hiken. "She succeeds in being funny because she plays these roles seriously."

There was a difference between Emma Ritzik and Lucille Toody. Emma was a mean woman - a hard battle-ax determined to save Rupert from Bilko's machinations. Underneath, she was a good and loving woman. Lucille was somewhat more sympathetic as a personality. She aspired to be cultured and elegant, having gone to Hunter College. Instead, she had to devote most of her time extricating her husband from a variety of messy situations.

In real life, Pons was an emotional, nervously talkative woman, further described by one columnist as possessing "an almost child-like friendliness and vivacity." Her real-life husband, David Ross, a professional radio and television announcer, was almost scared of her when she returned home on occasion in her television character, *sans* costume.

Born in Rhode Island in 1923, Pons was an elementary school teacher before making the transition to show business. She performed in a nightclub act called "Your Face is so Familiar," in which she did take-offs of such notables as Beatrice Lillie, Gertrude Lawrence, Lynn Fontanne and Helen Hayes. One critic hailed her performance as "brilliant." One evening, after a rough exchange with a heckler, her then fiancé said, "It's either them or me." She left the stage for him.

For 15 years she was a staple character in the radio series, *The Goldbergs*. In 1947, she began appearing in numerous guest spots on television anthologies. But after a few years on television, being labeled as "Miss Shrew, U.S.A.," she feared she would be typecast. "I've been turned down for ordinary character roles on the grounds that I'm too obvious," she explained. "If I appear in public without curlers and don't start shrieking at the top of my lungs, everyone is disappointed."

Memorable Lines:

Toody, talking to Muldoon over the phone, turns from the receiver to ask his wife if he may go fishing.

"Well," she shrills, "if fishing is more important to you than my happiness . . . If fishing is more important than your marriage . . . if fishing . . ."

"She says I can go!" says Toody over the phone.

Mickey Deems

Mickey Deems first came to the attention of New York theatergoers in the West Coast revue *Vintage 60*, after having established himself as one of the most popular nightclub entertainers in the country. Later, he delighted Broadway audiences with his performance in *Alive and Kicking* and his portrayal of the drunken signalman Taylor in *Golden Fleecing*. He was a standby for all seven of Sid Caesar's roles in the musical *Little Me* and played five roles of his own as well. Off-Broadway he appeared in *Kaleidoscope, Waiting for Godot* and played the Victor Moore role in the revival of Cole Porter's *Anything Goes*.

Mickey Deems began his professional career as a drummer with a touring band, cultivating his comic talents along the way. His switch from music to a comedy single led to successful engagements in nightclubs across the country, including New York's Blue Angel, Chicago's Palmer House, Las Vegas' Thunderbird and San Francisco's the hungry i.* On television he replaced Jackie Gleason for two weeks on *The Jackie Gleason Show* and appeared with Ed Sullivan, Garry Moore, Steve Allen and Jack Paar.

In addition to creating the role of Officer Fleischer on *Car 54*, Mickey Deems directed many of the segments (un-credited) and supplied additional dialogue. His spouse was Gertrude Black, secretary to Nat Hiken and Billy Friedberg. Deems' other talents included playing the piano and fixing broken television sets.

---

* *the hungry i* was intentionally spelled in lowercase.

Nipsey Russell

Nipsey Russell was known as the comedian whose one-liners and impromptu rhymes made him one of television's popular talk-show guests and game show panelists during the 1970s. Born Julius Russell in Atlanta, Georgia, on September 15, 1918, he moved to Cincinnati and lived with an aunt during his senior year in high school so he would be eligible to attend the University of Cincinnati tuition-free. A four-year enlistment in the Army - where he was commissioned as a captain in the field during WWII - interrupted his studies at the university. But he returned and earned a degree in English in 1946.

After college, he pursued his stage career in earnest, working black circuit clubs in the Midwest and on the East Coast before graduating to the Apollo in Harlem and top Catskills resort hotels like the Concord. It was his tenure at the Baby Grand, a Manhattan cabaret, however, that led to guest spots on Jack Paar's *Tonight Show*, and those national television appearances ignited his career in 1959. His catchy verse, aphorisms and gift of gab were perfectly suited for radio and television and soon he was making steady appearances on Arthur Godfrey's morning radio program and a variety of television shows.

His role as Officer Anderson, the switchboard operator, on *Car 54* demonstrated Nat Hiken's attempt to integrate African Americans as regular police officers on the series. "When I tried to break into television," Russell recalled, "I was told that white folks wouldn't understand what I was talking about." He described his position on the series as an "infinitesimal role." A year after *Car 54* went off the air, Nipsey Russell began performing on stage and soon caught the attention of columnist Gerald Nachman of the *New York Post*. In the Sept. 27, 1964 issue of the *Post*, Russell recalled his role on the series: "I'm trying to live that down, but I guess the part was so small I don't have too much to live down. In the act I always tell people, 'Yeah, I played a cop, but *I* didn't arrest anyone,' so at least it was good for a joke."

Phil Silvers

While Gwynne, Ross, Lewis, Reed and Pons were veterans of *The Phil Silvers Show*, the suspicious asked the inevitable: Why wasn't owlish Phil Silvers in the new series? Did he and Hiken have a falling out? Hiken explained for the October 1962 issue of *Pageant*, "We were just going in different directions. Phil had put four years into the Sergeant Bilko show. He wanted to go to Broadway, and he did. He starred in *Top Banana* and then *Do Re Mi*." No harsh feelings were found to exist, and the October 21, 1961 issue of *TV Guide* featured a photo of Phil Silvers on the set of *Car 54* with Ross and Gwynne in costume, and Nat Hiken standing behind Silvers, all laughing on the set.

Arthur Hershkowitz

Arthur Hershkowitz, Vice-President of Eupolis Productions, was a lawyer and brother-in-law of the late Fred Allen, with whom he was associated in radio production. Known as the business advisor, Hershkowitz was a quiet-spoken man who worked so closely with Nat Hiken that the men were often mistaken as brothers.

Filming on Location

Some television producers complained bitterly about filming shows on the streets of New York. While natural surroundings were preferred, city regulations hamstrung them, thus slowing up production. "I marvel at the police cooperation," Hiken explained. "What we do is get a three-day pass, leaving one day leeway for rain. Then, when we arrive on location the no-parking signs are up, the area is blocked off and four cops are on the scene. One thing, we have to be extremely careful about is not filming one of the 'Boys in Blue.' They might be accused of moonlighting if they inadvertently showed up on the show."

Also, celebrities from the West Coast were few and far between compared to sunny California. But Hiken found the solution simple:

a weekly cast of regulars who resided in New York (many of them performed on the stage in the evenings when *Car 54* was being filmed during the afternoon).

"Though you can't beat Hollywood for working conditions," says the Chicago-born Hiken, "I don't want to leave New York. I've been here for twenty-one years. But aside from that, my show is a New York show through and through."

"We've been all over the borough," Hiken told reporter Bob Lardine for the *Sunday News*. "The Bronx has a character all its own. Why, it has mountains unlike anything you've ever seen!"

In between filming production #3 for the series, on Saturday, June 22, 1961, *Show Business* reported that Nat Hiken was currently seeking all types of actors, all ages, all races, for dramatic extras and featured players. "If you have not already registered with Tom Ward, 1227 Sixth Ave., send photos, and résumés by mail only."

After the first six episodes were filmed, Hiken was interviewed by Art Woodstone of *Variety*, and explained his rationale: "There is a huge reservoir of offbeat, great talent here, and the faces are new to most of the country's television watchers. We had a meeting the other day. It was with the agency people, who watched six episodes and then asked me where I managed to find all those new faces. Those new faces were Paul Ford, Al Lewis, Gene Baylos and Maureen Stapleton."

"Nat Hiken, the producer and director, is a perfectionist, and he'll do a scene over and over until it's right," recalled Gwynne. "The tension really mounts on the fifth or sixth take. No curves or ripples or drops. Straight up. He's a great director. And somehow that quietness can be terrifying."

The Biograph Studios

In the middle of a residential block in the East Bronx stands the old five-story Biograph movie studio, the source of a series of two-reelers and feature films from the silent picture days. The site was temporarily an imaginary police station house.

The original studio was built in 1912 and was located at 11 East 14th Street in Manhattan. A year later, the Biograph Company decided to move their facilities uptown to 807 E. 175th Street, in the Bronx. The company produced a number of film shorts, but in 1916 (when income dropped off) Biograph ceased producing new films and began leasing out part of their studio space to other production companies.

As finances hardened, the studio was acquired by one of Biograph Company's creditors, the Empire Trust Company. In 1928 Herbert Yates took possession of the Biograph Studios properties and the film laboratory facilities and made it a subsidiary of his Consolidated Film Industries.

The studio was used to produce a large number of successful and non-successful features for the commercial market. *Woman in the Dark* (1934), *Midnight* (1934), *The Crime of Dr. Crespi* (1935), and *Manhattan Merry-Go-Round* (1937) were but a few. But even an eagle-eyed *Car 54* aficionado would not have recognized the movie sets on the TV show. Thirteen brand-new sets were built.

The Biograph studio ceased operations in 1939 and liquidated their inventory by offering film negatives (and the movie rights) to the general public. Mary Pickford bought the camera negatives of about 75 of her short films, and after a few other individual purchases, those remaining were donated to the film department of the Museum of Modern Art in New York City.

Empire Trust later assigned management of the property to one of its own subsidiaries, The Actinograph Corp., which held it until 1948. Martin Poll (who later became New York's Commissioner of Motion Picture Arts) restored Biograph Studios and reopened it in 1956 as the Gold Medal Studios, the largest film studio in America outside the Los Angeles area. Poll sold the property in 1961, when it was incorporated into a newer company, Biograph Studios, Inc. in 1961, unrelated to the original Biograph Company Corporation.

This is where *Car 54, Where Are You?* got involved. Eupolis Productions tracked down the owner of the landmark and made arrangements to pay a rental fee so the studio could go back into production. While street scenes were shot on location, almost all interiors of department stores, apartments (living rooms, bedrooms, etc.), and all the rooms in the police stations (including Block's office, the locker room, etc,) were shot on a total number of 15 sets.

The studio was run down, and problems occasionally occurred during filming, forcing the cast and crew to do their scenes again and again. "Great chunks of plaster came down every once in a while," recalled Fred Gwynne. "Just before we broke up for our spring vacation, you'd find people standing in places where the ceiling was showing signs of collapse. They were hoping to get the goods for a law case. For that extra vacation money, you know?"

In a memorandum dated Aug. 24, 1962 to all of the men on the crew, Sal Scoppa wrote: "As you know, last year we had trouble with leaks in the roof. The leaks have been repaired and it has been requested by the Studio owners that we do not put chairs, etc. on the roof. It would be very much appreciated if we refrain from any activity whatsoever on the roof, unless absolutely necessary to carry out a function of a job."

The condition of the building wasn't stable both structurally and financially. Biograph Studios went dormant again in the 1970s before the studio facilities burned down in 1980. Today, a New York Department of Sanitation depot stands in its place.

The Written Word

Hiken said the biggest criticism from the cop on the beat was, "Why don't you ever show the police on *Car 54* doing their work?" But, explained Hiken, that was not the show's intent. "What we want to do is depict the personal side of the average cop. That's why we never have any major crimes in our scripts. Besides, 98 percent of the crimes occurring in a neighborhood precinct are small stuff- and that's the way we write it."

During the first season of *Car 54*, Nat Hiken fully controlled the series and maximized his profits by taking on almost every aspect of production, from writing the scripts to directing. To help establish the format of the program, supervise the plots and direction the series would take week after week, Hiken sat down with all of the script writers in separate meetings to discuss each plot and how the finished script would appear on screen. "The important thing on a show of this kind is the plot," Hiken recalled. "If the plot is believable, you can go in any direction. And if you have something good, you build for residuals."

Another reason for writing at least one draft of each script (if not the final draft) was to keep the production costs down. "Back in my early days," Hiken said, "guys would write for nothing. They'd do anything until a big radio show spotted them and then they'd go to work for $50 a week, maybe tossing a joke into the script every three weeks. There used to be a lot of local outlets for their stuff. Now the union says the writers have to start at $750 a week. The guild minimum for a script is $1,200. Who's going to pay that kind of money to unproven youngsters?"

Whenever a story idea was accepted, script writers were assigned to write the scripts. On April 6, 1961, Marty Roth, Harold Flender, Art Baer and Ben Joelson were signing agreements regarding their plot outlines, and accepting script writing duties for the series, still tentatively entitled, "The Snow Whites."

Most of the script writers who worked on *Car 54* had a resumé from radio comedies. Art Baer began his career as a writer for radio programs including *The Robert Q. Lewis Show*. He teamed up for scores of television sitcoms, and they won an Emmy for *The Carol Burnett Show*. Baer was a gifted comedy writer whose material was used by Flip Wilson, Jonathan Winters, Perry Como and Victor Borge. *Car 54, Where Are You?* was his earliest contribution to television, but after the series ended, Baer wrote scripts for numerous other comedies including *Happy Days, The Andy Griffith Show, Hogan's Heroes, Good*

Times, Get Smart and *The Odd Couple*. Ben Joelson also got his television break on *Car 54, Where Are You?* and went on to co-script for the same television episodes and series with Art Baer.

Marty Roth wrote for other television comedies including *McHale's Navy, I Dream of Jeannie, Petticoat Junction* and *My Favorite Martian*. Harold Flender was also credited as Harold Flender for *Kraft Television Theater* and *I Spy*.

From the time a story was conceived to the finished product being put on celluloid (filmed on 35 mm), the process of creating the story and the script underwent numerous installments. The first was the submission. In order for a plot outline to be submitted to the Eupolis Productions and Nat Hiken, other than the form of a fan letter, the writer had to ask for a sign of release. Without this, any submission was considered "unsolicited" and subject to return without review.

The sign of release was a five-clause, two-page contract protecting both the writer and the television producers. The writer signed his or her name to the paper, the title of the plot outline, and under the following terms, submitted the plot outline with the signed contract.

1. The plot outline was being submitted voluntarily on the writer's behalf.

2. That the writer agrees to Eupolis' decision whether or not to use the story for the featured series and that the producers' decision was accepted as "final."

3. As a condition of permitting the writer to submit the plot outline, the writer agreed that the submission would be without prejudice to any of their rights and shall not raise any presumption that the producers made any use of the material.

4. If the producers accepted the material but no agreement was made between the writer and the produc-

ers, the plot outline would not be used, and the producers would not make any use of the material.

5.   The writer admits that the material is his or her own creation, not someone else's, and that they would hold the television producers harmless if any claim of infringement would be made after the material was telecast.

After the plot outline was submitted, the producers decided whether or not the outline would be feasible, and would be sent either a rejection letter or an offer to purchase the property. If the outline was accepted, the usual price was $500. Then the producers would assign a script writer to adapt the material into a shooting script. Each script would be given a brief meeting, discussed in detail between the script writer and the producers. The script would then be revised.

After a second meeting, a third revision (the final draft) would be typed out and submitted to Procter & Gamble and NBC's Broadcast Standards Department for censorship approval. Anything in question that could "possibly" bring about letters of complaints from viewers, or lawsuits, would be brought to the attention of Eupolis Productions, where the necessary changes would be made.

Example for production #60, "The Curse of the Snitkins"
Idea by Nat Hiken

First Conference Nat Hiken, Art Baer and Ben Joelson
Original Story by Nat Hiken, Art Baer and Ben Joelson
First Draft by Art Baer and Ben Joelson

Second Conference Nat Hiken, Art Baer and Ben Joelson
Second Draft by Art Baer and Ben Joelson

Rewrite of Second Draft by Nat Hiken

Final Script by Nat Hiken

Script writers were paid a required minimum according to the Writers' Guild, and the fee varied from one script writer to another, depending on how much Eupolis (and Nat Hiken) felt the task was worth.

THE SCRIPT WRITERS

The following is a complete list of all 60 productions. It includes who was officially credited for authorship, how much they were paid, and the check # from Eupolis Productions. If an author was paid twice for the same episode, the smaller amount was payment for the story, and the larger amount was payment for writing the script. Nat Hiken was not paid for his services, since he was the producer. His efforts are marked with $$$$$ and xxxxx. Tony Webster went on a weekly payroll half way through season one, so he was not paid a specific amount for each script he wrote. In many cases, Nat Hiken created the story proposal and someone else wrote the script. Hiken did not pay himself to create a story proposal - hence his name does not appear in most of the entries below. The list below represents *only* the payments made for each specific episode and who received that payment, as it was compiled for the Writers' Guild of America.

Small addendum: Gary Belkin wrote a story proposal and script entitled "Christmas Story." He was paid $2,000 for his services (check #3682) but the script was shelved, and never went into production.

Prod. #	Episode Title	Author	Amount	Check #
1	"Something Nice for Sol"	Nat Hiken	$$$$$	xxxxx
2	"Change Your Partner"	Tony Webster	$3,500.00	#1115
3	"Home Sweet Sing Sing"	Terry Ryan	$2,750.00	#1522
4	"Who's For Swordfish?"	Nat Hiken	$$$$$	xxxxx
5	"I Won't Go"	Gary Belkin	$1,250.00	#1521
		Gary Belkin	$500.00	#2048
6	"Muldoon's Star"	Harold Flender	$1,500.00	#1096
		Harold Flender	$500.00	#2617
7	"Gypsy Curse"	Tony Webster	$3,500.00	#1114
8	"The Paint Job"	Marty Roth	$1,500.00	#1097
		Marty Roth	$500.00	#2618
9	"Love Finds Muldoon"	Nat Hiken	$$$$$	xxxxx
10	"Thirty Days' Notice"	Art Baer	$875.00	#1524
		Ben Joelson	$875.00	#1525
		Art Baer	$250.00	#2616
		Ben Joelson	$250.00	#2615
11	"Catch Me on the Paar ..."	Terry Ryan	$2,750.00	#2038
12	"The Taming of Lucille"	Tony Webster	$3,500.00	#2040
13	"Put it in the Bank"	Syd Zelinka	$1,750.00	#3150
		Will Glickman	$1,750.00	#4432
14	"Get Well, Officer Schn ..."	Terry Ryan	$2,750.00	#2784
15	"Boom, Boom, Boom"	Syd Zelinka	$1,750.00	#3151
		Will Glickman	$1,750.00	#4433
16	"The Sacrifice"	Tony Webster	$3,500.00	#2039
17	"Toody and Muldoon ..."	Terry Ryan	$3,000.00	#3451

18	"Christmas at the 53rd"	Terry Ryan	$1,500.00	#3452
19	"How High is Up?"	Tony Webster	Weekly	xxxxx
20	"Toody's Paradise"	Syd Zelinka	$1,750.00	#4431
		Will Glickman	$1,750.00	#4434
21	"Toody and the Art World"	Nat Hiken	$$$$$	xxxxx
22	"What Happened to Th ..."	Tony Webster	Weekly	xxxxx
23	"How Smart Can You Get?"	Tony Webster	Weekly	xxxxx
24	"Today I Am A Man"	Terry Ryan	$3,000.00	#4430
25	"No More Pickpockets"	Tony Webster	Weekly	xxxxx
26	"The Beast Who Walked ..."	Terry Ryan	$3,000.00	#4738
27	"Courtship of Sylvia Sch ..."	Tony Webster	Weekly	xxxxx
28	"The Auction"	Syd Zelinka	$1,750.00	#5129
		Will Glickman	$1,750.00	#5128
29	"Quiet! We're Thinking"	Terry Ryan	$3,000.00	#5132
30	"I Love Lucille"	Tony Webster	$2,000.00	#2954
			$1,500.00	#5170
31	"A Man is Not an Ox"	Nat Hiken	$$$$$	xxxxx
		Billy Friedberg	$3,500.00	#5637
32	"Hail to the Chief!"	Tony Webster	Weekly	xxxxx
33	"... Sing Along with Mitch"	Buddy Arnold	$1,250.00	#5481
		Ben Joelson	$1,250.00	#5478
34	"Schnauser's Last Ride"	Tony Webster	Weekly	xxxxx
35	"One Sleepy People"	Terry Ryan	$3,000.00	#5947
36	"Occupancy August 1st"	Gary Belkin	$2,000.00	#5479
37	"Remember St. Petersburg"	Tony Webster	Weekly	xxxxx
38	"Toody, Undercover"	Terry Ryan	$3,000.00	#5272

39	"That's Show Business"	Gary Belkin	$350.00	#1098
		Gary Belkin	$2,000.00	#6269
40	"The Captain's Parrot"	Buddy Arnold	$1,500.00	#6364
		Ben Joelson	$1,500.00	#6365
41	"Star is Born in the Bronx"	Terry Ryan	$3,000.00	#6366
42	"Pretzel Mary"	Gary Belkin	$1,500.00	#6930
		Art Baer	$1,500.00	#6931
43	"142 Tickets on the Aisle"	Tony Webster	$2,000.00	#6179
		Tony Webster	$2,000.00	#6929
44	"J'Adore, Muldoon"	Ben Joelson	$2,500.00	#7132
45	"White Elephant"	Terry Ryan	$3,000.00	#7135
46	"Benny the Bookie's ..."	Gary Belkin	$1,500.00	#7417
		Art Baer	$1,500.00	#7418
47	"Stop, Thief!"	Tony Webster	$4,000.00	#7256
48	"Presidential Itch"	Robert Van Scoyk	$2,750.00	#4594
		Billy Friedberg	$3,500.00	#7641
49	"T&D Meet the Russians"	Billy Friedberg	$3,500.00	#7642
50	"Here We Go Again"	Gary Belkin	$1,750.00	#7643
		Art Baer	$1,750.00	#8037
51	"Star Boarder"	Terry Ryan	$3,000.00	#8038
52	"Biggest Day of the Year"	Lou Solomon	$1,500.00	#6823
		Bob Howard	$1,500.00	#6822
53	"Here Comes Charlie"	Nat Hiken	$$$$$	xxxxx
		Billy Friedberg	$3,500.00	#8294
54	"I've Been Here Before"	Terry Ryan	$3,000.00	#8168
55	"See You at the Barmitzvah"	Max Wilk	$3,500.00	#8169
56	"Joan Crawford Didn't ..."	Gary Belkin	$2,500.00	#8250

57	"Lucille is Forty"	Ben Joelson	$1,750.00	#0540
		Art Baer	$1,750.00	#0539
58	"Loves of Sylvia Schn ..."	Tony Webster	$4,000.00	#0467
59	"The Puncher and Judy"	Nat Hiken	$$$$$	xxxxx
60	"The Curse of the Snitkins"	Ben Joelson	$1,625.00	#9662
		Art Baer	$1,625.00	#9661

Music

As an author, producer and songwriter, Nat Hiken's musical col-laborators were Dick Stutz, Gordon Jenkins and George Bassman. Hiken composed "Close to Me," "Irving," and "Fugitive from Fifth Avenue." He was one of the writers of the Broadway review, *Along Fifth Avenue*. With John Strauss, he wrote the lyrics for the theme song, "Car 54, Where Are You?" (Strauss was married to Charlotte Rae at the time *Car 54* was being produced, and was responsible for the theme song for *The Phil Silvers Show* and *The Magnificent Montague* television pilot.)

Let the Filming Commence

It was agreed by Procter & Gamble, Howard Epstein and Nat Hiken that the pilot episode would be used as part of the 26 episodes con-tractually obligated to be filmed. The total production cost of the "Snow Whites" pilot was, as of March 4, 1961, $68,745.94. Addi-tional costs were added for transportation of the pilot to and from studios and additional paperwork, totaling $3,537.81. To round out the $75,000 cost stated in the agreement between P&G and Eupolis dated Nov. 21, 1960 (and rough draft of the agreement dated Nov. 4), Howard Epstein added $2,716.25 to cover the expense of Eupo-lis for services of producer, director and legal fees, making the grand total equal $75,000.

On May 4, 1961, Howard Epstein explained in writing to Richard

Zimbert (of the Leo Burnett Company, representative of P&G) that there would be a problem regarding the additional cost that Eupolis would incur because of the pilot. "Because of sponsor and agency urgency in seeing the rough print and then the necessity of getting out the current print instead of doing the normal processing of making one finished product, we are going to encounter additional costs because of the re-titling and scoring and the like including some minor re-shooting," Epstein explained. "It seems only fair and equitable that we be reimbursed for whatever these additional costs may be. It's true that in any event, we would have scored the pilot, but we would not have used the preliminary music nor the tentative titles, etc."

Procter & Gamble swiftly agreed to pay for the costs to rescore and re-titled the onscreen credits, which had yet to be decided.

The Laugh Track

Before television, audiences often experienced comedy, whether performed live on stage, on radio, or in a movie, in the presence of other audience members. When television producers attempted to recreate this atmosphere in its early days by introducing the sound of laughter or other crowd reactions into the soundtrack of television programs, this process was termed "laugh track," "laughter soundtrack," "laughter track" and most commonly, "canned laughter." The use of a separate soundtrack with the artificial sound of audience laughter for television comedies and sitcoms became common practice during the late 'fifties and early 'sixties. The first television show to incorporate a laugh track was *The Hank McCune Show* in 1950. By 1961, Ross Bagdasarian, creator of *Alvin and the Chipmunks*, refused to have a laugh track, reasoning that if the animated series was funny, there would be no need for the added laughter.*

---

* It has been put to print (though no verified source has been proven) that much of the "canned laughter" added to the sound tracks to television comedies and sitcoms was originally recorded during broadcasts of *The Red Skelton Show* and was used repeatedly for decades.

While recordings of laughter were available, Nat Hiken preferred to have a legit laugh track that matched the sequence of events in each *Car 54* film. Hiken ran an audience into a special studio and showed them the films. Their actual laughs at the on-screen situations were then recorded and later worked into the sound track. Rather than using "canned laughter," the track was more genuine.

The usual method producers arranged for live audiences for unknown shows was to contact the convention bureau, find out what convention was in town, and invite them to attend. For the pilot episode, Hiken found that the only group in New York was a convention of ministers. He was worried, but he needed an audience, so he issued the invitation. The ministers flocked to the screening. "We got so many long laughs that Nat had to take most of them out," recalled Fred Gwynne. "You couldn't hear the dialogue over the audience noise." Hiken had to arrange for the volume to be turned down for the sound track. This caused the episode, "Something Nice for Sol" to be pushed ahead a week, so the volume for the laugh track could be adjusted. Instead of being the first episode broadcast in the series, it was the second. A number of reviewers commented in their columns that the second episode was an improvement from the premiere, proving that Hiken's initial choice would have been excellent - had it not been for a large number of reviewers, who feeling that policemen were being disrespected on celluloid, would have made a negative comment either way.

With egg on his face, Frank Judge of the *Detroit News* commented, "The worst laugh track in television blights the show. Nothing, not even the sorely missed *Sgt. Bilko* series, could be *that* funny." Apparently he was unaware of how authentic the laugh track was. Another critic commented, "Last night the stain on plausibility was too great to be believed by the canned applause that began before the show did."

The Premiere: Critics Have Their Say

The same evening that *Car 54* premiered, Nat Hiken was not sitting in front of the television set. No telephone was close enough to receive the reports of viewer response. Hiken wasn't even working on a script or production of the next episode. Instead, he spent his hours at the Friars' Club, where the club gave a dinner in his honor - and jested about his television career. Phil Silvers was in attendance, as well as Joe E. Lewis, who sang a song about a gal who is giving her boyfriend "all your presents but the baby, because he's the only thing that you didn't give to me." Actor Gene Baylos, who appeared in the first episode of the series, told of his troubles with the management, throwing the blame on Hiken.

The first episode telecast, "Who's For Swordfish?," was not previewed for critics weeks in advance. "Something Nice for Sol" was previewed instead, which threw television critics for a loop when they saw an episode telecast that was of less quality than the one they previewed.

The former of the two was given a special press preview screening at the Friars' Club on Friday, September 8 in New York City. The reception was warm and the belly laughs plentiful as members of the press told both Nat Hiken and Howard Epstein that the episode was hilariously funny. Their true opinions, however, came out in their columns.

Every start of the fall season opens the door for television's "wise men," who engage in an annual guessing game: Pick the Hits. In doing so, they must name the misses as well as the hits, and the opinions they share for the favor of the audience. *Car 54, Where Are You?* received just as many positive reviews as it did negative. Common among critics, the split was almost equal for both opinions.

Columnist Jim Frankel of the *Cleveland Press and News* wrote, "I think *Car 54* could become the liveliest and funniest vehicle since the days of Phil Silvers' *Bilko* and Jackie Gleason's *Honeymooners*."

Lawrence Laurent of the *Post and Times Herald* (Washington,

D.C.) wrote in his column, "After seeing one episode, I wouldn't be surprised if Joe E. Ross and Fred Gwynne became the most celebrated comedy team since Abbott and Costello."

Another critic declared that "audiences don't like comedy cops any more than they like soap operas."

Terry Vernon of the *Long Beach Press-Telegram* commented in his September 23, 1961 column: "This series about two comedian cops got off to a funny start. It's broad comedy, unlike the household situation-type tripe we've been subjected to the past seasons. Overall prediction: A winner."

Paul Molloy of the *Chicago Sun-Times* wrote, ". . . Hiken might have had a hit. But he has sketched a preposterous (and sometimes cruel) caricature of the policeman. And it will be hard for some viewers, especially policemen, to be amused."

"I think it's going to be funny," quoted Fred Gwynne over the phone to columnist Russell W. Kane of the *Cleveland Plain Dealer.* "My wife is my most severe critic. She laughed all the way through the pilot."

Columnist and critic Frank Gagnard wrote, "The two patrolmen who are the central characters of the comedy series may not go down in folklore, but neither do they strive extravagantly for laughs."

After viewing the premiere episode, Bob Brock of the Dallas, Texas, *Times Herald* commented: "It is our painful duty to opine that TV lightning may not strike twice for Nat Hiken . . . The humor may be there, all right, but not much of it was showing . . ."

Bill Buchanan of the *Boston Record* remarked: "Despite my unusually good humor as I sat in my over-stuffed reviewer's chair, I'll go on record as saying that *Car 54, Where Are You?* will be the comedy hit of the TV season . . . How can a show which allows us to laugh at the police be anything but a hit?"

Hollywood Daily Variety commented: "Hiken had better not shoot in the streets. The cops will pinch him for obstructing traffic just to prove they're not dopes."

Milton R. Bass of the *Berkshire Eagle* (Pittsfield, Mass.) remarked: "It will be mostly humor and human nature, a nice relaxing half hour in the turmoil that is television."

Charles Denton of the *Los Angeles Examiner* wrote: "While certainly not an instant success, *Car 54* appears to have promise for lovers of the artful slapstick and conniving that made Bilko enduringly popular . . . If Hiken can come up with more of the same in the future, he could have a winner - allowing, that is, that New York's Finest don't sue him for defamation of character."

Bob Foster of the *San Mateo Times & News Leader* remarked: "All good television shows should achieve what they set out to do . . . *Car 54* does. It was intended to churn up a little laughter on the air lanes, and it most certainly did just that . . ."

Columnist Larry Wolters stated, "Suddenly, television is fun again."

The Battle Creek, Michigan, *Enquirer and News* reported: "Fred Gwynne, who looks like an emaciated center on a scarecrow basketball team, will probably be one of the major comedy 'finds' of the season."

Joe R. Mills of the *Columbus Dispatch* called the premiere "a piece of authentic slapstick."

Marie Torre of *The Herald* (Rutland, Vermont) commented the pilot was "a disappointment."

Eleanor Roberts of the *Boston Traveler* raved, "What Jackie Gleason and Art Carney did for *The Honeymooners* and Lucy and Desi did for *I Love Lucy*, Toody and Muldoon, as they're called, will accomplish for *Car 54*."

Variety, the leading Hollywood trade paper, previewed the opener in their Sept. 20, 1961 issue: "If Hiken can hurdle the existing obstacle of conveying that he's laughing at his supposedly dumb cops' foibles and weaknesses and inject a greater element of humaneness in their misdemeanors and escapades, he'll have himself a show."

The *Kansas City Star* wrote that *Car 54* "appears to be another winner."

Glen Graham of the *Argus-Courier* (Petaluma, California) commented: "I'm not particularly partial to any police department but recognize and respect its head in the community and certainly can't discount the quality of its men, which is about equal to the I.Q. found in the average business, newspaper, church or home. In other words, don't go along with the theory that nowadays policemen act like Keystone Cops. If anyone is going to have the laughing end of it, it might be officers who daily are called upon to meet mankind at its crummy worst. Now along comes *Car 54*, peopled by characters who garble the language and act like very unfunny small boys. Is anyone's I.Q. that low?"

Janet Kern of the *Chicago American* blasted the series, almost staking her reputation that "*Car 54* is not funny by any standard of humor of which this viewer is aware. It is, moreover, an insulting show . . . Insulting to every metropolitan policeman, and to the intelligence and taste of the viewers. Above all, it is nerve-wrackingly boresome."

Jerry Atkin of the *Post-Tribune* (Gary, Indiana) commented: "Of the five new series unveiling this weekend, Nat Hiken's *Car 54, Where Are You?* is most likely to succeed in a hurry . . . There's a well-planted rumor that Ross and Gwynne will be the Laurel and Hardy of the 60's. My husband thinks so. He laughed so hard he cried at a preview showing . . ."

Arch McKay of the *Alabama Journal* remarked that *Car 54* "appears to be an ill-conceived program thrown in for the benefit of the old Bilko fans, of which I was never a member. Fantastic people are placed into more fantastic situations with the expectancy of laughs . . . It is insulting to the law enforcement and to the general viewing public. To be truthful, *Car 54*, I couldn't care less where you are as long as you don't pop up on my TV screen again."

Some critics were not too observant. Jack Allen of the *Buffalo Courier Express* mistakenly said that *Car 54* was set in the Buffalo Police Department, instead of the Bronx.

The final verdict from the critics? Take it or leave it, the comedy was here to stay. Perhaps Jack Gould, famed television columnist for the *New York Times* summed it up when he wrote in his column: "Nat Hiken quite possibly is going to have the last laugh on the early detractors, including this corner, of *Car 54, Where Are You?* The extreme nonsense of the first show or two seems to have been wisely tempered and there is a lighter and more human touch to the proceedings; which is one way of saying perhaps Mr. Hiken had a better understanding of where he was bound than did some reviewers."

Critics Weigh In: The Second Episode

Of course, no TV critic should pass judgment on a series until at least three episodes are reviewed. For *Car 54*, the episodes varied too much in quality. When the second episode aired (the telefilm that was initially intended to be the premiere), critics took a second stab in their columns.

Anthony La Camera of *The American* commented this "was the pilot film which was previewed for us TV editors several weeks ago, and it proved just as entertaining the second time around. Since it's very funny in its own right, however, the Sunday-night series can do very well without all that raucous canned laughter. So here's hoping that producer-creator Nat Hiken puts a quietus on it very soon."

Columnist Fred Danzig of the *Berwick Enterprise* wrote: "For the record - a yarn titled 'Something Nice for Sol,' last Sunday's *Car 54, Where Are You?* on NBC-TV, was as hilarious as the most hilarious moments in the old Sgt. Bilko series, if not more so."

Block Party with Car 54

It was fiesta time in the Bronx when *Car 54* took to the streets.

"In the Bronx, nobody is shy," said Joe E. Ross. "When the kids want to know how a piece of equipment works, they don't ask questions. They pick it up and start taking it apart."

"They do ask for autographs," added Fred Gwynne. "They ask everyone - the cast and the crew. There's one kid they call Sylvester who must have had me sign 12 times. The last time he asked me to autograph his arm. He figured his mother wouldn't make him wash it off. How could I refuse?"

Filming on location wasn't difficult, as long as the spectators honored the crew's privacy to film without interruption. One afternoon, however, a lady in a fourth-story window hollered: "I've been on vacation in the mountains. Tell me the story so far and then I'll keep quiet!" For the premiere broadcast, repeated takes were made of a scene in which Joe E. Ross refused to write out a ticket. An irate citizen (the actor in the car) kept shouting, "Give me a ticket! Give me a ticket!" From a nearby window of a house came a voice saying, "So give him the ticket already and let me get some sleep!"

In one episode, when Ross and Gwynne did a scene in which they looked over a dozen dogs to find a runaway, there was a stir among the onlookers. "Soon the street was knee deep in mongrels," recalled Ross. "Everyone in the neighborhood hoped his dog would get in the scene."

The real policemen assigned to regulate traffic, so filming could commence without interruption, were often trying to crash the scene. Real cops were trying to figure out how to sneak into the show. One police officer supposedly told the crew, "It's about us; we've got a right." The show never used real policemen, even in crowd scenes. This was for both legal and financial reasons. First, the police officer would have to be paid for appearing in an episode. Second, the Screen Actors' Guild insisted that only actors with guild memberships could appear on screen - or the producers would face a fine. Everyone featured in all 60 episodes - including extras walking in the background - were hired actors, and not real New York police officers.

"We use big aluminum reflectors to focus the sunlight," explained Joe E. Ross. "One lady asked if she could borrow one to improve her daughter's sun tan. Why shouldn't she borrow something from us? We're neighbors."

Neighbors on East 175th Street took on proprietary interest in the show. When the crew was in front of the building to shoot street scenes, all of the nearby housewives settled down by their windows to watch the proceedings. One woman became the envy of her group when the curtains of her window showed in a shot.

On average the cast and crew usually consisted of 70 people, two trucks and a bus. When one episode demanded a traffic jam, the show created it by using the crew's own vehicles on a lonely stretch of parkway.

The Ratings War

Just two or three weeks after the premiere, newspapers were quick to report a "rating race" when long-time champ Ed Sullivan lost to *Car 54* by one Arbitron point, early on in the season. On Oct. 20, 1961, S.C. Potter of Procter & Gable sent Nat Hiken the following telegram:

> LAST SUNDAY'S SHOW WAS HIGHEST RATED OF ALL P&G SHOWS BEATING SULLIVAN BY OVER TEN SHARE POINTS IN THE 24 MAJOR MARKETS. FROM OUR COUNT, IT'S NUMBER SIX OF ALL SHOWS AND THE NUMBER TWO COMEDY ON THE AIR. THINGS LOOK VERY SOLID IF YOU CAN KEEP STRONG SCRIPTS COMING UP. NOTHING ELSE IS MORE IMPORTANT THAN SCRIPTS RIGHT NOW. HOPE TO SEE YOU IN A WEEK OR SO. AGAIN, CONGRATULATIONS AND REGARDS.

The Oct. 25, 1961 issue of *Variety* reported that "there are three half-hour comedy entries that have it made, regardless of their critical merits." The trade paper made sure to mention *Car 54* as being one of the most promising for NBC. By this time, *Car 54* was receiving a rating of 26.7 (tied in second place with *My Three Sons*), courtesy of a 24-city Nielsen study - with *Bonanza* being the only show to have a larger viewership than *Car 54*.

On that same day, Howard Epstein wrote to George Rosen of *Variety* to lodge a formal, written complaint. "We would like to call your attention to the 26.7 rating that *Car 54, Where Are You?* posted in the 24-City Nielsen, as set forth on page 27 of today's (25th) *Variety*; in the same listing, the Walt Disney rating is set out as 24.6. On page 25 of the same issue of *Variety*, *Car 54, Where Are You?* is used as an illustration of a show in a 'cradle' status. It is felt that it is hardly fair and statistically inaccurate to stigmatize in this way a program that increases its inherited rating by 2.1 points."

And the Offers Poured In . . .

Shortly after the series went before the cameras, an August issue of the *New Yorker* featured an article about the filming of *Car 54*, and this prompted a number of letters from residents of New York, including one dated Aug. 22, 1961, from Arthur T. Sheehan of City Island.

> Dear Mr. Hiken:
> Several times this summer I have watched your company shooting scenes for your new Car Fifty-Four show which the *New Yorker* says is to start this Sept. on NBC on Sunday nights. I hope you have the same success you had with the Bilko show.
> I've been coming to City Island with my family for eight years and often wondered why movie companies didn't use the locale, which is ideal. The Pearl White films [*The Perils of Pauline*, a 1914 silent movie serial] used to be filmed off High Island out here. The old owner used to make a good thing renting out his island for ship scenes.
> For eight years I superintended the making of CARE commercials so I became used to the problem of seeking locations and trying to think in terms of camera possibilities.
> Watching you shooting your scenes and getting the general format of your show from the *New Yorker*, the enclosed story line came into my mind as a possibility for you with City Island background.

The idea came from the story of the pirate Thwaite story. He was more notorious and cruel than Captain Kidd. He was never captured but finally retired as a gentleman to City Island where he built a fine estate and buried his ill-gotten gold. He was all set for the life of a country gentleman when a snake bit him and he died - probably the just retribution of all the victims he drowned. He never used to take prisoners.

Sincerely yours,
Arthur T. Sheehan

Nat Hiken took interest in the story idea, and acquired a release on the plot, but nothing ever developed from the story proposal.

Later in the year, Nat Hiken received a letter from Alan Dinehart of Hanna-Barbera Productions in Hollywood, California, dated Dec. 15, 1961.

Dear Nat,
Along with the Season's Greetings, let me congratulate you on *Car 54*. To my mind, there is no finer show on the air. I not only speak for myself, but also for Bill and Joe who were "hooked" on about the third show and now never miss it. Again, congratulations!

One of our staff writers who does *Yogi Bear*, *The Flintstones*, *Top Cat* and a number of other short cartoons for us, has written an outline for *Car 54*. I thought it was interesting enough to pass on to you. Let me hasten to add that you are under no obligation. Please feel free to read it. If you can use it, let me know. If not, he certainly will understand.

I wish you all success.

Sincerely,
Alan Dinehart

Apparently Howard Epstein was interested, and on Dec. 21, 1961, Alan Dinehart forwarded the release papers which Mr. Benedict was very happy to sign.

Ed Benedict had a list of credits to his name, including: two years with UPA writing Mr. Magoo shorts for theatrical release; he joined Hanna-Barbera approximately three years earlier writing half-hour episodes of *Huckleberry Hound*, *Quick Draw McGraw* and *Yogi Bear*; two years before, when it was decided to do *The Flintstones*, he contributed the major portion of these half-hour cartoons, and he had been a constant contributor on *Top Cat* (ironically a cartoon version of the *Bilko* series).

On Feb. 6, 1962, James J. Dowling of Philadelphia, Pennsylvania, submitted the following to Nat Hiken:

> Dear Mr. Hiken,
> I am sending you three prints from a cartoon panel I submitted to several syndicates four years ago. I called the panel *Officer Perry* and while most of the syndicates contacted felt it was "funny, cute and well done," they also believed *Perry* lacked "mass appeal."
>
> Since then *Car 54* has appeared and I've wondered whether *Officer Perry*, redrawn as *Car 54*, could be syndicated. I believe it can.
>
> Could some arrangement be made between you, N.B.C. and myself to put *Car 54* in the newspapers? I have in mind a gag panel, not a three or four panel strip. Presently, I have four reels "roughed" out and if you are interested, I will do the finished art and bring them to New York to show you. I realize, of course, that nothing can be done with *Car 54* without your and N.B.C.'s permission.
>
> In recent years two cartoon characters, Dennis [the Menace] and Hazel [the maid], have found their way into television, while a TV cartoon series, *The Flintstones*, has

made its way into the newspapers. Muldoon, Gunther, Schnauser and the boys should be the next. And can be.

Either way, *Car 54* is a very enjoyable half-hour. Keep it up.

Cordially,
James J. Dowling
222 E. Fisher Ave.
Philadelphia 20, Pennsylvania
GL 5 - 4564

Paul C. Ignizio of New York City wrote to Howard Epstein on April 24, 1962:

Dear Mr. Epstein:

I called at your office the other day to request a release form to submit an outline for a *Car 54* TV script, and was requested to send you information concerning my credits, which are as follows.

I believe I am thoroughly familiar with the characters of this story as I have been writing the *Car 54* comic book series for Dell Publications. Enclosed, you will find a copy of a *Car 54* comic book; the entire book (from cover to cover) was written by me. I have two more stories on *Car 54* which have been accepted but have still to be released.

In addition, I have written the entire book comic stories for *Laurel and Hardy*, *Diver Dan* and *The Twist*, all of which are published by Dell Publications.

My experience is not limited to cartoon stories. Previously, I have written TV scripts and although they did not consummate into sales, they were seriously considered by Mr. Ed Roerts of B.B.D.&O. and by Miss Pamela Ilott of CBS' *Lamp Unto My Feet*.

I will be looking forward to your reply.

Yours truly,
Paul C. Ignizio

On Nov. 13, 1962, the following was addressed to Nat Hiken of Eupolis Productions:

> Dear Nat:
> I understand you'll be employing live music, and I would like to recommend you use Skitch Henderson, who is an exceptional composer-conductor-arranger.
> I look forward to hearing from you.
> Best Regards.
>
> > Sincerely yours,
> > William Cooper
>
> P.S. He can also act!

On May 31, 1961, Christopher Sergel, Vice President of the Dramatic Publishing Company, wrote to Mr. Hershkowitz of Eupolis Productions, Inc., making an offer for the amateur theatre rights to the *Car 54* television series. "Before going into the details of our offer," the letter explained, "let me emphasize that it is limited to the amateur theatre rights, and that it has nothing to do with any other rights in the property such as motion picture, professional stage, radio, television and so forth."

The Dramatic Publishing Company was founded in 1885 by Charles H. Sergel, and had spent the past seventy-six years publishing such distinguished plays as Reginald Rose's *Twelve Angry Men*, Eric Hodgins' *Mr. Blandings Builds His Dream House*, George Bernard Shaw's *Caesar and Cleopatra*, and Irving Berlin's and Dorothy and Herbert Field's *Annie Get Your Gun*. Among the other television shows which the company handled similar subsidiary rights were *The Many Loves of Dobie Gillis*, *Father Knows Best*, *The Defenders* and *Bachelor Father*.

"What we would like to do is prepare a simple stage adaptation of *Car 54*, designing this stage version especially for the particular needs of the amateur market. Since the bulk of the amateur market is in the high schools, the show would be suitable for their use," the letter explained. "All of our adaptations are handled on the basis of the same royalty terms. This standard royalty contract provides that the owners of the original work receive 25 percent of the performance royalties and 5 percent of the playbook sale royalties. We offer these same royalty terms for the amateur rights to *Car 54*, and against these royalties we offer an advance of one thousand dollars."

The letter concluded with an explanation that the program *A Date with Judy*, which they published a number of years before, brought the original owner approximately a hundred thousand dollars from the amateur rights. Such earnings were quite exceptional and even then only arrived at over a period of many years. To date, there has been nothing to verify whether or not Mr. Hershkowitz approved of the idea, but since no such play was published, and no reports in local newspapers or national magazines reported of such a play, it is believed the proposal was rejected.

New York Produces More Than Broadway

Despite the abundance of police shows on television in the early 1960s, no two of them depicted the law enforcement officer in the same way. On *The New Breed*, the policemen had cultured college graduates who were trained in the use of sophisticated electronic gadgetry to track down criminals. On *87th Precinct*, the hard-bitten cops did not go in for such niceties, and instead used gunfire and a few grenades to hunt down criminals. The police depicted in *Naked City* had a human appeal - after chasing down their man for an hour, they might shed a tear over him because the unfortunate murderer never had a break.

These last two television programs were filmed in New York and premiered about the same time as *Car 54*, and had their equal share of criticism. The Sept. 27, 1961 issue of the *Boston Record* commented: "*Car 54, Where Are You?* makes the police look a little silly. But this show is taken for what it is - a farce. However, the *Precinct 87* show, which premiered Monday night, was supposed to be a serious version of *Car 54*. Unfortunately, it turned out to be nearly as funny."

It was a cliché-ridden effort that was even further hampered by corny dialogue."

Fred Danzig of the *Berwick Enterprise* remarked in his Sept. 26, 1961 column of "TV in Review" that *87th Precinct*, the new detective series that reached NBC-TV Monday night, "really scrambled some of my notions. Remember when I said *Cain's Hundred* was the worst of the new shows thus far this season? Forget it. Remember when I said *Naked City* was a good cops-and-robbers show, but not great? Forget it. *87th Precinct* makes them both look like Emmy winners."*

"The average TV crime show is no aid to police in commanding greater respect for law and order," quoted Deputy Police Commissioner Walter Arm of New York's finest, who didn't think *Car 54* was funny at all. "In these days of professionalism, it gives a poor and inaccurate picture of a New York policeman in the 1960s. Every man today must be a high school graduate. There are more than 1,200 New York City cops presently attending college. I can tell you for a fact that police chiefs around the country are saddened to see a couple of buffoons masquerading as policemen."

Patrolman John Pilewski of Flushing, N.Y., told columnist Bob Lardine of the *Sunday News*, "To me, it's just like the *Sgt. Bilko* show. The guys in it are lovable characters. They're not cops. Let's face it." Patrolman Will Kubon of Brooklyn told the same columnist, "I think it's a very funny situation comedy. It does to the police department what Sgt. Bilko did to the Army. I don't feel the least bit sensitive while watching it. I enjoy the show very much."

Was Car 54 Immoral?

"I want to show that cops are human beings," Nat Hiken explained. "They're regular guys, underpaid for the jobs they do, who have human failings and problems. But there is fun in their lives - as there is in anybody's life - and that's what I want to show more than any-

---

* The base of operations for *Naked City* was in lower Manhattan.

thing else." The filming of the episodes was done in an atmosphere resembling Sunday School class when compared to the boisterous on-camera sessions of the *Bilko* series. "With the Bilko show," said Hiken, "we used three cameras at once to get different angles of entire scenes that we later put together in the cutting room. With Phil Silvers' wild enthusiasm leading everybody along, it worked out well. With *Car 54*, though, we're using only one camera at a time in trying to make the show look as polished and professional as anything turned out in Hollywood. We're shooting only snatches of dialogue and action instead of whole scenes at once."

When the program was over and the laughs forgotten, some viewers began to question the wisdom of the whole thing. Was it "in the public interest" to portray law enforcement officials as clowns? What would be the ultimate effect of such portrayal?

Two days previous, an unnamed columnist for *The Courier*, a newspaper published from Candor, New York, debated:

"We're not being stuffy - we enjoy satire and take a fling at it ourselves now and then - but we feel that there is nothing to be gained by this type of program - nothing good, that is. To begin with, our country is in a touch-and-go situation regarding law enforcement. In many American cities, policemen have been mobbed when they tried to arrest an offender. Almost daily we read of law officers being killed in the routine performance of duty. Respect for law enforcement officials is at an all-time low, according to J. Edgar Hoover . . . Any program that tears down respect for policemen, even if it is intended to be funny, strikes us as being an open invitation to further disrespect for the law. If I were a policeman, I think that driving a prowl car and facing up to derisive taunts every time I showed up in public would be the last straw. Long hours, low pay, ever-present possibility of violence I could live with. But if every time I appeared in public, someone would shout derisively, 'Car 54, where are you?' and followed it with raucous laughter, I'd quit. Why add any more to the burden our policemen carry?"

Columnists were not the only ones to voice their negative opinions. The Sept. 23, 1961 issue of the *Utica New York Observer-Dispatch* featured a brief in "Badge Beat" column. According to Charles M. McCarthy: "The Police Conference of the State of New York Inc. has gone on record in opposition to a television program entitled *Car 54, Where Are You?* Conference officials said that letters of protest have been sent to the network and producers of the show, charging that the program was degrading to the police profession."

The New York Times Editorial

Nat Hiken received a stroke of good fortune when the *New York Times* featured an editorial praising the quality of the *Car 54* television series. The newspaper published thousands of articles, briefs, announcements and columns every year, but extremely few television programs were able to warrant an editorial over the past few decades. In the Thursday, Oct. 26, 1961 issue, the following went public:

> In recent months the lot of this city's policemen has indeed been an unhappy one. Beer-bottle barrages, near-riots, unsettled issues of pay and moonlighting, alleged interference in local politics have added to their burdens. Despite the earnest proposals made in their behalf, none seems more likely to give them air and comfort than a new television comedy series titled *Car 54, Where Are You?* which deals with two ingenious, warm-hearted gentlemen named Toody and Muldoon, who happen to earn their livings as members of the New York Police Department. The basic premise of its humor is that policemen are

people - a statement almost without precedent in American literature, yet one that conceivably could revolutionize our approach to policemen and theirs to life in general.

Our fiction has always given us lawmen who were either superhuman or subhuman. Our detective fiction is filled with allusions to "dumb cops" who are left twiddling ten thumbs while private investigators solve their murders for them. Cartoons and comic strips are stocked with fruit-filching policemen, incompetents who cannot even keep youngsters from sneaking under the ballpark fence. The proletarian novels of the Thirties gave us the hardened sadist who was the servant of private, not public, interests. Early movies gave us the Keystone Cops, delightful clowns, but crude caricatures incapable of serious accomplishment. More recently we have been given the monumentally efficient and perpetually heroic policeman.

We have been given, in short, every kind of policeman except the kind we pay to love, honor, identify with and obey. The standard images rarely convey the impression that police work is occasionally dangerous, usually dull, always underappreciated. Our men in blue long ago must have lost hope of acquiring understanding. They might well paraphrase Shylock saying, "Hath not a policeman eyes? Hath not a policeman hands, organs, dimensions, senses, affections, passions?" Those of us who would immediately concede that policemen do indeed share these attributes with the rest of mankind must also be prepared to answer affirmatively Shylock's question, "If you tickle us do we not laugh?" We are accustomed to laughing *at* policemen, not *with* them. Surely it cannot be that every occupational group on earth except policemen encounters humor in their daily lives.

Our respect for policemen is increased, rather than diminished, by a portrait that reveals a grin in place of the customary scowl. The searchlight of humor can illuminate without binding. For the average citizen, personal contact with the police is quite limited. Very few of us have ever been gangland chiefs, gold smugglers or international jewel thieves. The first policeman most of us encountered was the man who guarded the street crossing outside the elementary school, a pleasant symbol of our entry into a grown-up world. We who have little to fear from the police have nothing to fear from seeing them as part of the human comedy. As for the juvenile and adult delinquents who have demonstrated their disdain for the law, there is even less to be lost. Conceivably a humanized portrayal of policemen can soften their hostility.

It is significant that public respect for New York's Finest reached new heights a year ago, when the presence of Khrushchev, Kadar and other Iron Curtain representatives necessitated long hours and more tedious duty. But it was not deeds of epic heroism that inspired this change. It was sympathy for men who had been stuck with a dreary job. Respect for human beings comes more easily than respect for automatons. The warm humor generated by the heroes of television's mythical Bronx precinct can have the same effect, for they make the force seem like a happy place. The program might well be the soft answer that turns away the wrath of the bottle-wielding rioters and rebalances the skewed public image of the New York police.

Joe Wolhandler of public relations of the Eastern Division of the Audience Building Counselors, sent the editorial to Nat Hiken, with the following message: "It is unprecedented for the *New York Times* to discuss a television comedy series on its editorial page, and we thought you would like to see this unusual praise of *Car 54, Where Are You?*"

Nat Hiken, upon reading the editorial, sent copies of it to every police chief within New Jersey, New York, and the surrounding states. The replies to Hiken were all praises, and revealed just how many members of law enforcement felt strongly for the program. As Hiken explained in his letter that accompanied the copy of the editorial, "We try to present a warm, entertaining comedy that shows policemen as people -- their jobs, family life and personal interests. Although our stories are imaginary, we try to make every effort to portray the police procedures accurately. We are lucky to have as our Technical Advisor, Detective (Retired) Harold Reidman, a veteran of many years in the N.Y. Police Department."

Joseph P. Darcy, Chief of Police for the City of Fitchburg, Mass., wrote to Nat Hiken on Jan. 4, 1962, thanking him for the program. "This program is a favorite of mine and my family," he wrote, "and each Sunday night we turn from Ed Sullivan's program to *Car 54*, and get a great deal of enjoyment from viewing it. The *New York Times* editorial will benefit all police departments, and cause many people to alter their opinions about the members of these organizations, resulting, I hope, in better public relations."

Charles F. Zanzalari, acting Chief of Police for the Department of Public Safety, City of Perth Amboy, New Jersey, wrote to Hiken on Dec. 29, 1961. "From the many comments by the members of our department and citizens of our community, the consensus of opinion is that your program is a warm, delightful, entertaining comedy that shows the brighter side of our chosen law enforcement profession and tends to create better public relations."

Early Problems with "Car 54"

Based on the Nielsen early December report, *Car 54* had moved down to a 24.1 rating, number 20 on the top 20 list of highest-rated television programs. While the series dropped from number 3 to number 20 in two months, it was still on the top 20 list, making *Car 54* a proud forefront for NBC in the three-network competitive rating race . . . and Ed Sullivan was still losing out in the ratings when competing against *Car 54*. "We're the first show to knock Sullivan off in 14 years," Fred Gwynne told a reporter for the *Houston Post*.

By November, 1961, the ratings for *Car 54* started to slip. Competition was strong. On Dec. 3, 1961, Hal Wickliffe wrote to Nat Hiken. "For curiosity sake," he wrote, "I've been probing people who have stopped watching *Car 54* to find the reason why. In the main, their answers reveal that there simply is not enough police work in the show as they were led to believe."

"Let's not kid ourselves," Wickliffe continued. "The majority of the tax-paying public maintains definite illusions about policemen, expecting them to be dedicated and courageous men - and you can't tell me that they don't honestly resent having these illusions shattered. With the Bilko series, it was another story and you were operating on a different premise. There you had a wider latitude as people are aware that soldiers goof off, gamble, chase women and horse around. If you are continually going to write about Toody and Muldoon's home life, their plans to leave the police or using the force to their own selfish advantage, it could easily rub the public the wrong way. You must remember that the average, law-abiding citizen looks upon a policeman as a public servant and if you stray too far from his area of responsibility on the series, there's bound to be more and more objections. Personally, it never struck me as wise at trying to underestimate the intelligence of viewers, for fear of it backfiring right in my face."

Other problems raised issues with production. For the holiday offering, "Christmas at the 53rd," director Al De Caprio attempted to film the entire episode in two days - making it the shortest film shoot for the series. On the morning of Nov. 30, 1961, at the Biograph Studios, preparations to shoot a scene for that episode required nine extras consisting of men, women and children. As Arthur

A. Hershkowitz, Vice President of Eupolis Productions explained in a letter drafted to the Screen Actors' Guild, "[I]t was discovered that, in order to obtain the proper artistic values in the shot, additional extras would be required to serve as background." It was determined that seven additional adults would suffice. The entire building was canvassed and four members of the Screen Actors' Guild were found who were available to be added. Three more were needed. Byrnie Styles, a talent agent, made a number of frantic calls to Screen Actors Guild members whom he knew resided in the Bronx; he hoped they could get to the studio quickly enough so the production would not be held up. Not one was available.

As explained by Hershkowitz in the same letter: "In desperation, three mothers were recruited to serve as background. They were present in the studio due to the fact that their children, who are members of Screen Actors Guild, were being utilized in the show."

Through channels unknown and unexplained, the Screen Actors Guild in New York learned of the violation, and slapped Eupolis Productions with a fine of $645. Hershkowitz drafted a letter to Paul Giles of SAG, hoping to levy the fine to a total of $72.78, citing a restriction of $24.26 per mother, rather than the damages assessed in the Guild's notice dated Dec. 4, 1961: "We humbly submit that putting these mothers, who are not members of your organization, into the scene was a violation, born however out of desperation. They were hired, moreover, not as players but as atmosphere."

The Police Are After "Car 54"!

According to the Feb. 2, 1962 issue of *The Washington Post*, the executive director of the National Police Hall of Fame, Frank J. Schira, had been spending his winter months sending his protest to 800 Chiefs of Police, 1,000 newspapers, members of Congress, police associations, sponsors of the program and the F.C.C. Schira had what columnist Lawrence Laurent referred to as "a splendid display of spleen" in an editorial that was then being circulated. Schira protested:

"If we, as policemen, acted in any way as the men in *Car 54* do, we would be fired immediately or committed to an institution. Yet, both young and adult minds are subjected to the weekly antics of these well-paid actors (who never have had to face the dangers of really doing patrol). It is degrading to us. The kids who chant 'Car 54, Where Are You?' as the patrol car passes by are not amusing. It leads to disrespect of law enforcement officers. Respect for the badge is being laughed out of existence."

One critic believed that the badge wasn't likely to be "laughed out of existence" because television paid too much homage to policemen. The 1961-62 television season offered 31 programs in which a law enforcement officer is the hero. (This statistic included reruns of syndicated programs such as *Highway Patrol*.) The viewing schedule showed only one program in which a sheriff is a villain, and that was *Robin Hood*, and the sheriff was neither contemporary nor American.

Ironically, the day before *The Washington Post* reported this news, a dispatch from the United Press International's Fred Danzig reported that actors Joe E. Ross and Fred Gwynne "have become honorary members of the New York Police Department's Honor Legion, indicating acceptance of their series by New York's finest."

If anyone questioned the popularity of the *Car 54* series during the two years the program aired over the NBC prime-time slot, the March 12, 1962 issue of the *New York Post* put that question to rest. The paper printed a news brief from the Associated Press about two policemen of Valley Park, Mo., who found themselves on foot investigating the theft of the town's one and only police car. The cruiser was stolen while the officers were in a café drinking coffee. The auto was found after three hours of searching, parked in weeds about half a block from where it had been stolen. The theft was probably the work of pranksters. *The New York Post* headlined the brief, "Car 54, Where Are You?"

The Automobiles

The "Car 54" Toody and Muldoon drove was painted dark red and white to destroy any resemblance to New York's official dark green and white squad cars. "Cab drivers are always passing by and pointing out the car to their passengers. They tell them it's a Police Department experiment in color schemes," recalled Joe E. Ross. "The people in the Bronx are the last of the rugged individualists. They're interested in what we're doing, but they are now over-awed."

The use of automobiles in each episode, naturally, had to be cleared with the manufacturer for trademark legalities. After a number of phone calls and letters exchanged between Arthur Hershkowitz, the vice president of Eupolis Productions, and Byron Avery, Manager of the West Coast promotion office of Chrysler Corporation during the month of May, the Chrysler Corporation drew up a contract (dated June 5, 1961) in agreement with Eupolis Productions, Inc. The contract stated quite clearly that Chrysler would furnish, for approximately one year from the date of delivery, four automobiles for the use of the series. In return, Chrysler received substantial promotion during the closing credits.

Hershkowitz also agreed to periodically furnish the automotive corporation with publicity stills showing Chrysler's cars in use so the corporation could use them for promotional purposes.

Eupolis Productions registered the cars in their name, paying for the costs, and agreed to hold Chrysler harmless from any Federal, State or local excise, sales or use of other taxes which could be levied as a result of the transfer or use of the vehicles. Chrysler was also held harmless for any damage to property or injury to people (including death), arising out of the possession or use of the vehicles. Eupolis also provided, at their expense, insurance coverage. A policy was taken for $50,000/$250,000 bodily injury, $100,000 property damage, and $50 deductible collision insurance. A copy of that insurance policy was forwarded to Chrysler so the corporation could feel assured that they were held free of any liability as a result of the television production.

On June 29, 1961, Arthur Hershkowitz signed the contract and during the first week of July, the following four automobiles were delivered to Eupolis Productions:

1. 1961 Plymouth Belvedere, 4-door sedan   Serial # 3211-180010

2. 1961 Plymouth Belvedere, 4-door sedan   Serial # 3211-177546

3. 1961 Dodge Dart, 4-door sedan   Serial # 5112-176283

4. 1961 Plymouth, 4-door sedan*   Serial # 3711-180088

After filming of the first season episodes was completed, the vehicles were returned to Chrysler at a certain dealership in New York City. Since the television program was, by January 1962, renewed for a second season, an amendment for the purpose of deleting the four 1961 Chrysler Corporation vehicles covered in the Letter of Agreement dated June 5, 1961, was drawn up. The amendment, dated Jan. 25, 1962, was approved and accepted by Eupolis Productions, with the same terms as above, with the exception of the vehicles - seven 1962 vehicles were now replacing the four 1961 vehicles. The new replacements were as follows:

1. 1962 Plymouth Belvedere, 4-door sedan   Serial # 3226-145398

2. 1962 Plymouth Belvedere, 4-door sedan   Serial # 3226-145410

3. 1962 Plymouth Fury, 2-door hardtop   Serial # 3326-155476

4. 1962 Plymouth Fury, 4-door station wagon
Serial # 3726-154178

5. 1962 Plymouth Fury, 4-door station wagon
Serial # 3726-155980

---

* This was a 9-passenger Sport Suburban used not for on-camera filming, but for the transportation of cast and crew to various locations in New York.

6. 1962 Dart 330, 4-door sedan   Serial # 5226-156056

7. 1962 Chrysler New Yorker, 4-door station wagon
                                                   Serial # 8723-152507

If production for the first season was made possible with four vehicles, then it begs the question: "Why three additional vehicles?"
The answer was simple. Nat Hiken wanted the 1962 Chrysler New
Yorker (No. 7 above) for personal use as a fringe benefit for the hard
work that went into the day-to-day production of *Car 54*. The automobile was under Eupolis Productions' insurance policy, and had to
be returned within a year of the vehicle's initial delivery.

This fringe benefit was carried over for both Joe E. Ross (No. 3)
and Fred Gwynne (No. 5), so the actors could commute to work.
Car number 6 was issued to Duke Farley, who played Patrolman
Reilly on the series - also a fringe benefit.

The first two vehicles (Nos. 1 and 2), the red and white Plymouth
Belvederes, were used as background props for all garage scenes,
and whenever it was called upon for location shots. These are the
very automobiles used as police cars in all of the requisite scenes
filmed for the second season episodes. Car number 4 substituted the
Sport Suburban used during the first season, so equipment, cast and
crew could be transported to locations in New York.

A similar agreement between Eupolis Productions and General
Motors granted the permission (and furnishings) of a 1962 Chev-
rolet Sedan to be used as a prowl car for a number of episodes.
This fact was disclosed to the West Coast Promotion Manager of
Chrysler, who had no objection to the use of a competitor's product
in the episodes. General Motors also supplied a 1962 Greenbriar
Convar for J.C. Delaney, set decorator for the series, to be used for
productions (though this car never appeared on screen in any of the
60 episodes produced).

In July of 1962, the automobiles were revised again. The two police cars remained on the premises, and Nat Hiken and Duke Farley kept the vehicle used as a fringe benefit. All other cars were turned over to a Plymouth Corporation representative. Joe E. Ross and Fred Gwynne had to relinquish their vehicles, but those were replaced with the following convertibles for the summer months:

Plymouth Fury - white convertible

Serial # 3326-216794 (Joe E. Ross)

Plymouth Fury - red convertible

Serial # 3326-216940 (Fred Gwynne)

A Plymouth Fury, 4-door station wagon was added to the production, listed among production paperwork as "pick-up car" used to transport cast, crew and equipment to locations in New York City. A Valiant V-200, 4-door station wagon was added to the production, listed among production paperwork as "props car," also used for transportation of cast, crew and equipment for location shooting. For the first time since the series began production, a third police car was made available (instead of the usual two): a Dart 300, glade green 4-door sedan. Serial numbers for these additional vehicles are listed below:

Plymouth Fury, 4-door station wagon   (Pick-Up Car)
Serial # 3726-215639

Valiant V-200, 4-door station wagon   (Props Car)
Serial # 1726-199103

Dart 300, 4-door sedan   (Police Car)
Serial # 4226-159803

The latest 1963 models from Plymouth were offered to the production crew and delivered on Dec. 27, 1962. According to an amendment dated Jan. 9, 1963, (signed on Jan. 17, 1963, by Howard Epstein, president of Eupolis Productions), the following were the last of the vehicles used for filming the final episodes of the series:

1. Plymouth, 4-door sedan   (red & beige)   Serial # 3236-111732

2. Plymouth, 4-door sedan   (red & white)   Serial # 3236-103276

3. Plymouth convertible   (light blue)   Serial # 3336-129745

4. Plymouth station wagon   (light blue)   Serial # 3736-130434

5. Plymouth station wagon   (medium blue) Serial # 3736-132884

6. Dodge, 4-door sedan   (vermillion)   Serial # 4132-126551

7. Dodge, 4-door sedan   (turquoise)   Serial # 4132-127997

8. Dodge station wagon   (medium blue) Serial # 4536-129416

9. Chrysler station wagon   (oyster white)   Serial # 8733-156329

Cars numbered one, two and seven were police cars used for on-screen filming. The convertible was a fringe benefit for actor Joe E. Ross. Car number five was a fringe benefit for Fred Gwynne. Car number nine was a fringe benefit for Nat Hiken, replacing the 1962 New Yorker he had "borrowed" for the past year. Car number four was labeled as the "pick-up car" and number eight was labeled as the "props car." Car number six was featured on the final few episodes of the second season, as well as the detective's car.

The License Plate Numbers

For legal purposes, license plate numbers of real vehicles caught on camera were not allowed to be captured on screen, for fear of liability from a non-member of the production. However, Eupolis Productions did arrange with the state of New York to acquire a number of license plates that were authentic, and could be featured on camera. These plates were often reused on multiple cars lent to the production from Plymouth.

The license plate numbers for the two detective cars featured on the series were 3N 1219 and 1C 5907. As for the numerous police cars (1961, 1962 and 1963 models) that appeared on screen for the series, the following license plates were used: 1N 3514, 1C 5908, 4N 9847, 6N 8572, and 1C 5905. (The license plate number 1C 5905 was featured on a Plymouth Belvedere and a Dodge 4-door Sedan, both of which were used as a police car in separate episodes!)

The Procter & Gamble "Car 54" Contest

In 1962, Procter & Gamble, the program's sponsor, offered an unusual contest which would award 54 contestants $1,000 each, and one lucky winner a grand prize of $10,000. Contestants were asked to imagine that Toody and Muldoon wanted to drive around the country and visit each of the 33 locations represented by dots on the contest's six-by-eight-inch map. The object was to find the shortest route.

Merchandising

About the time the second season of *Car 54, Where Are You?* began airing over the NBC-TV network, eight different items were being officially merchandised and targeted to young children. Three comic books were published by Dell, coloring books, punch-out books, activity books, marionettes and puppets, a *Car 54* box game, miniature molded plastic figures of Toody and Muldoon, and a leather holster set. To give an idea of the money both NBC and Eupolis Productions were making in royalties for the merchandise, the following statement was issued on merchandising income from *Car 54, Where Are You?* from inception through Dec. 31, 1961.

Gross Income

Allison Industries - Advance Royalty $2,000.00

Dell Publishing - Advance Royalty $1,000.00

Standard Toykraft Products $1,000.00

Total Gross Income $4,500.00

Under contract, NBC's merchandising retained 40 percent of the gross profits. Eupolis received $2,700 total, which was then divided among the various actors and administrators who were contractually entitled to a percentage of profits.

NBC had a marketing department that handled such approvals, and made sure that they received an advance royalty up front, followed by five per cent of the net profits for future royalties. This percentage varied more or less with certain merchandise, but NBC did insist with all manufacturers that a $1,000 minimum royalty payment be made at the time agreements and contracts were signed. (In case sales were lackluster, NBC's initial "minimum royalty payment" compensated for the time and trouble spent drawing up the contracts and paperwork.) After deducting their share of the royalties, NBC forwarded a financial statement and 60 percent to Eupolis Productions. It was Eupolis' responsibility to divide the royalties to actors Fred Gwynne and Joe E. Ross, whose likenesses and images were portrayed on much of the packaging. The likenesses of the two leads were used only in connection with the articles licensed, and prior approval of NBC and Eupolis Productions, Inc. was needed before going to the assembly line.

Even after the *Car 54* series ceased airing, the actors, producers and network were still receiving royalty checks on merchandise. Case in point: While Fred Gwynne was in Universal City, California, working on *The Munsters*, he received a check for $54.15 for his share of *Car 54* merchandising sold during the third quarter of 1964, ending Sept. 30, 1964.

This is not a bad figure when you consider that during the fourth quarter of 1962 (ending Dec. 31) Eupolis Productions earned $1,555.52 in net profits from merchandising. A breakdown:

Gross Income

A.A. Records - Advance $1,000.00

Allison Industries - Royalties $386.40

Dell Publishing - Advance 1,000.00

      Royalties . . . . $206.14 . . . . $1,206.14

Total Gross Income $2,592.54

Under contract, NBC's merchandising retained 40 percent of the gross profits. Eupolis received $1,555.52 total, which was then divided up under stipulation of contracts, to the various actors and administrators who were entitled to a percentage of profits.

One bit of merchandise that never came to light was a battery-operated, remote-controlled *Car 54*, intended to retail at approximately $2.98. James P. Forbes of Louis Marx & Company, Inc., manufacturers of mechanical toys, steel and plastic toys and trains, proposed the idea to executives at NBC in the fall of 1962. Eupolis and NBC agreed that such a toy would help promote the television series, and on Nov. 30, 1962, a contract was drawn up. Louis Marx, however, did not sign the contract, stating in a letter dated December 12: "Since we are working on this Remote Control Car in Hong Kong (and it usually takes about 12-18 months to finalize anything when you are working on an overseas basis), we do not want to tie you up - or bind you, in any way, in the interim."

On Nov. 15, 1961, a contract was drawn up with Standard Toykraft Products, Inc. in Brooklyn, New York, for the manufacturing and sale of colored pencil sets to sell at a suggested retail price ranging from 29 cents to $7.50, depending on the various sets sold. This toy was apparently never manufactured.

Among the toys manufactured and stocked on department store shelves was a leather holster set. Manufactured by Milner Leather Products Ltd. (100 Richmond Street East, Toronto 1, Ontario, Canada), the police-style holster wrapped around the waist of young children, so they could pretend to be play "cops and robbers," Muldoon and Toody style. This product was licensed only to the Dominion of Canada, and contracts were drawn up and signed on Dec. 8, 1961. Months after the leather holster sets hit the stores (in early August of 1962), the NBC Merchandising Department terminated negotiations with Milner Leather Products. The Canadian company had to change its plans because of the limitations imposed by the Canadian government on the flow of cash out of the country.

On Sept. 15, 1962, A.A. Records, Inc. signed an agreement with NBC to produce phonograph records identified with the television program. The term of the agreement was for a period of three years from the date of release (no later than Feb. 1, 1963). Like the comic books and other products merchandised using the *Car 54* television series, NBC furnished the record company with photographs and materials for A.A. Records to use for promotional advertisements, album covers, and exploitation of the records. NBC received the $1,000 minimum royalty payment, and three percent of the net profits from the record sales.

The Comic Books

On May 23, 1961, an agreement was drawn up and signed between Dell Publishing Company, Inc. (located at 750 Third Avenue, New York, N.Y.) and the National Broadcasting Company for the publishers to produce and sell comic books using the names and characters from *Car 54, Where Are You?* The agreement granted Dell a one-year term beginning Sept. 1, 1961. Dell paid NBC $1,000 as a minimum royalties guarantee on the signing of the agreement, and a 3/8 cent on each copy printed. On foreign editions by parties other than Dell (should Dell option to license the comic in other countries to other

comic printers), 50 percent of the sum received by Dell after the de-
duction of commissions, taxes in foreign countries, cost of reproduction material, and other "out-of-pocket" costs were applicable.

Dell furnished NBC with a certified statement of copies printed
when paying the royalties to NBC every six months beginning October 1. Dell was solely responsible for the content of the comic books,
and had the option to borrow plot devices from previously broadcast
episodes. NBC sent Dell representative television scripts, and photographs and Kodachromes of the actors and actresses, but after looking
over the material, Dell chose to feature original stories in the comics.

Dell had the option to extend the agreement for an additional
year on the same terms, if they chose to notify NBC of their intention
to extend, and pay another $1,000 fee by May 1, 1962. This option
was never exercised, suggesting that after the three issues were published, sales figures were not up to Dell's expectations, and were not
financially worth renewing another year.

On Oct. 19, 1961, Howard Epstein of Eupolis Productions wrote
to Norman Lunenfeld of the NBC Merchandise & Sales Division, regarding his opinions on the preliminary material for comic book
distribution. "Overall, I think the material is generally good and I
hope that it reaps us royalties, as well as giving us promotion for our
show," Epstein wrote. However, Epstein had two concerns. The first
was his opinion that many of the frames did not have faithful repro-
ductions of the facial qualities of Muldoon and Toody. "Some of
the frames were fine, so we know it can be done," he explained. The
second was of some merit: "We feel it is bad policy to condone the
gang code that classifies one who turns over a criminal to the police
as a 'stool pigeon.' This is what is being done in the story line when
the gang refuses the boy membership because they believe that he
captured the jewel thief and turned him over to the police."

"These comic books are geared for children and we could be
censured for treating the 'stool pigeon' doctrine as a correct one;
that the philosophy does exist in teen gangs does not make it right,"

Epstein concluded. "We feel it is difficult enough to do a television show based on comic policemen without leaving ourselves vulnerable to the charge that we are publishing and distributing a wrong moral concept to children."

The issues went to print with very little (if any) changes from the input of Howard Epstein or NBC. The retail price (newsstand price) was twelve cents for each of the issues.

No. 1, March-May 1962
Dell Publishing Co., Inc.
Copyright 1961, Eupolis Productions, Inc.
Title: "Outside the Ritz Hotel" (32 pages)
Plot: Gunther gets the Medal of Honor when he helps recover valuable diamonds stolen from a maharaja, and helps his nephew win a ball game at the same time.

No. 2, June-Aug, 1962
Dell Publishing Co., Inc.
Copyright 1962, Eupolis Productions, Inc.
Title: "Indian Givers" (32 pages)
Plot: Gunther and Toody raid an illegal gambling establishment, proving their worth as police officers.

No. 3, October 1962
Dell Publishing Co., Inc.
Copyright 1962, Eupolis Productions, Inc.
Title: "The Vanishing Furniture" (33 pages)
Plot: Gunther and Toody arrest cowboys and Indians, who then make a mess of the station before the captain wants them back out on the streets.

Was There Going to Be A "Car 54" Spin-Off?

Very little information has been uncovered on the proposed *Car 54* spin-off (featuring the character of Patrolman Wallace, as played by series regular Fred O'Neal). The only tangible evidence of this concept is the following letter to Nat Hiken from George Norford of the National Broadcasting Company. It is dated May 4, 1962:

Dear Nat:

It is heartening to have your interest and support in developing a "Car 54 . . ." program that will feature Wallace and later serve as a pilot for the contemplated series involving his family.

Basic to the whole effort is your understandable concern that the pilot script do justice to the high humor and hilarity that are hallmarks of your series, while at the same time show enough of the Wallace family in their own environment to excite interest in the possibilities of a series involving them.

You know broadly my contemplated approach to the material, having read the script I have developed and the outlines suggested for future shows in the projected series. With your expert knowledge of what will sell in the TV market, you can determine what must be done to give this first script the charge it must have to make the necessary impact and stir the necessary interest.

With this advice and assistance from you I can whip the script into the shape required for inclusion in your series. At the same time I hope to invest it with enough of the Wallace family flavor to suggest where a series based on their life can lead. How much of the program should be devoted to the Wallace family is, of course, something we shall have to establish.

We share the conviction that television and the national

audience have reached the level where such a "Car 54 . . ." program and such a series, properly executed can rouse a critical and commercial acceptance of great size. At the same time, like you, I am also convinced that the first introduction of this family, in the context of your service, must have the tender, loving care and the expert handling to make sure that this acceptance is attained. Your interest in the project is the best sort of insurance a man can have to guarantee this happy result. It is an interest that I trust will continue far beyond the pilot phase.

I have the happy feeling that television and its audience at home and subsequently abroad, will remember for a long time to come, and with the fondest regard those associated with this pioneering venture.

I am looking forward to our meeting on Monday, May 14, at which time I hope to discuss the foregoing with you as well as our respective interests in this property from the proprietary and financial standpoints and in terms of my services as writer of the pilot.

Sincerely,
George Norford

Memorandum to All Departments

The following are letters written to members of the cast and production during filming. They reveal an insight to the series and the production.

August 7, 1962
Memorandum to All Departments
From: Sal Scoppa
It is the policy of Eupolis Productions, Inc., and will be the policy for the future, to permit visitors on the set. However, in order not

to crowd the set and possibly interfere with shooting, it is requested that anyone desiring visitors on the set should first submit names and dates to Sal Scoppa, so that the [number]of visitors on the set for any given day can be properly controlled. This, we hope, will result in more enjoyment for the visitors and will not make it difficult for the shooting.

November 2, 1962
Memorandum to the Regular Members of the Cast
From: Arthur A. Hershkowitz
Every Monday the production, at its own cost, provides a barber to give haircuts and/or trims to the regular members of our cast. It is imperative that each regular member make arrangements with the barber to have the work done during the hours of 12:30 and 3 p.m. Please co-operate by having your hair cut every Monday.

The Emmy Awards

The Emmy Awards—honoring programs telecast between April 16, 1961 and April 14, 1962—were held at the Hollywood Palladium, the Astor Hotel in New York, and the Sheraton-Park Hotel in Washington, D.C. Broadcast over NBC, the awards ceremony was, as usual, a star-studded affair. To be nominated for the award was indeed an honor, but the night did not look so grand for *Car 54. Car 54, Where Are You?* It lost to *The Bob Newhart Show* for "Outstanding Program Achievement in the Field of Humor." Nat Hiken, Tony Webster and Terry Ryan lost to Carl Reiner (*The Dick Van Dyke Show*) for "Outstanding Writing Achievement in Comedy." But the big moment came when Lucille Ball came out on stage to present the award for "Outstanding Directorial Achievement in Comedy." Nat Hiken won the statuette for his efforts on *Car 54, Where Are You?*, beating out John Rich for *The Dick Van Dyke Show* and Seymour Berns for *The Red Skelton Show*.

On May 26, 1963, the annual Emmy Awards came up again and Nat Hiken only won one nomination for the *Car 54* series. It was for "Outstanding Writing Achievement in Comedy." For the second year in a row, Hiken lost out again to Carl Reiner for *The Dick Van Dyke Show*.

Summer Publicity

In June of 1962, Joe E. Ross and Fred Gwynne shared the spotlight with Gene Krupa's Quartet at Freedomland's Moon Bowl.

On June 3, 1962, the newspaper comic strip "Pottsy," featured a seven-panel strip in which the title character, a patrolman, observes the filming of *Car 54* and races over to the patrol car to meet Muldoon and Toody, asking "All right, you guys, lemme have your operator's license!"

According to tax returns for Eupolis Productions, Inc., the total income generated by the first season's worth of *Car 54* television episodes, (including summer reruns up to Aug. 31, 1962, merchandising fees, personal appearance fees, and space and facilities rental) was $2,070,877.74.

Car 54 Day

On Sept. 16, 1962, Joseph F. Periconi, President of the Borough of the Bronx, issued a proclamation declaring the 16th of Sept., 1962 as "Car 54 Day," and urged the citizens "to share in the enjoyment of the wonderful world returning to us this Sunday evening with Officers Toody and Muldoon and their fellow officers."

According to the proclamation:

> WHEREAS: the role of our Police Officer has often been portrayed from drab routine to incredible dangers with emphasis on the Officer's martinet-like disassociation from the community in which he is assigned; and

WHEREAS: in fact it is those Officers who have identified and involved themselves with the communities they serve who have contributed most to making The Bronx a better place in which to live; and

WHEREAS: Officers Toody and Muldoon and their fellow officers in *Car 54, Where Are You?* have brought into the homes of The Bronx and the rest of the nation a picture of Police Officers with all the warmth and humor we identify with the Police Officer who guided us across our first grade school crossing.

The Second Season

The timing could not have been better - because the premiere of the second season of *Car 54* aired over NBC-TV that evening, with an episode entitled "Hail to the Chief!" Critics, though, remained divided about the show's intrinsic merit.

Columnist Leo Burnett reviewed the season opener in the Wednesday, Sept. 19, 1962 issue of *Variety*: "*Car 54*'s second tour of duty initialed with laughs generously planted, but the so-so story on the opener suggests the same format and general plot liner of last season . . . Scripter Tony Webster seized on a premise pregnant with yucks . . . Some of the gags were obvious, but there were enough snappy lines and some solid performances to serve the session with its needed lift . . ."

For the first season, Nat Hiken wrote virtually all 30 scripts himself, but the pressure of time and his desire to put more effort into direction (for which he had won an Emmy) now forced him to bring in other writers for season two. In addition to producing and directing the first season episodes, he took on almost every job but acting. (In one episode, when Hiken needed a pencil sketch in a hurry for one scene, he made it himself.)

For the second season, Hiken took on Billy Friedberg as chief script-writer to ease the labors that were taking a toll on his health. Friedberg had written several scripts for Phil Silvers' series, and had worked with Hiken on the radio series, *The Magnificent Montague*, so he was familiar with Hiken's writing style.

The stars of the series, Joe E. Ross and Fred Gwynne, were content with filming a second season - especially since the pay was more and Chrysler threw in a temporary automobile for the actors to travel from home to work - a fringe benefit that was a pleasant luxury.

"It's good to be back for the second season," Ross commented. "Last year we started with a twenty-six-week contract. The time slot bugged me - opposite Ed Sullivan on Sunday nights. We did fine, though."

The production crew, actors and producers all received complimentary toothpaste from Procter & Gamble, as a "thank you" from the sponsor, for the hard work they were about to put into the second season. Al Lewis recalled receiving "enough toothpaste to brush my teeth for eight or ten hours."

Hank Garrett, a physical culture enthusiast and night club comedian, portrayed the role of Officer Nicholson on the series. "I'm a headliner now because of *Car 54*. For me the show is paying off in all directions," he remarked for an interview with the *Milwaukee Journal*. "The other day my car was stolen. I found it when the police couldn't. I scouted the neighborhood, quizzed the kids. Just like we'd do on the show."

Fred Gwynne had also been a fixture on the night club circuit for years. While his combined audience number never exceeded 20,000 people, the television series was reaching an estimated 40 million with each broadcast.

The public had clearly identified with the show. When a police squad car in Nyack, N.Y., was stolen from its parking place in front of the police station, the townspeople and police immediately dubbed it "Car 54." In Akron, Ohio, the two detectives who drove a Cruiser No. 54 petitioned their captain to please make the other patrolmen quit calling them "Toody" and "Muldoon," and to order police radio dispatchers to refrain thenceforth from calling, "Car 54, where are you?" Over in Dayton, Ohio, the department dropped the number 54 from its fleet.

Across the Rockies, in Berkeley, California, a police bulletin quoted witnesses who described a man who held up a supermarket as being a double for "Officer Muldoon." A high-ranking New York police official, who insisted that he not be identified, told a reporter for *TV Guide* that he would like to see *Car 54* canceled because it made all policemen appear to be morons. "Being a policeman is a grim and humorless business, not at all funny," he said frankly.

The New York official's reaction was seconded by some police officers across the country, while the fan mail delivered to Nat Hiken made it clear that there were many police officers who saw the lighter side of their occupation. There were sensation-seeking TV columnists who disregarded the series as an unfavorable parody, and their opinions were sometimes carried away as public opinion. "The same thing happened with Bilko [*The Phil Silvers Show*]," recalled Nat Hiken. "The Army was behind the show from the start, and offered us cooperation. Then a New York columnist wrote: 'ARMY BIG BRASS UPSET BY BILKO.' It just wasn't true. We tried to trace the source but couldn't."

Though the Pentagon could easily have been offended by the weekly irreverence for Army brass, they stated officially that they not only enjoyed the series, but regarded it as an invaluable tool for the Army's recruiting program.

One of the few other official blasts against *Car 54* came in San Antonio, Texas, where the Police Officers' Association passed a resolution to the effect that the show "makes us look stupid." According to *Variety*, the show-business weekly, a copy of the resolution was sent to NBC President Robert E. Kintner, asking that the series be discontinued. But the association's house organ, The Badge, said later that the resolution had been "ramrodded" through - to the distress of some San Antonio police.

The captain of the 48th Precinct publicly stated that he and his men found the show amusing, and discussed the comical situations often in their squad room. He also said that the presence of *ersatz* policemen in uniform (the *Car 54* actors) on the streets of his precinct had created no confusion among either his men or the area's residents.

Nat Hiken, however, recalled the morning a Bronx housewife came down the street and in through the front door of the studio, screaming, "Help, police! My husband is beating me!" The *Car 54* people quieted her down, then called legitimate police to her rescue. Others made a similar mistake. An irate man demanded justice because his car had been ticketed unfairly, unaware that the men in uniform were actors. "Of course, we simply took down the 53rd Precinct sign and put the old Biograph Studio sign back up," Hiken said.

Policemen wrote to the cast and the producer explaining how the *Car 54* scripts reflected their own experiences. One detective recalled an episode in which Toody and Muldoon gave rides to precinct residents, delivered groceries and did similar small favors. "I used to do that all the time," explained one officer. "What do you do when you see a guy waiting in the rain for a bus and you know it isn't coming for half an hour? You give him a lift, of course!"

On one evening, Fred Gwynne and his wife were driving away from a Broadway theater when they were approached by "the two most steely-eyed, iron-jawed police officers I'd ever seen." He was certain they would chew him out for some traffic violation. Instead, as they walked by, one winked at the other, exclaiming, "Ooh, ooh!" - one of Officer Toody's catch-phrases on *Car 54*.

"I find some of the local Bronx police saluting me, all in good fun," recalled Paul Reed. "In the Bronx I was taken for a tour of Philadelphia in a prowl car after the [Broadway] show."

Joe E. Ross, driving his own car, attempted to make a left turn in a no-left-turn area. A policeman spotted him, but merely waved him on, with, "You really didn't make the turn, Toody, and besides I'd hate to ticket a fellow policeman." Ross even recalled a moment when he took his girlfriend to the Radio City Music Hall: "There was a long line at the box office. We didn't have to wait, though. A cop who was on duty there spotted me and said, 'Hi, Toody,' and brought me up to the front of the line. Most of the cops I talk to seem to get a kick out of the show. I'm not so sure about the brass in the police department."

Publicity: Fact or Fiction?

A number of trade papers printed articles and columns regarding the *Car 54* program and/or the cast and crew, knowing that additional papers would be sold because of the program's popularity. In return, the television series received additional promotional pieces to attract reader attention - free advertising for the network, sponsor and producer.

Regrettably, however, many of the articles that appeared in print were fictional - created by the network's publicity department. Newspapers and magazines accepted almost any item sent to them from an official source, no matter how off-beat or unrealistic it may appear. Case in point: The Oct. 9, 1962 issue of *The Long Island Press*. This newspaper was released in Jamaica, New York with a circulation of 286,371 (Evenings) and 371,566 (Sunday). The article, penned by columnist Joseph Finnigan, reported the following:

HOLLYWOOD (UPI) — Joe E. Ross, bumbling "Gunther Toody" of *Car 54, Where Are You?*, wandered about 3,000 miles off his Bronx police beat and ended up in "Marshal Matt Dillon's" hoosegow today. Jim (Marshal Dillon) Arness collared Toody as the make-believe New York cop arrived on *Gunsmoke*'s Dodge City set.

"I found him loitering on the streets of Dodge," kidded Arness, looking down at his visitor. "I got a wire from his partner saying this guy ran off the job. Now I've got to extradite him back to New York where he belongs." Toody is a puny, five-feet-ten inches tall compared to Arness' six-feet six. Next to Arness he looks like Khrushchev shaking hands with Sonny Liston.

The only other lawman who has dared show his head around "Dodge City" since Arness took over was that town's real marshal. He was treated royally compared to Toody's arrest. Here was an obvious reason Dillon looked suspiciously on Toody's wanderings. Matt works for CBS while Toody's show is an NBC product. Network television's a very competitive business and Toody is lucky Arness let him out of the clink.

Toody protested his innocence when Arness hauled him into the bucket. "I wanted to ask directions from a fellow officer," explained Toody. "All I do is walk across Dillon's street and he nabs me for jaywalking. If I get caught jaywalking two more times they take away my shoes." Toody's pleadings swayed Dillon who freed the errant easterner. To make sure Toody didn't go back with a bad impression of western sheriffs, Arness took him over to *Gunsmoke*'s Long Branch saloon, ordered series bar owner Kitty to pour and everybody celebrated.

Shaking off Dodge City's dust, Toody left the set, convinced that he's much better off getting lost in New York City. "The police cooperate with us back there," he said, his attitude one of a sophisticated cop looking down at his country cousin lawman.

Naturally, the above reprint is pure hokum, and created merely for publicity purposes for two separate television programs on two separate networks. There were many such articles composed for publicity, and many readers took the printed fiction as the gospel.

The Sept. 23, 1961 issue of the Roanoke, Virginia *Times* featured a column about Patrolman Gunther Toody and Patrolman Francis Muldoon that, while disclosing the fact they were characters on a television program entitled *Car 54* (the column never gave the program's complete title), it was cleverly written to give readers of that paper the impression that Toody and Muldoon were real New York City patrolmen.

Numerous trade papers featured brief columns supposedly written by actors Fred Gwynne and Joe E. Ross. While many fans believe that these columns were really penned by the actors, the reality is that the publicity department created the briefs, and submitted them to various newspapers and magazines with the intent of creating some publicity for the series.

Progress Report

During the brief fall hiatus between filming *Car 54* episodes, Joe E. Ross taped *Art Linkletter's House Party,* which was telecast on October 29, and appeared on *Your First Impressions,* which aired October 4.

On Sunday, October 28, Fred Gwynne and Al Lewis (substituting for Joe E. Ross, who was out of town) were "surprise" guests at a dinner of the Columbians, a national organization of policemen and other civil servants. Governor Rockefeller was the main speaker. The boys had a pre-arranged skit with the Governor, written by Nat Hiken, performed for the amusement of the attendees, despite the Governor's incessant interruptions to say, "You boys are great."

The November 1962 issue of *Allegro* reported continued success resulting from the American Federation of Musicians' drive for the use of live American-made music in television films. For the second season of the series, contract negotiations were completed for *Car 54, Where Are You?,* whereby producers of the show agreed to use live music for musical scoring on the same terms and conditions recently signed with the A.F.M. by Hollywood producers. This contract meant that virtually every telefilm company in both Hollywood and New York had now signed up for the A.F.M. for the use of live music in their productions.

On November 9, Joe E. Ross, Fred Gwynne and other actors on the show became so popular among New York cops that their Legion of Honor organization, staging a benefit, invited the bogus policemen to be honored guests. After receiving word of something important, the host walked off stage, after introducing the actors, leaving them with nothing to do - a real-life situation that was in keeping with the television show. Finally, Horace McMahon, star of television's *Naked City*, who was also a guest, grabbed a microphone and bellowed to the audience, "These guys aren't from my precinct. Do you know where they belong?" The responding roar of laughter from the audience indicated they knew.

On November 18, Hank Garrett, who played the role of Officer Nicholson on *Car 54*, appeared at the Hackensack, New Jersey Police Department's Turkey Shoot.

Sometime during the month of November, Duke Doucette of the production company appeared on *To Tell the Truth* as a "liar" and *Car 54, Where Are You?* received full program credit. Eupolis also arranged for Fred Gwynne to return to the daytime program, *Password*, as the guest of the week, beginning December 31. Gwynne had been a guest for the television program a year before. His appearance was taped during the Christmas break.

How Healthy Are the Actors?

On Oct. 19, 1962, Eupolis Productions arranged for Dr. Joseph Harkavy to administer anti-influenza shots to all the employees of *Car 54, Where Are You?* According to an October 17 memo, addressed to all personnel: "We urgently request that everyone employed at the Biograph Studios submit themselves to the inoculation for his or her own benefit, as well as the continued good health of fellow employees." This medical treatment was paid for by the company, but not everyone on the staff wanted to receive the shot, which was optional.

Everyone in the cast and crew agreed except for the following: Edith Hamlin, Joan D'Incesceo (already had hers), Peter Garafalo (already had his), Bob Snavely, Walter Jones (already had his), Paul Reed (already had his) and Marie Montague.

The Thanksgiving Day Parade

For the televised Macy's Thanksgiving Day Parade in 1962, *Car 54* was one of the many featured highlights, though circumstances almost kept the show from being represented. Eupolis Productions had a firm commitment from Macy's early in the fall and there were no problems until, at the eleventh hour, the store raised the question of the make of the *Car 54*. Macy's was committed to using only Buick vehicles in the parade; Eupolis was committed to using only Chrysler cars. Neither party would concede. The promotion was all but lost until Howard Epstein suggested a compromise: Neither a Chrysler nor a Buick would be used; instead, the stars (Gwynne and Ross) would be seen in a neutral vehicle. "It was important that the public see Ross and Gwynne, not a police car," explained Epstein, "We won everybody's consent to this solution."

On the day of the parade, everything was set to have Ross and Gwynne ride triumphantly in an English taxi (not a Buick). On camera, the boys were to hop out of the taxi and present a ticket to a fire engine bearing clowns, and then find that their own vehicle had gone on without them. An NBC representative was to brief them on the morning of the parade.

Thanksgiving Day in New York was a day of heavy rain and strong winds. Faced with its first bad weather in eight years, the parade was thrown into total chaos. The NBC representative never showed up. Neither did the fire engine. The English taxi set off at the head of the parade, without Ross and Gwynne. A member of Eupolis' staff, assigned to assist Ross and Gwynne with the press and parade officials, quickly arranged for the actors to be brought down to 35th Street (a block before the camera position) by limousine. After seeing that they were given raincoats, overshoes and shelter, arrangements were made for them to *walk* into camera range and do a bit with the plastic raincoats and an umbrella (which was conned out of the hand of an innocent bystander, who spoke only Spanish).

"Joe E. Ross and particularly, Fred Gwynne, were wonderfully helpful in creating the act, on a street corner in the rain, ten minutes before air," recalled Epstein. When it appeared that there would be no Macy's manpower to carry the *Car 54* sign on camera, another member of Eupolis' staff climbed into the sandwich board and led Ross and Gwynne down Broadway. Twenty seconds before air time, the English taxi materialized, but not the fire engine. The boys went ahead with the piece of business that had been worked out. "All reactions to their bit had been excellent," Epstein continued. "Our favorite comment was 'They did a very funny bit, but how could you count on it raining?'"

While the calamity was going on, each newspaper, radio reporter and cameraman covering the Macy's Parade, was contacted on the street by Eupolis' staff and given the full report on what had happened. The NBC announcer was given a special copy. Among the breaks resulting from this was the photograph that appeared in the *New York Post* showing the boys under the umbrella. The Associated Press obtained similar photos.

On December 8, Joe E. Ross and Al Lewis appeared at the opening of a new shopping center in Philadelphia. Before the opening, it was arranged for them to visit Philadelphia's newest precinct station. There they were photographed for the event, and the shopping center took large ads to announce their appearance.

On December 9, Joe E. Ross went to Baltimore to headline the Multiple Sclerosis Telethon on WBAL-TV. On December 18, Al Lewis played Santa Claus at the Union City, New Jersey Christmas Party for blind children.

The Al Lewis Promotional Tour

Utilizing the cast's Christmas vacation, Al Lewis agreed to participate in a three-day publicity tour for *Car 54, Where Are You?* For maximum mileage from this short period, Eupolis Productions chose Boston and Chicago. The trip was the most productive use of space and of on-the-air exposure. Since the tour was close to the "Presidential Itch" episode that would be broadcast weeks after, Lewis wore Toody and Muldoon buttons at all times. Thus, his interviews had to inquire about the buttons. For television interviews, Lewis had to present buttons to his hosts.

On the morning of January 3, Lewis went to Boston. The first activity was a visit to the *Boston Globe*. This resulted in a news-page photograph which was used the next day, and a full feature with art by TV editor Elizabeth Sullivan. While at the *Globe* offices, Lewis and the Eupolis staff learned that the paper's "Visiting Our Neighbors" department had come across an interesting story that the owner of Massachusetts #54 had his plates stolen. They were able to verify the plate owner's claim of having known Fred Gwynne in his Harvard days, so the story was serviced to AP and UPI. The former owner of the license plates found himself the unlucky victim of national press coverage since the story was carried on the radio-TV news broadcasts serviced by the wires, and to all subscribing papers in the Northeast.

Over lunch, Lewis was interviewed by the city's other TV editors, who were given exclusive art and an individual angle for his story. In attendance were Arthur Fetridge (*Herald*), Tony LaCamera (*American*), Eleanor Roberts (*Traveler*), Percy Shain (*Globe*), Don Mannering (*Christian Science Monitor*) and Guy Livingstone (*Quincy Patriot-Ledger*).

Lewis was also scheduled to appear on WBZ-TV, in a special segment for the station's popular children's program, *Clubhouse*. That 15-minute segment, devoted entirely to the *Car 54* show, aired on January 4.

In Chicago, Lewis appeared on three television shows, two radio shows, and three press interviews, and participated in the production of promos. Upon arrival in Chicago, Lewis went directly to WMAQ, where he did a 20-minute interview on *The Jack Eigen Show*. On January 4, his schedule was as follows:

10:00 A.M.	*Chicago Tribune* - photo session in the Color Studio, and interview with Marion Purcelli.
11:45 A.M.	WNBQ - Lewis (in uniform) was the guest of the day on *The Dorsey Connors Show*.
12:30 P.M.	*Gary Post-Tribune* - telephone interview with Gerrie Atkin.
1:00 P.M.	WNBQ - taping one 10-second and two 20-second promos.
2:00 P.M.	WCFL - interviewed on the *Bob Elson Radio Show*.
3:00 P.M.	Visit to Leo Burnett.
4:00 P.M.	Telephone interview with Irv Kupcinet (Kup).
6:00 P.M.	*Chicago American* - dinner with Bill Irvin, for a cover story.

On January 5, Lewis was taped for the *Kup Show*, aired later that evening on WBKB. Immediately thereafter, he taped *The Jack Eigen Show*, which aired on January 6 on WNBQ TV. His appearance on *The Kup Show* was mentioned in Kup's column, and in the newspaper ads for the show.

The first two months of 1963 were filled with activities designed to reinforce *Car 54*'s image as good citizens and friends of the nation's police. The events were valuable in themselves and as pegs for news. The National Safety Council honored *Car 54* and its stars with a plaque for their "distinguished public service." Photographs were taken of the plaques and the stars in uniform, and released to the press.

In January, Joe E. Ross appeared on *The Tonight Show* to talk about *Car 54*. In that same month, Ross entertained at the installation dinner of the Honor Legion of the New York Police Department.

The following week, Al Lewis and Hank Garrett entertained at the Traffic Squad Benevolent Association dinner. In the weeks that followed, Paul Reed was guest of honor at a dinner for New Jersey newsboys, which was a project of local police groups. Al Lewis was a guest at the New Jersey State Police Headquarters. Along with Paul Reed, Lewis was a guest of the Patrolmen's Benevolent Association in Ewing, New Jersey. Such appearances were covered by the press.

In a major promotion with *The Price is Right*, a contestant on that program won a walk-on role in *Car 54*. The late-January/early-February broadcast was promoted at the time of the winning and when the episode aired. The winner became the peg for national publicity. Ross and Gwynne made a guest appearance on that show as part of NBC's cross-promotion. Their appearance was heavily promoted by the network, both on the show itself and in promotional spots.

The Treasury Department

During the late 1950s and early 1960s, the U.S. Treasury Department expanded their annual Savings Bond campaign by distributing a short promotional film to organizations, schools, employee groups, and civic and church groups. Every year the Department contacted the producers of a television program and proposed a charitable contribution in the form of a film ranging from 16 to 26 minutes in length, using the same actors portraying the characters best associated with the television viewing audience.

These films played just like any ordinary television episode, complete with opening credits and theme song. In the past such shows as *Father Knows Best, Mister Ed, Leave it to Beaver* and *The Life of Riley* were utilized, while *Lassie* and *The Lone Ranger* chose to broadcast their special film as part of the weekly television series.

In November of 1962, the U.S. Treasury department expanded their 1963 drive by contacting Howard Epstein of Eupolis Productions, for the possibility of using the cast and crew of *Car 54, Where Are You?* for a promotional film. Hiken originally pursued the possibility of this in conjunction with Procter & Gamble paying the cost of the filming, an estimated $10,000. Because Procter & Gamble assumed the cost of a similar film only two years before, it was felt that the company should not repeat the contribution.

Epstein convinced the Treasury people to utilize the stars without P&G underwriting the production. The matter was briefly discussed with Nat Hiken in November, but because of his pressing schedule during December, Epstein chose not to pursue the matter until after the first of the year. Regrettably, scheduling became an issue and the film was never produced. Joe E. Ross and Fred Gwynne, however, officially launched the 1963 Freedom Bond Drive in Washington in April, and were honored guests of the Treasury Department. A testimonial luncheon for the stars was given by the Advertising Club of Washington.

The Radio Contest

On Feb. 13, 1963, CBS Radio (KNX, Los Angeles) received permission from Howard Epstein of Eupolis Productions, Inc. to employ the title "Mobile Unit 54, Where Are You?" in connection with a KNX promotional campaign and contest.

The plans for the promotion and contest are as follows: Clues as to where KNX's Mobile Unit No. 54 was located would be broadcast throughout the day, and radio listeners would be instructed to send postcards to the station if they felt they knew where the Mobile Unit was located. Postcards would be drawn at random by station personnel and a telephone call placed to the writer of the card. The first caller who correctly identified the location of Mobile Unit 54 would win a Dodge automobile; others would win consolation prizes. The words "Mobile Unit 54, Where Are You?" was used extensively in the promotion and conduct of the contest. The title was widely circulated and promoted in all forms of media. The contest began Feb. 25, 1963, and Harfield Weedin, program director of CBS Radio arranged for rights clearances so the contest could go through without a hitch - awarding the winner a brand new Dodge.

Conflict Behind the Camera

During the filming of both seasons, Joe E. Ross never took the time to learn the lines written in the scripts. Often improvising whenever the scene called for it, Ross would not stick to the script. Used to burlesque and stand-up comic performances, Ross did not deliver his lines exactly as it read in the scripts. As a result, Ross clashed with Nat Hiken on a number of occasions, and even threatened to walk off the set. Fred Gwynne recalled for a 1990 issue of *Television Quarterly* how Ross had to be "beaten every so often" to be reminded that he could be replaced. During the second season, scripts were written to focus primarily on the characters of Leo Schnauser and his wife, Sylvia, so less dialogue and scenes were written for Ross. At one point, according to Gwynne, Hiken was going to fire Ross, and replace him with Al Lewis. The ex-burlesque actor cried and begged to keep his job. Hiken "relented."

THE CLOSER

In the Aug. 14, 1963 issue of *Variety,* summer reruns of weekly television programs dominated the top 15 shows on the National Nielsens (for the two-week period ending July 14). *Car 54, Where Are You?* received a rating of 16.9, putting the show in the number 14 slot, beating such programs as *Ben Casey* and *Password,* which were formerly on the top of the rating chart. While CBS dominated with 12 of the top 15 shows, only two programs broadcast over NBC had higher ratings than *Car 54 - Bonanza* (24.1) and *Hazel* (17.5). This meant that even during the summer months, *Car 54* was the third-highest-rated program on the NBC network.

According to Fred Gwynne, Nat Hiken was under an enormous strain to write, produce and direct the series, and if the network decided not to renew *Car 54,* Hiken did not pursue a renewal with the network, knowing it would only be asking for more stress.

The Aug. 25, 1963 issue of the *New York Times* reported that Nat Hiken would not be active in the medium the coming season. Hiken publicly commented to reporters: "I'm playing golf. I may move to California. I have been offered good working conditions out there." While NBC moved forward with their plans to replace the time slot with *Grindl,* starring Imogene Coca, Hiken quietly made plans to fly to the West Coast in what was really an attempt to sell the 60 *Car 54* films to a studio that would grant him control over a new television series without the restraints from the East Coast. *

In late September, the trade papers started leaking news about Desilu's negotiations with producer-creator-writer Nat Hiken, in what was possibly a deal that would alter the future of the *Car 54* series. A number of Hollywood studios had contacted Hiken while he was in New York, over the past year, and though he acknowledged that Four Star made an offer, it was Desilu that struck his interest.

Hiken flew to Los Angeles on what he termed as an "exploratory" trip, which blossomed into two prolonged talks with Desilu production chief Jerry Thorpe, involving not only his services for future television productions, but also the company's ownership of the 60 negatives of *Car 54*. Founded by Desi Arnaz and Lucille Ball in 1950, the Los Angeles production company had profited from a number of television series including *I Love Lucy, The Untouchables* and *The Andy Griffith Show*. Their strong point was their ability to profit from reruns, syndication by its sales arm, Desilu Sales. The studio wanted to sign Hiken as a creator of a new series, though the terms of the proposal never went public.

Hiken continued to hold onto the *Car 54* films, retaining their use as reruns, either on a network - or in syndication - until he was certain of his prospects in California. The deal with Desilu collapsed and Hiken made a quick effort to negotiate with NBC, just days after his return to New York.

Earlier in the year, Hiken created a half-hour pilot film, *The Great Montague*, starring Myrna Loy and Dennis King, adapted from his 1950-51 radio program, *The Magnificent Montague*, which starred Monty Woolley. This was not the first time Hiken had attempted to develop the radio program to television. He managed to lure Monty

---

* The situation comedy, *Grindl*, never met NBC's expectations, and was canceled after one season.

Woolley into a contract to reprise his radio role for a television series beginning in the fall of 1956. After this failed, he went and made a second attempt with Sir Cedric Hardwicke and Vivienne Segal, according to the March 23, 1958 issue of *TV Guide*. The second proposal was intended to premiere in September of 1958, but that deal also fell through.

NBC apparently suffered no ill feelings for Hiken attempting to strike a deal with Desilu (though Hiken publicly denied having any conversation with a Desilu rep) - they struck a deal to buy out Hiken's *Car 54, Where Are You?* interest, with Hiken on board to produce a number of pilots for the network. While the network wanted to purchase the *Car 54* series, they would not meet Hiken's terms, and as a result, the *Montague* series never fleshed out beyond the pilot stage. *

The NBC deal fell through; Hiken and the network parted ways. Weeks later, Hiken turned to lawyer and negotiating exec Howard Epstein, of Eupolis Productions, to sell the series outright to Telesynd, a division of Wrather Corp, to be sponsored in local markets by another Wrather division, toymaker A.C. Gilbert, for a possible product tie-in. This too, fell through.

It was believed that one of the reasons for the fold of the Telesynd deal was the financial difficulties encountered in late 1963 by A.C. Gilbert, as reported in the financial press. A Telesynd executive was quizzed by reporters, but he would only say that A.C. Gilbert was interested in *Car 54* as a vehicle. The series was to be sold to local stations with a built-in A.C. Gilbert commercial buy, but Gilbert hauled in on big promotion plans slated for various toys and games.

Wrather subsequently refused to guarantee Gilbert's sponsorship, causing a stalemate with the property of 60 *Car 54* films.

NBC execs read about the conflict, and made Howard Epstein of Eupolis Productions an offer to buy the films outright. George A.

---

* Hiken took the pilot (Hiken's third attempt to bring *The Magnificent Montague* to television in nine years) to CBS. The network viewed the film and declined.

Graham Jr., board chairman of NBC Films and NBC International, and Morris Rittenberg, president of NBC Films, patted themselves on the back for securing the *Car 54* films - this time without any of Nat Hiken's terms to guarantee a number of future television programs under his production. The deal was struck; the contract was dated January 3, 1964.

The series was offered a market-by-market basis for U.S. syndication immediately. In New York City, WABC-TV was the first buyer; the *Car 54* reruns began airing on January 4, 1964. (Episodes were scheduled for a 10:30-11:00 p.m. time slot.) By August of the same year, Rittenberg reported that NBC Films sold more than 7,500 hours of programming during the first six months of 1964, a 15 percent increase over the same period last year. Most in demand were half-hour comedy series. *Car 54, Where Are You?* was (by August) sold in 27 markets, making it the top program sold for syndication.

In early 1964, Procter & Gamble executives were shocked to discover that when *Car 54, Where Are You?* was being run in syndication, their company logo and/or products, which appeared on screen during the closing credits, was missing. (Everyone who has seen the series knows that the credits during the close of each episode, wrapped around a space that remained blank in the corner.) Originally, when the television programs aired, a product of the Procter & Gamble company was displayed on the screen. Since P&G were not the sponsors for the syndicated runs, any references to the company were removed. In mid-April, Mr. Slater of Leo Burnett & Company, representatives of P&G, expressed written disapproval of the syndicated openings and closingstoward the neutral syndicated openings and closings. By April 20, Howard Epstein worked out an agreement with P&G to use the syndicated opening and end titles for a payment of $1,000. An agreement was drawn up between P&G/Leo Burnett and NBC covering rights in perpetuity on the openings and closings.

The American Bankers Association

In 1963, U.S. currency in the form of coins (pennies, nickels, dimes, etc.) began to vanish from circulation at an alarming rate. The U.S. mint blamed the shortage on coin collectors and began a campaign to encourage the general public to put their coins back into circulation. (The real cause of the shortage, according to a number of historians, was the growing popularity of vending machines, parking meters and phone booths that accepted coins.)

On July 20, 1964, Howard Epstein, President of Eupolis Productions, Inc. talked to Robert W. Barron of the American Bankers' Association, located at 90 Park Avenue in New York City. The A.B.A. had intentions of producing a series of radio broadcast announcements to help the United States Treasury focus national attention on the current coin shortage. To catch the attention of radio listeners, the Association wanted to employ the theme, music, characters and general format of the *Car 54* show in 60-, 30-, 20- and 10-second radio "spots." Their intention was to inform the public about the acute coin shortage and enlist their cooperation in alleviating the epidemic.

On July 22, 1964, Howard Epstein mailed a written confirmation to Robert G. Howard, the Director of Public Relations Committee for the A.B.A., granting them permission to use the "spots" for the national circumstances cited above. These were heard across the United States for the duration of the coin shortage.

Reprinted below is the 60-second public service announcement, produced by the U.S. Treasury/American Bankers Association.

SOUND:	(MUSIC: *Car 54* theme followed by . . .)
SOUND:	SIREN AND CAR ENGINE (UNDER)
VOICE:	(FILTER MIKE) Calling all coins! . . . Calling all coins!
SCHNAUSER:	Hey, Gunther, what's this "Calling all coins" stuff?
GUNTHER:	That's about the coin shortage, Schnau-

	ser. Remember Thursday, the candy store couldn't give you change for an ice cream pop?
	That's 'cause there's not enough coins to go around.
SOUND:	SIREN OUT
SCHNAUSER:	Where'd they go?
GUNTHER:	Well, a lot of them are in piggy banks . . . just resting. And some people save coins in paper rolls.
SCHNAUSER:	So what? Saving's good.
GUNTHER:	Sure, Schnauser, but not at home. The country needs coins moving around. That's why the Treasury wants us to ask everybody to exchange their coins at the bank for bills.
SCHNAUSER:	Hey, if there's a shortage, coins'll be worth more. I'm gonna save them!
GUNTHER:	Don't be stupid, Schnauser — they won't be worth more. And remember, we need our coins circulating till the government has time to make enough to go around so . . . (EXCITEDLY) Hey, pull over to that bank!
SCHNAUSER:	Trouble?
GUNTHER:	Naw, I want to exchange this roll of quarters . . .
VOICE:	(ON FILTER) Calling all coins! . . . Exchange them at your local bank . . . Please!
ANNOUNCER:	This was an announcement of the American Bankers' Association and the United States Treasury.

A Bit of Irony . . .

In 1966, four years after *Car 54, Where Are You?* went off the air, the NYPD Movie/TV Unit was formed. In a city that is dense with vehicular and pedestrian traffic, the unit formed a relationship with the NYPD, to assist television and movie producers, with complex shooting situations. The unit assists camera crews to get the scenic shots needed of bridges, highways, or busy intersections, controls traffic to ensure that companies can get shots that may otherwise be impossible, and monitors child work permits, stunts, prop firearms, placement of equipment, pedestrian safety and parking. The service was - and still is - free to productions filming within the city limits.

Had *Car 54* continued for another four years, Hiken's job might have gotten a little easier . . .

The Years after Car 54

In 1966, Universal Studios released a theatrical movie, *Munster, Go Home!* with the majority of the show's stars reprising their television roles. Towards the end of the movie, Herman (Fred Gwynne) and Grandpa (Al Lewis) are shouting for help. Herman cries "Call Batman!" A second later he shouts, "Car 54, where are you?"

After filming *The Munsters* in Universal City, California, Fred Gwynne returned to New York City. From 1975 to 1982, he made a total of 79 guest appearances on *The CBS Radio Mystery Theater*, a series of audio chillers syndicated over hundreds of radio stations across the country. Gwynne played the role of a sheriff in the episodes entitled "The Sealed Room Murder" (originally broadcast Oct. 23, 1975), "In Another Place" (Jan. 16, 1978), "If a Body" (Dec. 10, 1979) and "Kill Now - Pay Later" (Aug. 20, 1980). He played the role of an ex-police sergeant in "Second Sight" (Oct. 6, 1980). In the episode "Ninety Lives," (Aug. 29, 1979), Gwynne did not play the role of a law officer, but the name of the character he played was "Muldoon."

In his varied career, Gwynne also did voice-overs for commercials, a job he called "the sweetest, most generous thing that could happen to an aging actor." As an author and actor, Gwynne admitted: "As I grew up, I saw that the fine arts were not for me, because I knew I'd never make enough money to support a goldfish." The gentlest of giants died in Baltimore on July 2, 1993, because of complications of pancreatic cancer. Just days before his death, Al Lewis had a long telephone conversation with him, but they did not discuss Gwynne's illness. "We just talked about life in general," recalled Lewis. "I have been a performer for seventy years and my four most pleasant years were with Fred Gwynne. I'm glad I could tell him that."

The *Batman* television series offered Joe E. Ross an opportunity to reprise his trademark "Ooh! Ooh!" in the episode, "The Funny Feline Felonies," originally telecast on Dec. 28, 1967. Ross played the role of a talent agent and, in one scene, issued his verbal *Car 54* trademark. Just a year before, Ross played the role of a caveman in the short-lived comedy series, *It's About Time*, about two astronauts whose space capsule lands in the Stone Age. In 1976, Joe E. Ross played the role of an unnamed patrolman in *Slumber Party '57*.

Joe E. Ross died of a heart attack on Aug. 13, 1982. He was stricken while performing in the clubhouse of his apartment building in Van Nuys and was pronounced dead at St. Joseph Medical Center, Burbank, California. He was 67 years old. Inscribed on his tombstone were the words "This Man Had a Ball." Ross had a provision in his will that he be given a comical send-off. Attending the service were several comedians, including *Car 54* alumnus Larry Storch.

Nat Hiken did not believe in visiting a doctor unless it was absolutely necessary. Chain smoking and poor eating habits eventually took a toll on his health, and his close friends were greatly concerned. On December 7, 1968, while watching a basketball game on television, he suffered a heart attack and died. Years later, in an interview for *Television Quarterly*, a journal of the National Academy of Television Arts and Sciences, his widow Ambur, recalled just how taxing the *Car 54* series had been on her husband's health: "I once asked him if it was kind of tough following Bilko. He said it was murder."

One year after *Car 54,* Al Lewis and Fred Gwynne appeared together in *The Munsters,* taking up residence at the fictional 1313 Mockingbird Lane. Decades after the show's two-year run, strangers still greeted him on the street with shouts of "Grandpa" and "Schnauser." Unlike some television stars, Lewis never complained about getting typecast and made appearances in characters for decades. "Why would I mind?" he asked in a 1997 interview. "It pays my mortgage." Jane Fonda credited Al Lewis with getting her politically active when they met during the shooting of the 1969 movie, *They Shoot Horses, Don't They?*

Al Lewis' acting career was just one of his many exploits - he was a basketball talent scout, ran a Greenwich Village restaurant, and at age 75, ran as the Green Party candidate against incumbent Gov. George Pataki. He didn't defeat Pataki, but managed to collect more than 52,000 votes.

"Some people thought his antics were over the top, such as when he remarked at a Capitol press conference that the way to get rid of PCBs in the Hudson was to get a big spoon and feed it to the CEOs of G.E.," recalled Mark Dulea, the party's campaign manager at the time. "He told me later, 'You have to get the media to write about you. But the real people, the people on the streets, they understand what you are saying when they hear the joke.'"

Lewis was especially outspoken about reforming New York's strict drug laws, and John McDonagh recalled, "He was very hard on the police in brutality cases. But when the police held a rally at City Hall for a pay increase, he spoke there. I remember he came back to the station with an honorary PBA card that said 'Car 54.' He was very proud of that."

Many years after *Car 54* was into syndicated reruns, Lewis hosted a radio program on WBAI in New York. At one point during the 1990s, he was a frequent guest on the Howard Stern radio show, once sending the shock jock diving for the delay button by leading an undeniably obscene chant against the Federal Communications Commission.

One of the more popular lines expressed by fans, upon meeting Al Lewis, was "I thought you were dead." Lewis, however, took it in great stride. When he celebrated his 77th birthday at his Italian eatery, Lewis delivered the evening's best line to clear another Munster misconception. After a fan gushed about how much she enjoyed *The Munsters*, especially when the hand came out of the box ("Thing" on *The Addams Family*), Lewis leaned over and whispered, "That was the other — show!"

In 2003, Mr. Lewis was hospitalized for an angioplasty. Complications during surgery led to an emergency bypass and the amputation of his right leg below the knee and all the toes on his left foot. He spent the next month in a coma. On Feb. 3, 2006, New York resident Al Lewis passed away.

Hanna-Barbera produced eight animated shorts based on the *Car 54* television sitcom in 1972. Joe E. Ross supplied the voice for Gunther Toody. They were originally shown on a rotating basis, with other animated shorts, on another cartoon show entitled *Wait 'Til Your Father Gets Home*. The cartoon began as a one-shot animated segment on Paramount's *Love American Style* series on ABC-TV in 1972. Entitled "Love and the Old-Fashioned Father," it served as the pilot for the syndicated 1972-74 series. The pilot was originally purchased by the NBC owned stations to help fill up the then new FCC prime-time access rule time slots.

Reruns of *Car 54, Where Are You?* premiered on the Nickelodeon cable network on July 1, 1987, and received a warm welcome from a few newspaper columnists, including Marvin Kitman of *Newsday*. In the spring of 1990, under the Republic label, the first 16 episodes (in chronological order by airdate) were released on eight separate volumes on home video. In June of 2004, on the grounds of the New York City Police Museum, the fourth annual Vintage Car Show offered everything from former patrol cruisers to the Batmobile. Among the displays was one of the original police cars used on *Car*

54, Where Are You?

On Jan. 28, 1994, Orion Pictures theatrically released a feature-length motion picture entitled, *Car 54, Where Are You?* Adapted from the television series of the same name, the motion picture was filmed on location in Toronto, Canada and New York City in 1990, and was not released for four years. While the characters of Toody and Muldoon were portrayed by actors David Johansen and John C. McGinley, Nipsey Russell reprised his role of Police Chief Dave Anderson. Al Lewis reprised his role of Leo Schnauser (in the hospital scene was watching an episode of *The Munsters* on the television screen). The *Car 54* movie, like the television series, received an almost equal share of negative and positive critiques. During Gunther Toody's dream sequence, he is wearing the same uniform that was worn by his character in the original show.

EPISODE GUIDE

Extreme care has been made to ensure that the information listed below is accurate. Rather than consulting Internet websites (which has proven in the past to contain inaccurate material), this author chose to consult the original archival production material. Scripts, production reports, contracts, inter-office memos, and other paperwork were cross-referenced and double-checked to ensure all the dates and titles are accurate. Example: the episode "Lucille is Forty" is spelled correctly, *not* "Lucille is 40." "Get Well, Officer Schnauser" has a comma in the title. The dates each episode was filmed were referenced with a calendar to ensure that no typographical errors were made on the production sheets.

Every script written for the series was submitted to the Broadcast Standards Department of NBC (30 Rockefeller Plaza, NYC, NY) to be checked and verified that the content of each script would prevent NBC from being sued and from complaints from television viewers. They would, on occasion, submit suggested revisions. Under each episode I listed "NBC Review" for the date each script was read by the staff of this department. The date does not constitute the Program Department's approval, only the date the script was read and reviewed. George Norford, Alys Reese, Jane Crowley, Dorothy McBride, and Rod Egan were among the staff that looked over the scripts to verify that none of the contents would or could make NBC liable for a lawsuit.

THE STAFF AND CREW OF EUPOLIS PRODUCTIONS, INC.

While not all of the names listed below were credited on screen during the opening or closing credits, the men and women responsible for the 60 *Car 54* productions were committed to their tasks, whether it be transportation of equipment for location shots or secretarial paperwork. A few people such as Sal Scoppa, moved up in ranks or performed multiple tasks to keep production running smoothly, so they are credited accordingly with their tasks.

There were a few people who worked on the pilot (production #1) and never worked on any other episode of the series. For those exceptions, their credit is marked accordingly.

Acct. & Legal	Herskovits & Epstein
Accountant	Leo Ascher
Agency Liaison	George L. Vales
Art Director	Richard Jackson
Assistant to Mr. Friedberg	Gertrude Black
Bookkeeper	Suzanne K. Farley
Boom Man	Walter Jones
Camera Operator	Richard Kratina
1st Asst. Camera Op.	Robert Snavely
2nd Asst. Camera Op.	Paul Slivka
Casting Director	Edith Hamlin
	Lou Melamed (billed on screen as "Associate Producer")
Casting Secretary	Joan D'Incecco
	Marilyn Schlossberg

Carpentry	Edward Egan
	Tommy McDermott
Comedy Director	Mickey Deems
Co-Producer	Billy Friedberg
Costume Designer	Kay Morgan
Director	*Listed accordingly under the episode entries.*
First Asst. Director	Mickey Rich
First Asst. Director	Pete Scoppa
Second Asst. Director	Gerry Rich
Second Asst. Director	Sal Scoppa (also First Assistant Director on occasion)
Second Asst. Director	Bob Vietro
Second Asst. Director	Mike Wyler (pilot only)
Director of Photography	J. Burgie Contner (pilot only)
	George S. Stoetzel, a.s.c. (entire series except pilot)
Doctor	Joseph Harkavy, M.D.
Driver	Joseph Cariero
Editors	Anne Busch
	J.B. Oettinger
	John Strauss
Asst. to Editor	George Loughran
Asst. to Editor	Kevin O'Neil
Electricians	John Begley
	Fred Clare
	Harry Ford
	William Shaw
	Thomas Siracusa
Expeditor	Duke Doucette
Grip	John Delaney, Sr. (billed on screen as "John Delaney Sr.")
	Thomas Egan
	Edward Gardner

	John Harrigan
	Walter Pluff, Sr.
	Kenneth Thompson
	Joseph Williams
Hairdresser	Caryl Forrest
Head Carpenter	Lester Drambour
Head Electrician	Harry Ford (billed on screen as "Chief Electrician")
Makeup	Peter Garofalo
	Stan Lawrence (pilot only)
	Richard Willis
Music Supervisor	John Strauss
Nat Hiken's Secretary	Gertrude Black
Producer	Nat Hiken
Production Assistants	Duke Doucette
	Louis Hall (also listed as Lewis Hall)
Production Manager	Martin Leichter
	Sal Scoppa
Production Secretary	Mary K. Tosto
Production Supervisor	Howard Adelman
Props	John Cuomo
	Edward Kammerer
	Russell Tice
	John Wright
Props Assistant	Hubert J. Oates, Jr.
Property Master	Fred Ballmeyer
	Francis Brady (pilot only)
Scenic Artists	Conrad Maranzano
	Cosmo Sorice
Script Supervisor	Barbara Robinson
Set Decorator	Fred Ballmeyer
	J.C. Delaney

Set Designer	Al Brenner
	Robert Gunlach (pilot only)
Sound Mixer	Richard (Dick) Gramaglia (also billed as
	"William Gramaglia" on screen credits)
Steno-Typist	Barbara Rock
Supervising Film Editor	Marie Montagne
	Ray Sandiford
Technical Advisor	Harold Reidman
Typist	Rita Nunez
Vice President	Arthur A. Hershkowitz
Wardrobe	Vincent Stewart
	Thauma Seid

SEASON ONE

Production #4 "WHO'S FOR SWORDFISH?"
Copyright Notice: Eupolis Productions, Inc. © September 17, 1961;
LP21510
Filmed: Thursday, Friday and Monday, August 3, 4 and 7, 1961
Openings and Closings for the series, 1-4 and Thurs, August 10, 1961
Initial Telecast: September 17, 1961.
Teleplay scripted by Nat Hiken.
Directed by Al Di Caprio.

Cast: Milo Boulton (*the Inspector*); Shelley Burton (*Officer Murdock*); Duke Farley (*Reilly*); Hank Garrett (*Officer Ed Nicholson*); Jim Gormley (*Officer Nelson*); Jerry Guardino (*Officer Antonnucci*); Fred Gwynne (*Officer Francis Muldoon*); Al Henderson (*Officer O'Hara*); Sybil Lamb (*Helen O'Hara*); Jock McGraw (*Fishing Captain*); Fred O'Neal (*Officer Wallace*); Beatrice Pons (*Lucille Toody*); Paul Reed (*Captain Paul Block*); Joe E. Ross (*Gunther Toody*); Ralph Stantley (*Conroy*); and Joe Warren (*Officer Steinmetz*).

Plot: When Toody and Muldoon observe O'Hara on his brother-in-law's yacht, Toody longs for the opportunity to go sword fishing. Applying scheme after scheme to convince O'Hara to let them go for a ride on the yacht - which includes bribing Captain Block with Swordfish steaks - Toody succeeds. But days before their scheduled departure, Toody and Muldoon accidentally pull over a citizen for failing to stop at a stop sign, and realize that if they give a ticket, they will have to appear in traffic court and miss their chance for sword fishing. And it would be just their luck that the citizen loves to go to court so he can argue about his rights . . . and demands the ticket.

Trivia, etc. There is a line delivered in this episode, "This is a police report, not a script for Milton Berle," was actually an in-joke. Nat Hiken had been a writer for Berle's radio program in the late 1940s.

While it was not intended to be the series opener, this episode introduces the police officers that would appear frequently on the program, including Officers O'Hara, Nicholson and Wallace. The second half of this episode concerns Toody and Muldoon's attempt not to give a ticket to a citizen for a traffic violation, so they can avoid going to traffic court and, hence, be off work the day they are scheduled to take a ride on a yacht for a little sword fishing. The interplay with words between the police officers and the citizen, and other police officers who arrive on the scene, is reminiscent of old vaudeville sketches. The Battle Creek, Michigan, *Enquirer and News* reported: "There's one particularly funny scene showing a wayward motorist vainly pleading for a ticket. Though it's not a driving technique recommended to all viewers of this program, it does get the required guffaws."

Variety reviewed the series opener: "If Nat Hiken disciplines himself (and it's a pretty safe bet, based on past performance, that he'll find the remedy), it's still possible that *Car 54 - Where Are You?* can emerge as a funny lampoon on the men in blue."

Production #1 "SOMETHING NICE FOR SOL"
Copyright Notice: Eupolis Productions, Inc. © September 24, 1961; LP21511
Filmed: Monday to Friday, January 16 - 20, and Monday, January 23, 1961.
Initial Telecast: September 24, 1961
Mimeo script, dated August 23, 1961
Teleplay scripted by Nat Hiken.
Directed by Al Di Caprio

Cast: Gene Baylos (*Habidashery Harry*); Tony Carrado (*the poolroom proprietor*); Mildred Clinton (*Sandra*); Mark Dawson (*Corbett*); Diane Deering (*Dowager*); Duke Farley (*the policeman*); Janet Fox (*the mother*); Bryant Fraser (*the boy*); Nathaniel Frey (*Abrams*); Mike Gorrin (*the painter*); Jerome Guardino (*Officer Antonnucci*); Fred Gwynne (*Officer Francis Muldoon*); Albert Henderson (*Officer Steinmetz*); Gerald Hiken (*Webster*); George Kane

(*Officer Murdock*); Dave Kurlan (*Officer Kissel*); Judith Lowery (*woman in store*); Charles Mayer (*the store proprietor*); Harold Norman (*Reilly*); Elba Ocampo (*the Spanish woman*); Fred O'Neal (*Officer Wallace*); Paul Reed (*Captain Paul Block*); Joe E. Ross (*Gunther Toody*); Nipsey Russell (*Officer Anderson*); Joseph Warren (*Dubrow*); and Bernie West (*Harry*).

Plot: Toody has been voted in as head of the Brotherhood Club. His first act is to help the men decide what to get Sgt. Abrams, who is about to celebrate his 25th anniversary on the force. At first they decide on a gold watch, but there isn't enough money. Then they decide to get him an identification bracelet, but he already has one. Finally, Toody hits upon the perfect idea: a pair of orthopedic shoes. After all, Abrams has problems with his feet, hence the reason he is a desk sergeant. But when Toody and Muldoon discover that orthopedic shoes have to be custom made, the challenge isn't getting hold of Abrams old pair of shoes - it's getting a plaster mold made without the sergeant suspecting anything . . .

    Trivia, etc. The character of desk clerk Kissel was originally going to be played by actor Lou Polan. Dave Kurlan played the role for the pilot, but when it came time to film the series as a regular, Kurlan was unable to commit, so Bruce Kirby took over and stayed on as Kissel for the entire series. This was also the only episode George Kane played the role of Officer Murdock. Shelley Burton played the role throughout the rest of the series. Albert Henderson played Officer Steinmetz in this episode - Joe Warren played the character for the duration of the series.

    Gerald Hiken, who played the role of Webster in this episode, was producer/director/writer Nat Hiken's real-life cousin. Gerald had the recurring role of Mr. Katz, the butcher in Sector 3 (the section Muldoon and Toody patrol) in a number of episodes. Gerald Hiken would, years later, be nominated for a "Best Actor" Tony Award in 1980 for his role on Broadway's *Strider*.

    The June 28, 1961 issue of *Variety* discussed the series briefly, months before its official premiere. The pilot film was previewed and one critic commented that the plot made "for some of the most hilarious sequences TV has ever seen. And it matters not a whit to us that such a situation would happen in real life about once a millennium."

Talent Fees: The pilot was produced separately from the regular series, and for all intents and purposes, was a separate production. For example, while Nathaniel Frey was paid $500 for his role of Sgt. Abrams in this episode, when it came time to sign up as a recurring character, he was paid $315 for each episode filmed thereafter. Gerald Hiken was paid $500 for his appearance as Webster in the pilot; when appearing in the recurring role of Mr. Katz, the butcher in future episodes, his salary was $315 per episode. The talent fees for the pilot episode are listed below and reflect only what the actors were paid for this episode, not the rest of the series:

Nipsey Russell $225
Mildred Clinton $315
Nathaniel Frey $500
Paul Reed $350
George Kane $315
Fred O'Neal $315

Gene Abydos $650
Mark Dawson $420
Gerald Hiken $500
Albert Henderson $315
Hal Norman $315
Bernie West $500

Production #3 "HOME SWEET SING SING"
Copyright Notice: Eupolis Productions, Inc. © October 1, 1961; LP21512
Rehearsal: none
Filmed: Thursday to Wednesday, July 20, 21, and 24 - 26, 1961
Mimeo script dated August 6, 1961
NBC Review: July 14, 1961
Initial Telecast: October 1, 1961
Teleplay scripted by Terry Ryan and Nat Hiken.
Directed by Nat Hiken.

Cast: Gene Baylos (*Benny*); Edwin Bruce (*the nephew*); Shelley Burton (*Officer Murdock*); Mildred Clinton (*Mrs. Abrams*); Nathaniel Frey (*Abrams*); Hank Garrett (*Officer Ed Nicholson*); Jerome Guardino (*Officer Antonnucci*); Fred Gwynne (*Officer Francis Muldoon*); Al Henderson (*Officer O'Hara*); Ruth Masters (*Mrs. Muldoon*); George McCoy (*the detective*); Fred O'Neal (*Officer Wallace*); Beatrice Pons (*Lucille Toody*); Paul Reed (*Captain Block*); Joe E. Ross (*Gunther Toody*); Nipsey Russell (*Officer Anderson*); and Michael Vale (*Klein*).

Plot: "Backdoor Benny" is released from prison and, fulfilling his promise from years before, he pays Toody a visit for a chance of rehabilitation. Benny, however, has developed habits such as sleeping in a room with minimum furniture, walking the yard and asking for his letters to be censored. Longing for the life he had behind bars with his friends, Benny gains their confidence long enough to pull a job and get arrested. Down at the station, he enthusiastically gives a full confession, complete with fingerprints. His multiple attempts fail when Muldoon and Toody discover his motive, and do what they can to prevent him from going back to prison. Benny, though, is one step ahead: He has stolen Captain Block's watch, which will surely land him a place in prison.

Trivia, etc. In the opening scene, Toody comments, "Sergeant Abrams! Guess who we stopped for speeding! Rocky Graziano! Did you hear me? Rocky Graziano! He was heading for . . ." Originally the script referenced Mickey Mantle. NBC's legal department, however, advised Nat Hiken's office that unless Hiken could secure a release from Mantle, the ball player's name should not be used. Arthur Hershkowitz, the script contact for the series, talked to Hiken, who was close friends with Rocky Graziano from the television series *The Martha Raye Show*, and contacted a representative of Graziano. With permission, they made the substitution.

More Trivia, etc. Gene Baylos is listed as "Special Guest" in opening credits.

Production #2 "CHANGE YOUR PARTNER"
Copyright Notice: Eupolis Productions, Inc. © October 8, 1961; LP21513
Filmed: Thursday to Tuesday, July 13, 14, 17 and 18, 1961
Initial Telecast: October 8, 1961
Final draft dated July 7, 1961.
Teleplay scripted by Tony Webster and Nat Hiken.
Directed by Nat Hiken.

Cast: Arthur Anderson (*clerk #1*); Beatrice Pons (*Lucille Toody*); Shelley Burton (*Officer Murdock*); Duke Farley (*clerk #2*); Dan Frazer (*Bradley*); Nathaniel Frey (*Abrams*); Hank Garrett (*Johanson*); Bruce Glover (*Reilly*); Jim Gormley (*Officer Nelson*); Jerome Guardino (*Officer Antonnucci*); Fred Gwynne (*Officer Francis Muldoon*); Al Henderson (*Officer O'Hara*); Phil Kennedy (*Benton*); Bruce Kirby (*Hamilton*); Ruth Masters (*Mrs. Muldoon*); Fred O'Neal (*Officer Wallace*); Paul Reed (*Captain Paul Block*); Joe E. Ross (*Gunther Toody*); Nipsey Russell (*Officer Anderson*); and Joe Warren (*Officer Steinmetz*).

Plot: Most patrolmen paired together last about nine months on average before they request re-assignment. Wondering why Toody and Muldoon have spent the past nine years together without a single request of transfer, Captain Block plants a notion in their heads that causes the men to request new partners. After a week of re-assignments, most of the men in the precinct demand the Captain assign the two back together again.

Trivia, etc. This episode was supposed to be a three-day shoot, but filming took a day longer than scheduled, causing the production to complete on Tuesday instead of Monday. Paul Reed was paid $450 for the three days he was needed. Dan Frazer was paid $250 for the three days he was needed.

Production #5 "I WON'T GO"

Copyright Notice: Eupolis Productions, Inc. © October 15, 1961; LP21514
Filmed: Thursday, Friday, Monday and Tuesday, July 27, 28, 31 and August 1, 1961
Initial Telecast: October 15, 1961
Teleplay scripted by Gary Belkin and Nat Hiken.
Directed by Nat Hiken.

Cast: Milo Boulton (*O'Malley*); Matt Crowley (*Brady*); Fred Gwynne (*Officer Francis Muldoon*); Douglas Herrick (*the grandfather*); Will Hussung (*Benton*); Dave Kerman (*Berger*); Al Lewis (*Mr. Spencer*); Vincent Lynch (*the boy*); Mona Moore (*Mary Henderson*); John O'Leary (*Carmody*); Molly Picon (*Mrs. Bronson*); Paul Reed (*Block*); Joe E. Ross (*Gunther Toody*); Maurice Shrog (*Ellison*); and Van Dexter (*Birchfield*).

Plot: Toody and Muldoon (along with representatives of practically every other city department) are asked to do what they can to "encourage" sweet little old Mrs. Bronson to leave her old, city-owned brownstone so that it can be removed to make way for a new approach to the George Washington Bridge. She has been served a number of summonses, but she refuses to budge, and they hate to forcibly evict her for fear of incurring the wrath of the various "citizens' committees" who make front-page headlines of such situations. Toody and Muldoon finally question Mrs. Bronson, and ask her why she refuses to move. Winning her confidence, she explains that she is waiting for her runaway dog to come home. The officers search the city and find him alive and well, and Mrs. Bronson goes happily to a new residence.

Trivia, etc. Throughout the series, there was the realism of life in a politician's play land, the big city. In this episode, when apartment buildings were condemned to make way for a new approach to the George Washington Bridge, during an election year, Mrs. Bronson refused to move. Offering coffee and cake to Toody, Muldoon and various process servers, Mrs. Bronson explained the delicate truth: "They wouldn't put a nice grandmother in the street. In an election year with the Democrats worried about the Bronx, especially they wouldn't put a nice Jewish grandmother in the street." These lines had to get by P&G's censor - an ad man who kept a sponsor's eye on *Car 54* scripts - and they didn't go unnoticed.

Salley DeMay was a stand-in for actress Molly Picon (who was listed in the opening credits as "Special Guest") during the first two days of filming. Though the name of the dog with Mr. Finkelstein was called "Prince," Mrs. Bronson refers to the pooch as "Queenie." The dog's real name (off-screen) was Queenie.

Al Lewis, who was then in the Broadway hit musical *Do Re Mi*, was cast in the relatively brief role of a construction foreman, and was paid $225 for his appearance in this episode. His classic delivery of his tag line "Arrivederci Mrs. Bronson" made such a hit that Hiken was determined to write Lewis in as a regular on the series. The role turned out to be that of Officer Leo Schnauser, the sergeant who was permanently perched on the brink of hysteria.

This episode was supposed to be a three-day shoot, but ran over an extra day. Actor John Garrett O'Leary was paid $225 the same for his appearance in this episode. Paul Reed was paid $450 for the three days he was needed.

Production #6 "MULDOON'S STAR"
Copyright Notice: Eupolis Productions, Inc. © October 22, 1961; LP21515
Rehearsal: Friday, August 11, 1961
Filmed: Monday to Wednesday, August 14 - 16, 1961
Initial Telecast: October 22, 1961
Teleplay scripted by Harold Flender and Nat Hiken.
Directed by Nat Hiken.

Cast: Tom Ahearne (*the police captain*); Amelia Barleon (*old woman #1*); Richard Blackwell (*Stag*); Bill Cameron (*Al*); Arthur Clark (*the newscaster*); Sally DeMay (*old woman #2*); Nancy Donahue (*Cathy Muldoon*); Hank Garrett (*Officer*

Ed Nicholson); Fred Gwynne (*Officer Francis Muldoon*); Al Henderson (*Officer O'Hara*); Lisa Loughlin (*Theresa "Tessie" Tangiers*); Ruth Masters (*Mrs. Muldoon*); Helen Parker (*Peggy Muldoon*); Beatrice Pons (*Lucille Toody*); Wood Romoff (*Verdon*); Joe E. Ross (*Gunther Toody*); and Joe Warren (*Officer Steinmetz*).

Plot: When a Hollywood starlet named Tessie Tangiers arrives in New York City to escape the media frenzy, Gunther Toody picks her up at the airport. With the help of New York's finest he keeps the fans at bay, but quickly realizes that the hotel would be of no value in security. Deciding to do his partner a favor (knowing Francis worships the screen actress), he arranges for Tessie to stay with the Muldoons. Later that evening, Toody and his wife take Tessie out with Francis, in the hopes of pairing the two - but Francis has never been on a date. The evening comes to a close when Tessie observes a woman imitating the actress, in mocking jest. The actress leaves in tears, but Francis assures her that while actors come and go, people like her will be immortalized by people like him, who enjoy her pictures. On the way back to the airport, Tessie realizes that Francis makes a valid point: she may have a job that forces her to escape the overwhelming popularity from time to time, but she will have to endure the fame and fortune since her success has grown from the people who admire her for who she really is.

Trivia, etc. This episode was supposed to be a two-day shoot, but ran over an extra day. Of the first nine episodes filmed, this was the only one without Paul Reed. During the shooting in mid-August, Reed was appearing in the new musical, *How to Succeed in Business Without Really Trying*, at the Shubert Theater in Philadelphia. Pages of the script were tossed out and a new scene was rewritten to accommodate the actor. The result was the elimination of the character altogether for this script. Reed would have been out of two more episodes had Hiken not decided to discontinue shooting for two weeks. During the final two weeks of the musical's five-week run in Philadelphia, Reed had to commute between the Bronx and Broad and Spruce streets. (Reed signed up for the stage play three months before *Car 54* was definitely booked by NBC for the season.)

Stage actress Lisa Loughlin made her screen debut in this episode of *Car 54*, and would return in a later episode. These would be her only television appearances.

Production #8 "THE PAINT JOB"

Copyright Notice: Eupolis Productions, Inc. © October 29, 1961; LP21516
Filmed: Thursday, Friday, Monday and Tuesday, August 17, 18, 21 and 22, 1961
Initial Telecast: October 29, 1961
Teleplay scripted by Marty Roth and Nat Hiken.
Directed by Nat Hiken.

Cast: Jimmy Archer (*the tough guy*); Shelley Burton (*Officer Murdock*); Al Ensor (*Lefty*); Everett Everett (*Joe*); Alan Frank (*man #1*); Hank Garrett (*Officer Ed Nicholson*); Jim Gormley (*Officer Nelson*); Larry Gaynes (*the young man*); Harry Gresham (*Lucas*); Fred Gwynne (*Officer Francis Muldoon*); Al Henderson (*Officer O'Hara*); Al Lewis (*Al, the paint shot employee*); Stella Longo (*woman #2*); John Murphy (*the boy*); Fred O'Neal (*Officer Wallace*); Iris Paul (*Leona*); Maria Pinckard (*elderly woman*); Paul Reed (*Captain Paul Block*); Pat Ripley (*woman #1*); Joe E. Ross (*Gunther Toody*); Nipsey Russell (*Officer Anderson*); Billy Sands (*Lou*); Sonny Sands (*man #3*); Claire Waring (*middle-aged woman driver*); Joe Warren (*Officer Steinmetz*); and Wayne Wilson (*elderly man*).

Plot: Because the precinct only has two squad cars, and one of them was recently put under for repairs, Gunther and Muldoon try their best to keep Car 54 from going into the shop. Their efforts are wasted when a pedestrian accidentally damages the car. Toody gets an idea to have the damaged fender replaced within the next hour so no one at the station will ever know. Muldoon, fearing the beat they would walk if it is reported that the car was damaged, agrees - unaware that the garage they take the car to is being operated by crooks who run a stolen car ring. After a few mishaps and the wrong paint job, Toody and Muldoon realize who the crooks are and arrest the guilty parties.

Trivia, etc. This episode was supposed to be a three-day shoot, but ran over an extra day. Iris Paul was described as "the Kim Novak look-alike" by columnist John David Griffin for the *New York Mirror*, in his brief about this episode of *Car 54*.

Production #9 "LOVE FINDS MULDOON"

Copyright Notice: Eupolis Productions, Inc. © November 5, 1961; LP21517
Filmed Thursday to Wednesday, August 24, 25, and 28 - 30, 1961
NBC Review: August 21, 1961

Initial Telecast: November 5, 1961
Final script dated July 23, 1961.
Teleplay scripted by Nat Hiken.
Directed by Nat Hiken.

Cast: Nancy Donahue (*Cathy*); Hank Garrett (*Officer Ed Nicholson*); Alice M. Ghostley (*Bonita*); Fred Gwynne (*Officer Francis Muldoon*); H. Kadison (*the counterman*); Ruth Masters (*Mrs. Muldoon*); Helen Parker (*Peggy*); Beatrice Pons (*Lucille Toody*); Paul Reed (*Captain Paul Block*); Joe E. Ross (*Gunther Toody*); and Nipsey Russell (*Anderson, the policeman*).

Plot: Lucille Toody thinks it is about time that Muldoon, her husband's partner, got married and settled down. She thinks he would be just right for Bonita, a former school mate who is still very attractive and moreover, is eager to get married. In her early years, however, Bonita had a crush on Ramon Navarro, whom she never met. The crush soured and since then, any man who even remotely reminded her of Navarro was to be shunned. Unwittingly, Muldoon commits the unforgivable crime and his flourishing courtship with Bonita is brought to an abrupt end.

Trivia, etc. Filming for this episode was originally scheduled to be completed on Tuesday, August 29, but production ran a day behind so it took five days instead of four to film. Alice Ghostley is billed during the opening credits as "Special Guest."

Production #7 "THE GYPSY CURSE"
Copyright Notice: Eupolis Productions, Inc. © November 12, 1961; LP21518
Rehearsal: Monday, September 25, 1961
Filmed Tuesday - Friday, September 26 - 29, 1961
NBC Review: August 11, 1961
Initial Telecast: November 12, 1961
Teleplay scripted by Tony Webster and Nat Hiken.
Directed by Nat Hiken.

Cast: Maurice Brenner (*Kramer*); Lance Cunard (*Griswald*); George Del Monte (*the gypsy man*); Ivy Ellen (*the gypsy girl*); Hank Garrett (*Officer Ed Nicholson*); Fred Gwynne (*Officer Francis Muldoon*); Jack Healy (*Rodriguez*);

Mark Hunter (*the gypsy boy*); Beatrice Pons (*Lucille Toody*); Paul Reed (*the Captain*); Joe E. Ross (*Gunther Toody*); Nipsey Russell (*Officer Anderson*); Maureen Stapleton (*the gypsy woman*); and Joe Warren (*Officer Steinmetz*).

Plot: Officer Toody, in plain clothes, gets the goods on an old gypsy woman for fortune telling. Out of spite, the old woman puts a "curse" on him. His partner, Muldoon, dismisses the curse as a lot of foolishness, but Toody believes his health and family life are really being affected by it. Even Lucille, Toody's wife, begins to believe it until the old gypsy woman herself proves there is no such thing.

Trivia, etc. Originally titled "Gypsy Woman," this episode changed title to "The Gypsy Curse" after discussions between Arthur Hershkowitz and the NBC Broadcast Standards Department stated that the old woman must be presented as an individual and not representative of all gypsies. Muldoon's line "Gunther, you're crazy, Lucille is the most wonderful woman in the world," was altered so the word "crazy" would not be said during the episode.

More Trivia, etc. Maureen Stapleton, who was given a "Special Guest" credit on screen during the opening credits for this episode, was paid $2,000 for her appearance. Her most memorable line in this episode was a curse she placed in one scene: "May all your teeth fall out the day before Thanksgiving."

Production #10 "THIRTY DAYS NOTICE"
Copyright Notice: Eupolis Productions, Inc. © November 19, 1961; LP21519
Rehearsal: Monday, October 2, 1961
Filmed Tuesday - Friday, October 3 - 6, 1961
NBC Review: September 26, 1961
Initial Telecast: November 19, 1961
Teleplay scripted by Ben Joelson, Art Baer and Nat Hiken.
Directed by Nat Hiken.

Cast: John Alexander (*Judge Schweitzer*); Dort Clark (*the District Attorney*); Virginia De Luce (*the blonde*); Sally DeMay (*the grandmother*); Fred Gwynne (*Officer Francis Muldoon*); Jerry Jarrett (*Bernie*); Henry Lascoe (*Mr. Corfu*); George McCoy (*Detective Manzer*); Mike O'Dowd (*the prisoner*); Lou Polan

(*Mr. Morris*); Beatrice Pons (*Lucille Toody*); Joe E. Ross (*Gunther Toody*); Ralph Stantley (*Lt. Morgan*); and Michael Vale (*Al Cooper*).

Plot: Toody is continually complaining to Lucille about their rent-frozen apartment. When the landlord comes to collect $50 rent, Toody gives him an ultimatum - either fix the problems with the apartment or they will leave. The landlord gratefully accepts their 30-day notice. Toody agrees, and says he will find another apartment. When he starts to find a new place, he discovers the horrible truth - no apartment is available for less than $125. He finds a crook that is (he thinks) going to jail. Toody strikes a deal with him to take over his apartment. After much finagling, they finally move into the crook's apartment, but the first night the supposed crook's wife shows up and she provides her husband's alibi, and Toody and Lucille luckily get their old apartment back again.

Trivia, etc. Filming for this episode was originally scheduled for a three-day shoot, but production ran a day behind.

Production #11 "CATCH ME ON THE PAAR SHOW"
Copyright Notice: Eupolis Productions, Inc. © November 26, 1961; LP21520
Filmed Monday to Wednesday and Friday, October 9 - 11 and 13, 1961
NBC Review: October 6, 1961
Initial Telecast: November 26, 1961
Teleplay scripted by Terry Ryan and Nat Hiken.
Directed by Nat Hiken.

Cast: Joe Alfasa (*Wilson, the tailor*); Rick Colitti (*Crook*); Mickey Deems (*Officer Charlie Fleischer*); Hugh Downs (*as himself*); Hank Garrett (*Officer Ed Nicholson*); Tom Geraghty (*Winchell, the butcher*); John Gibson (*Father Flannagan*); Jerry Guardino (*Officer Antonnucci*); Fred Gwynne (*Officer Francis Muldoon*); Al Henderson (*Officer O'Hara*); Abby Lewis (*woman in butcher shop*); Gloria McCarty (*Mrs. Killgallen, the mop shaker*); Fred O'Neal (*Officer Wallace*); Beatrice Pons (*Lucille Toody*); Shelly Post (*woman's V.O.*); Paul Reed (*Captain Paul Block*); Joe E. Ross (*Gunther Toody*); and Nipsey Russell (*Officer Anderson*).

Plot: Toody thinks his fellow officer Charlie Fleisher is the funniest man alive and should be on *The Jack Paar Show*. Toody meets Hugh Downs who is substituting for Paar and arranges an appearance on the show. The big night arrives and Fleisher gets on camera and freezes. Toody moves into the breech and proves to be very funny on the show. A reappearance for Toody is arranged, by popular demand, but when his big day comes, Toody freezes in front of the camera. Muldoon, Toody's partner, takes over and breaks it up. But when it comes his time to star, the outcome is clear.

Trivia, etc. Just a month before this episode went into production, Nat Hiken was interviewed by Art Woodstone for *Variety*, and the subject of Jack Paar came up. Hiken, who had a deep respect for Paar, regarded the TV personality as "a guy who keeps things stirred, a guy who keeps America awake." After the script was conceived, a discussion between Arthur Hershkowitz, representative of Eupolis Productions, Inc, the program's packager, and Paul Oor, Paar's producer, helped make it possible to use Jack Paar's name on the program, and Hugh Downs billed as a "Special Guest."

The original script initially called for Lucille and Captain Block to use the word "idiot" in separate scenes, but the NBC Broadcast Standards Department suggested the use of that word be dropped or substituted. There was also caution on invading the right of privacy when mentioning names of celebrities in this episode - Joey Bishop, Phyllis Diller, Jonathan Winters, Frank Sinatra, Dean Martin, Doris Day, William Holden, Walter Winchell, Earl Wilson and Zsa Zsa Gabor.

More Trivia, etc. Actor John Gibson went down for costume fitting for his role of Father Flannagan in this episode, and according to the Screen Actors' Guild, he was entitled to one hour of pay ($11.25). Since he was not paid for his hour and no one was advised of the fitting, the matter was brought to the attention of Mary K. Tosto of Eupolis Productions, Inc., who arranged for a check for $11.25 to be mailed to Gibson a week after filming completed.

John Banfield was Hugh Downs' stand-in. Hugh Downs for "Catch Me on the Paar Show" was paid $1,500.

This was Mickey Deems' first of many appearances as Officer Charlie Fleischer on *Car 54*. Deems was also given status as "Comedy Director" behind-the-scenes, even though his name never appeared in the closing credits unless he played the role of the officer.

Production #12 "THE TAMING OF LUCILLE"
Copyright Notice: Eupolis Productions, Inc. © December 3, 1961; LP21521
Rehearsal: Monday, October 16, 1961
Filmed: Tuesday - Friday, October 17 - 20, 1961
NBC Review: October 18, 1961
Initial Telecast: December 3, 1961
Teleplay scripted by Tony Webster and Nat Hiken.
Directed by Al De Caprio.

Cast: Carl Ballantine (*Al*); Martin Brooks (*Petruchio*); Hank Garrett (*Officer Ed Nicholson*); Martha Greenhouse (*Rose*); Fred Gwynne (*Officer Francis Muldoon*); Al Henderson (*Officer O'Hara*); Fred O'Neal (*Officer Wallace*); Beatrice Pons (*Lucille Toody*); Albert Quinton (*Baptista*); Joe E. Ross (*Gunther Toody*); James Valentine (*Gremio*); Joe Warren (*Officer Steinmetz*); Jane White (*Katherine*); and Elaine Winters (*Bianco*).

Plot: Toody and Muldoon share special duty in the park where they see a performance of Shakespeare's *The Taming of the Shrew*. Toody decides Lucille is henpecking him too much and decides then and there that "there'll be some changes made." In the meantime, Lucille is at home watching *Craig's Wife* [a 1936 film starring Rosiland Russell as a domineering woman]. She makes up her mind that she will change her ways. Meanwhile, Toody lays the law down - he's going to stay out until two in the morning. He soon gets tired of this newfound freedom. Muldoon, sensing Toody's discontentment, quietly tells Lucille that her husband is "cutting up" with other women. When Toody returns home, he finds his wife taking over her old ways, and Toody is happy again.

Production #13 "PUT IT IN THE BANK"
Copyright Notice: Eupolis Productions, Inc. © December 10, 1961; LP21522
Rehearsal: Monday, October 23, 1961
Filmed: Tuesday, October 24 - 27, 1961
Initial Telecast: December 10, 1961
Final script dated July 28, 1961.
Teleplay scripted by Will Glickman, Sydney Zelinka and Nat Hiken. *
Directed by Al De Caprio.

---

*   The spelling of the writers' names was not consistent throughout the series. Sydney Zelinka was also spelled Sydney Zelenka and Sid Zelinka. Will Glickman was also spelled William Glickman.]

Cast: John Alexander (*Cartwright*); Arthur Anderson (*Henry Ford*); John C. Becher (*Clark*); Heywood Hale Broun (*Wayne*); Walton Butterfield (*bank president*); James Dukas (*Fink Foster*); Hank Garrett (*Officer Ed Nicholson*); Larry Gaynes (*elevator boy*); Harry Gresham (*broker #1*); Fred Gwynne (*Officer Francis Muldoon*); Al Henderson (*Officer O'Hara*); Al Lewis (*Leo Schnauser*); Gilbert Mack (*Tony Shoeshine*); Sylvia Mann (*woman in bank*); Tom Mahoney (*J.D. Rockefeller*); John O'Leary (*Haskell*); Fred O'Neal (*Officer Wallace*); Lou Polan (*Edwards*); Ken Roberts (*Teller's V.O.*); Joe E. Ross (*Gunther Toody*); and Joe Warren (*Steinwetz*).

Plot: When Toody is voted as treasurer of the police fund, Muldoon advises him to put the funds in the bank. Toody, however, gives in to temptation and convinces the men that the stock market is a better investment. Shortly after Toody puts all $800 plus dollars into International Sulfur stock, he suspects that the investment may not have been solid. To quell his concerns, Toody repeatedly visits the man in charge of the corporation. The frequency of the policeman's inspections cause witnesses unrest, and a sell-off occurs. This causes others to spread rumors and the value of the stock plunges. When an investigation uncovers the cause, Toody is personally given a check for $1,500 for the purchase of his stock, under the advice of the Secretary of the Treasury who personally tells Toody to "put it in the bank."

Trivia, etc. During production, the script and production went under the title "The Wizards of Wall Street," before it was changed to "Put it in the Bank."

In the opening credits, Sydney Zelinka was credited as Sid Zelinka. Regardless of the true spelling of his first name, Zelinka's credits included writing scripts for *The Phil Silvers Show*, *The Jackie Gleason Show*, *The Honeymooners*, *The Flintstones*, *Bewitched* and *Get Smart* (and his name was spelled both ways on the various programs).*

Production #14 "GET WELL, OFFICER SCHNAUSER"
Copyright Notice: Eupolis Productions, Inc. © December 17, 1961; LP21523
Rehearsal: Monday, October 30, 1961
Filmed: Tuesday to Friday, October 31 and November 1 - 3, 1961
NBC Review: October 30, 1961
Initial Telecast: December 17, 1961

Teleplay scripted by Terry Ryan and Nat Hiken.
Directed by Al De Caprio.

Cast: Lawrence Fletcher (*the bank president*); Jim Gormley (*Officer Nelson*); Fred Gwynne (*Officer Francis Muldoon*); Bruce Kirby (*Officer Kissel*); Al Lewis (*Officer Leo Schnauser*); Frank Marth (*Cunningham*); Fred O'Neal (*Officer Wallace*); Dick O'Neill (*guard #1*); Anita O'Shayne (*the nurse*); Paul Reed (*Captain Paul Block*); Joe E. Ross (*Gunther Toody*); Billy Sands (*the thief*); and Mary Tahmin (*Miss Berger*).

Plot: There is only $9.52 left in the Get Well Fund and Officer Schnauser has three broken toes. Since Toody is the treasurer, the blame is put on his shoulders when Schnauser isn't going to get the funds needed. Since Toody happens to have been a classmate of a bank robber who is expected in their district, Toody is assigned to try to identify him. Through a mix-up, $30,000 is put in the bag for Schnauser, but in the course of events, it is returned and the bank insists upon a reward of $100, which is promptly given to Schnauser.

Trivia, etc. During production, the script and production went under the title "The Big Bank Robbery," before it was changed to "Get Well, Officer Schnauser."

Production #19 "CHRISTMAS AT THE 53ᴿᴰ"
Copyright Notice: Eupolis Productions, Inc. © December 24, 1961; LP21524
Rehearsal: none
Filmed: Thursday and Friday, November 30 and December 1, 1961
NBC Review: November 30, 1961
Initial Telecast: December 24, 1961
Teleplay scripted by Terry Ryan and Nat Hiken.
Directed by Al De Caprio.

Cast: Robert Ader (*Joe, Reilly's kid*); Billie Allen (*Anderson's wife*); Carl Ballantine (*Al*); Phil Carter (*Feldman*); Mickey Deems (*Officer Charlie Fleischer*); Duke Farley (*Reilly, the desk sergeant*); Hank Garrett (*Officer Ed Nicholson*); Alice Ghostley (*Bonnie Kalsheim*); Duane Grant, Jr. (*Anderson's boy*); Martha Greenhouse (*Rose*); Fred Gwynne (*Officer Francis Muldoon*);

Jack Healy (*Rodriguez*); Al Henderson (*Officer O'Hara*); Al Lewis (*Officer Leo Schnauser*); Scotty Moore (*the little boy, fingerprinting*); Fred O'Neal (*Officer Wallace*); Beatrice Pons (*Lucille Toody*); Paul Reed (*Captain Paul Block*); Sindee Richards (*the little girl, fingerprinting*); Joe E. Ross (*Gunther Toody*); Nipsey Russell (*Officer Anderson*); and Joe Warren (*Officer Steinmetz*).

Singers: Milton Chapman (*Miller*); Jerry Graff (*Pucci*); Noah Hopkins (*unnamed*); Edwin Lindstrom (*Jones*); Arne Markusson (*Moskowitz*); Alan Sokoloff (*Clark*); Robert Spiro (*unnamed*); Leonard Stea (*unnamed*); and David Vogel (*unnamed*).

Plot: The policemen of the 53rd Precinct, their families and friends come together at the precinct for the annual Christmas party. Policemen with talent - and those without - perform a number of musical songs, for the entertainment of those at the precinct. A group of the patrolmen, led by Schnauser, recite the creed of the precinct's Brotherhood Club, getting into an argument in the process. Captain Block helps the women at the precinct observe the dress code for their men in uniform. But when all the fun and games is over, the phones continue to ring and the patrolmen go out on their beat to keep in the merry mood of Christmas . . . revealing that even on a festive holiday, the men in blue never rest.

Trivia, etc. The title on the earliest drafts of the script was "Christmas Show." This episode may have had the shortest production schedule of the series - it took only two days to film. (See page 62 regarding a citation issued from the Screen Actors' Guild for the use of three women in this episode that were not members of the Guild.) Actress Alice Ghostley, who was billed as "Special Guest" in the opening credits, was paid $1,500 for her services in this episode.

"Christmas at the 53rd" featured the song "You're Nobody 'Till Somebody Loves You," written by Russ Morgan, Larry Stock and James Cavanaugh, and published through the Southern Music Publishing Co., Inc. Payment for use of the song (and a five-year agreement for reruns and syndications) was $350.00.

Fred Gwynne really could play the guitar, as demonstrated in this episode. "He very rarely got excited," recalled Al Lewis. "I would scream and yell on the set and he would play the guitar or draw caricatures."

"He was fabulous, absolutely terrific," said Charlotte Rae of Fred Gwynne. "He had a wide range of talent and acting styles."

Paul Reed, who sang on stage in *Guys and Dolls* and *Hold It*, performs a musical *tour de force* in this episode.

Carl Ballantine wasn't always a comedian. After attending many Saturday matinees at a local theater which lured juvenile patrons with free magic tricks, he developed a magic act of his own. Magic, plus the movie projector he earned selling gum, made him the most popular lad in the neighborhood. He put on magic and movie shows in the basement of his home, charging two cents admission.

While in high school, he performed at many functions. Then, with a tuxedo and several magic tricks, he was booked into several night spots on the West Coast. Carl felt he was now ready for the vaudeville circuit. But vaudeville, it seemed, was not ready for Ballantine. He had honed his comedy-magic act to perfection. With a fanfare, resplendent in top hat and tails, he would stride on stage and proceed to work up to his stellar tricks with frills, gestures and flourishes. The audience would be on edge, ready to be amazed. But the tricks never worked.

"This was just the way I'd planned the act," recalled Ballantine, "but the audience just thought I was an awkward magician. I bombed in Atlanta, then Holyoke, then Des Moines." Finally, in 1942 at the State Lake Theatre in his home town of Chicago, he gave the act a last chance. "They flipped. It was the same act, but the audience knew what I was driving at this time and loved it."

The Amazing Mr. Ballantine spent a career in theaters, night clubs and industrial shows. Best known for his role of "Gruber" in the television comedy, *McHale's Navy*, he played the recurring role of Al on *Car 54*. In this holiday offering, he got the opportunity to demonstrate a few magic tricks in front of the camera.

RERUN
December 31, 1961 featured a rebroadcast of the episode, "I Won't Go."

Production #16 "THE SACRIFICE"
Copyright Notice: Eupolis Productions, Inc. © January 7, 1962; LP22541
Rehearsal: Monday, November 13, 1961
Filmed: Tuesday - Friday, November 14 - 17, 1961
NBC Review: November 8, 1961

Initial Telecast: January 7, 1962
Teleplay scripted by Tony Webster and Nat Hiken.
Directed by Al De Caprio.

Cast: John Becher (*the motorist*); Phil Bruns (*Benedict*); Phil Carter (*the desk sergeant*); Michael Conrad (*Smasher*); Nancy Donahue (*Cathy*); James Dukas (*the repair man*); Bryant Fraser (*the little boy*); Fred Gwynne (*Officer Francis Muldoon*); Al Lewis (*Officer Leo Schnauser*); Ruth Masters (*Mrs. Muldoon*); Beatrice Pons (*Lucille Toody*); Paul Reed (*Captain Paul Block*); Joe E. Ross (*Gunther Toody*); and Nipsey Russell (*Officer Anderson*).

Plot: Toody believes Muldoon has sacrificed a promotion to detective in order to keep their "team" on the force intact. Toody tries to build up Muldoon's confidence by having his colleagues remind him of his past heroic deeds. The efforts remind Muldoon of an old injury which makes him ineligible to become a detective anyway. Everyone is happy that he'll be staying on the old job.

Trivia, etc. John Becher, who played the minor role of the motorist, had a double for some of his scenes.

Production #15 "BOOM, BOOM, BOOM"
Copyright Notice: Eupolis Productions, Inc. © January 14, 1962; LP22542
Rehearsal: Monday, November 6, 1961
Filmed: Tuesday to Friday, November 7 - 10 and Monday, November 13, 1961
Initial Telecast: January 14, 1962
Teleplay scripted by Nat Hiken, Will Glickman and Sydney Zelinka.
Directed by Al De Caprio.

Cast: Arthur Anderson (*Boden*); Toni Darnay (*the nurse*); Diane Deering (*Miss Heffington*); Jim Gormley (*Officer Nelson*); Harry Gresham (*Grover*); Fred Gwynne (*Officer Francis Muldoon*); Gerald Hiken (*Mr. Katz, the butcher*); Leon Janney (*Dr. Sturm*); Jerry Jarrett (*the producer*); Al Lewis (*Officer Leo Schnauser*); Jan Murray (*as himself*); Paul Reed (*Captain Paul Block*); Florence Robinson (*Mrs. Katz*); Joe E. Ross (*Gunther Toody*); and Truman Smith (*the doctor*).

Plot: A barbershop quartet singing contest is held for the benefit of city departments, including the transit bureau, the school board, the health department and the police precincts. Comedian Jan Murray is one of the three judges. Before the elimination round is completed, Murray suffers a severe case of nerves after hearing the same "boom, boom, boom" refrain 63 different times. After a little rest and relaxation, Murray overhears the men from the 53rd Precinct practicing in the studio next door, and suspects he is going out of his mind. Resting in a quiet section of a hospital, he then overhears Muldoon and his men practicing in the room down the hallway, and finally cracks under the strain.

Trivia, etc. The routine with Florence Robinson playing the role of Mrs. Katz, asking her husband, "Are you alright Sam?" was later restaged for the episode entitled "Benny the Bookie's Last Chance." According to an inter-office memo, dated Oct. 23, 1961, the former title for this drama on the first draft of the script was "Harmony." Jan Murray was paid $1,500 for his guest appearance.

More Trivia, etc. The music featured in this episode, like any television series, required clearance in advance. The composition, "By the Light of the Silvery Moon," was licensed from the Remick Music Corporation for $200, under the stipulation that only three partial visual vocals and two partial background vocals be used. The license was for a period of 10 years, after which, reruns on television would require the contract to be renewed for an additional fee.

"Love's Old Sweet Song," which carried the bars - "boom, boom, boom" - that make up the humorous refrains in this episode, was composed by J.L. Molloy and Clifton Bingham, and published by Boosey & Hawkes, Inc. For the use of the one visual vocal (partial use approximately four bars), was licensed for $150. Agreement between Eupolis and the agent representing the song writers was made between November 1961 and February 1962. A five-year renewal for the same fee was dated Jan. 27, 1964.

Production #17 "TOODY AND MULDOON CRACK DOWN"

Copyright Notice: Eupolis Productions, Inc. © January 21, 1962; LP22543
Rehearsal: none

Filmed: Friday, November 17, 1961, Monday to Wednesday, November 20 - 22, 1961
NBC Review: November 20, 1961
Initial Telecast: January 21, 1962
Teleplay scripted by Terry Ryan and Nat Hiken.
Directed by Al De Caprio.

Cast: Florence Anglin (*the mother*); Mildred Clinton (*Mrs. Colby*); Everett Everett (*Harry*); Duke Farley (*the desk sergeant*); Lawrence Fletcher (*the Chief Inspector*); William Fort (*Hogan*); Fred Gwynne (*Officer Francis Muldoon*); Gerald Hiken (*Mr. Katz*); Jake LaMotta (*Seaman*); Gilbert Mack (*Callucci, fruit store owner*); Paul Reed (*Captain Paul Block*); Robby Reed (*the little boy*); Joe E. Ross (*Gunther Toody*); and Helen Verbit (*Mrs. Callucci*).

Plot: A new Chief Inspector makes his rounds and checking up on sector three, Toody and Muldoon's section of the Precinct, finds all kinds of violations in the streets. He lodges his concerns to Captain Block, who promptly relocates our two boys from sector three to the waterfront. On closer scrutiny, the Chief Inspector discovers that in the nine years since Toody and Muldoon took over, the entire sector has been free of crime, and he finds that the minor violations (obstruction of sidewalks, loud speakers in the streets, etc.) are not important in comparison to the good work the boys have done - such as keeping major crime in their section non-existent. When the Chief Inspector returns to compliment the Captain, Block seeks out Toody and Muldoon, and takes their place on the waterfront before the Inspector discovers Block's error.

Trivia, etc. Recurring character Mr. Katz, the local butcher, makes a brief appearance in the beginning of this episode. The role of the little boy was played by Robby Reed, the son of actor and series regular Paul Reed.

On Monday, December 4, the crew shot Rear Projection scenes for this episode with Joe E. Ross, Fred Gwynne, Lawrence Fletcher and William Fort.

Production #20 "TOODY'S PARADISE"
Copyright Notice: Eupolis Productions, Inc. © January 28, 1962; LP22544
Rehearsal: Monday, December 4, 1961

Filmed: Tuesday to Friday, December 5 - 8, 1961
NBC Review: December 1, 1961
Initial Telecast: January 28, 1962
Teleplay scripted by Will Glickman, Sid Zelinka and Nat Hiken.
Directed by Al DeCaprio

Cast: Florence Anglin (*Olive*); Elizabeth Fraser (*O'Brien*); Martha Greenhouse (*Rose*); Fred Gwynne (*Officer Francis Muldoon*); Will Hussung (*Inspector Kleinmetz*); Al Lewis (*Officer Leo Schnauser*); Ruth Masters (*Mrs. Muldoon*); Paul O'Keefe (*the kid*); Thelma Pelish (*Bertha*); Beatrice Pons (*Lucille Toody*); Paul Reed (*Captain Paul Block*); Joe E. Ross (*Gunther Toody*); and Loretta White (*Elsie Block*).

Plot: After taking Lucille to the movies one too many times, Toody realizes his wife longs for romance. She especially admires Alec Guinness in *The Captain's Paradise* - the story of a man with a different sweetheart at two different ports. Hoping to build himself up in the eyes of his wife, Toody volunteers for special dragnet duty. The Inspector, knowing Toody's capacity for getting things generally mixed up, puts him on an undercover assignment in Brooklyn with a female officer, trying to catch purse snatchers. A few nights later, Lucille and her sister Rose observe Toody sitting in the park with the blonde (an undercover policewoman). Lucille packs her bags, starting a chain of events that can only be resolved when his undercover duty is explained. Lucille comforts her husband, commenting he looks like a hero to her - and always will.

Trivia, etc. According to an inter-office memo, dated Oct. 23, 1961, the former title for this drama on the first draft of the script was "Platinum Blonde Cop."

On Monday, the same day rehearsals were conducted, the crew shot Rear Projection scenes for Production #17, "Toody and Muldoon Crack Down" with Joe E. Ross, Fred Gwynne, Lawrence Fletcher and William Fort.

Production #18 "HOW HIGH IS UP?"

Copyright Notice: Eupolis Productions, Inc. © February 4, 1962; LP22545
Filmed: Friday, November 24, Monday to Wednesday, November 27 - 29, 1961
Various pickup shots filmed Thursday, December 7, 1961.
Initial Telecast: February 4, 1962
Final draft dated: November 21, 1961.
Teleplay scripted by Tony Webster and Nat Hiken.
Directed by Al De Caprio.

Cast: Alice Beardsley (*Gloria Harper*); Sorrell Booke (*Commissioner Harper*); Phil Carter (*Feldman, the fat policeman*); Arthur Clark (*Quazey*); Duke Farley (*the desk sergeant*); Hank Garrett (*Officer Ed Nicholson*); Lucy Greeno (*Mrs. Walsh*); Fred Gwynne (*Officer Francis Muldoon*); Fred Harper (*the salesman*); Al Lewis (*Officer Leo Schnauser*); Shari Lewis (*Melinda*); Ruth Masters (*Mrs. Muldoon*); Fred O'Neal (*Officer Wallace*); Paul Reed (*Captain Paul Block*); Joe E. Ross (*Gunther Toody*); Nipsey Russell (*Officer Anderson*); and Noel Thomas (*McCabe*).

Plot: Commissioner Harper is determined to root out the physically weak patrolmen in the force - especially those who are overweight and too tall - giving the police force a bad reputation. Muldoon panics when he discovers that his height might disqualify him from the force. The maximum height is six foot six, and Muldoon just learned he is six foot seven. Knowing that the Commissioner plans to attend the benefit dance to inspect the officers of the 53rd Precinct, Muldoon decides not to go to the dance. He changes his mind when his mother hooks him up with a young lady named Melinda, who, as it turns out, is very short. Fearing the worst if he escorts the young lady to the dance, Muldoon rejects Melinda until his conscience plagues him. Commissioner Harper pulls Muldoon aside, and thanks him for taking the attention away from him and his wife. While the Commissioner is short in height, his wife is the same size as Muldoon!

Trivia, etc. Production notes stated Al Lewis, Sorrell Booke and Paul Reed had Broadway show commitments and therefore, were unavailable for shooting on Wednesday, the last of the four days of filming.

Shari Lewis is billed in the opening credits as "Special Guest," and was paid $700 for her appearance.

The original title for this production was "Muldoon Grows Taller," when submitted to Eupolis Productions, and the title was changed when Nat Hiken took the mimeographed copy and rewrote the script.

Production #21 "TOODY AND THE ART WORLD"
Copyright Notice: Eupolis Productions, Inc. © February 11, 1962; LP22546
Rehearsal: Monday, December 11, 1961
Filmed: Tuesday to Friday, December 12 - 15, 1961
NBC Review: December 7, 1961
Initial Telecast: February 11, 1962
Teleplay scripted by Nat Hiken.
Directed by Al DeCaprio.

Cast: Rick Colitti (*the thief*); Severn Darden (*Karpathia*); Diane Deering (*Dowager, with dog*); Duke Farley (*the desk sergeant*); Dan Fraser (*the kid*); Hank Garrett (*Officer Ed Nicholson*); Fred Gwynne (*Officer Francis Muldoon*); Al Henderson (*Officer O'Hara*); Al Lewis (*Officer Leo Schnauser*); Fred O'Neal (*Officer Wallace*); Beatrice Pons (*Lucille Toody*); Charlotte Rae (*Mrs. Schnauser*); Paul Reed (*Captain Paul Block*); Joe E. Ross (*Gunther Toody*); and Shepperd Strudwick (*Pennington*).

Plot: Toody and Muldoon attempt to evict an eccentric artist from an old building. Toody becomes enamored with one of the abstract paintings, which he seems to understand thoroughly. This so impresses the artist that he makes a present of it to Toody. Lucille, however, will not have the painting in her house, nor will anybody else for that matter as the abstract is mistaken for junk. Toody spends the next few days passing the painting on to a number of friends, each of whom attempts to get rid of it. When the true value of the painting becomes known, Toody and Muldoon discover to their horror that the last possessor was Sylvia Schnauser, who didn't like the canvas and threw it into the incinerator.

Trivia, etc. This marked the first of many episodes to feature Charlotte Rae as Schnauser's wife. On Monday, December 11, during rehearsals, the production crew took advantage of the opportunity to shoot photographs with Lewis and Rae, for the publicity department.

A viewer of the *Car 54* series, Edward A. Dickson of Los Angeles, California, wrote to Nat Hiken, proposing they do an episode about Muldoon and Toody safeguarding a precious and valuable painting. "I thought that the present publicity given to the arrival of the famed and priceless 'Mona Lisa' affords tremendous possibilities for use in your series," Dickson wrote. "Can't you just see the need of a police guard for the Mona Lisa and the burden of such protection to fall on the shoulders of the Precinct 53 and the good, persevering Captain having no one else available but Toody and Muldoon? . . . Prior to this you could just imagine the Mona Lisa being stolen and the news broadcast stating - 'Ladies and Gentlemen, today a great tragedy fell on these United States, The Mona Lisa has been stolen' . . . Toody, hearing this, turns to his wife and says, 'Ooo-ooo did you hear that? Some poor girl has been kidnapped, wonder who her parents are?'"

While his plot idea was never used on the series, this episode marks Toody and Muldoon's only venture into the art world.

More Trivia, etc. The featured painting in this episode that causes all the conflict was done by Fred Gwynne, made especially for this episode. "Fred's an extremely talented guy - one who can write, paint and script," Joe E. Ross said. "His painting ranges from complete realism to the wildest abstract stuff you've ever seen." Gwynne explained "If I could devote a year to my painting, I'd come up with a solid style." Gwynne's real-life passion for art mirrored some of the scenes in this episode.

Production #22 "WHAT HAPPENED TO THURSDAY?"
Copyright Notice: Eupolis Productions, Inc. © February 18, 1962; LP22547
Rehearsal: Monday, December 18, 1961
Filmed: Tuesday to Friday, December 19 - 22, 1961
NBC Review: December 14, 1961
Initial Telecast: February 18, 1962
Teleplay scripted by Tony Webster and Nat Hiken.
Directed by Al DeCaprio.

Cast: Jim Boles (*first man*); Duke Farley (*Reilly*); Hank Garrett (*Officer Ed Nicholson*); Martha Greenhouse (*Rose*); Fred Gwynne (*Officer Francis Muldoon*); Bruce Kirby (*Officer Kissel*); Al Lewis (*Officer Leo Schnauser*); Aphena Lords (*first woman*); Fred O'Neal (*Officer Wallace*); Beatrice Pons (*Lucille Toody*); Charlotte Rae (*Mrs. Schnauser*); Paul Reed (*Captain Paul Block*); Joe E. Ross (*Gunther Toody*); and Nipsey Russell (*Officer Anderson*).

Plot: For a number of years, the Schnausers have a habit of getting into a fight every Thursday evening. No one can comprehend why it's always on a Thursday, but the neighbors have started to complain and Muldoon and Toody are getting tired of trying to break up the married couple. Toody comes up with a crazy idea - a plot to have Officer Schnauser think it is Friday, instead of Thursday, in an effort to give the couple a week without fighting. With the assistance of Muldoon, the men successfully trick Schnauser into believing it's Friday. Their efforts, however, throw the whole Station House into a state of confusion, when Captain Block also falls for the switcheroo, and the officers start making the adjustments. In the end, the plan backfires when Sylvia, believing Schnauser is trying to confuse her à la Charles Boyer in *Gaslight*, starts a fight loud enough for the neighbors to call in another complaint.

Production #23 "HOW SMART CAN YOU GET?"
Copyright Notice: Eupolis Productions, Inc. © February 25, 1962; LP22548
Rehearsal: none
Filmed: Tuesday to Friday, January 2 - 5, 1962
NBC Review: January 3, 1961
Initial Telecast: February 25, 1962
Final Script was dated January 3, 1962 (suspect the date was typed wrong)
Teleplay scripted by Tony Webster, from a story by Tony Webster and Nat Hiken.
Directed by Al DeCaprio.

Cast: Duke Farley (*Reilly*); Fred Gwynne (*Officer Francis Muldoon*); Al Henderson (*Officer O'Hara*); Gerald Hiken (*Katz*); Al Lewis (*Officer Leo Schnauser*); Richard Morse (*Corrigan*); Fred O'Neal (*Officer Wallace*); Beatrice Pons (*Lucille Toody*); Paul Reed (*Captain Paul Block*); Richard Roat (*Garfield*); Joe E. Ross (*Gunther Toody*); and Nick Saunders (*Kushman*).

Plot: When the background of each officer is studied in an effort to match patrol car partners who have the same intellectual capacity and taste, Toody and Muldoon are separated. A young rookie who graduated with the highest marks ever recorded at the police academy is assigned to Car 54 to ride with Muldoon, also a college graduate and intellectual. Toody, his partner of nine years, is unhappy about the separation. But no more so than the captain of the precinct when Car 54 and its new team cruises past hold-ups, accidents and fires without notice. Finally, Muldoon pleads for Toody's return. In the car, Toody talks nonsense and Muldoon doesn't have to listen and therefore can keep his mind on police work. The new rookie, however, brought up such intelligent subjects that he had to keep his mind on what the guy was saying, at the expense of his police work. Toody and Muldoon team is promptly reunited.

Trivia, etc. The rookie's credentials in this episode (a Harvard graduate and Phi Beta Kappa) are the same actor Fred Gwynne possessed in real life.

Production #24 "TODAY I AM A MAN"
Copyright Notice: Eupolis Productions, Inc. © March 4, 1962; LP22549
Rehearsal: Monday, January 8, 1962
Filmed: Tuesday to Friday, January 9 - 12, 1962
NBC Review: January 12, 1962
Initial Telecast: March 4, 1962
Teleplay scripted by Terry Ryan and Nat Hiken.
Directed by Al DeCaprio.

Cast: Nick Colasanto (*Marty*); George Del Monte (*Club Captain*); Howard Freeman (*Mr. Parker*); Fred Gwynne (*Officer Francis Muldoon*); Bob Hastings (*Sanders*); Al Henderson (*Officer O'Hara*); Sybil Lamb (*Priscilla Parker*); Al Lewis (*Officer Leo Schnauser*); Ruth Masters (*Mrs. Muldoon*); Paul Reed (*Captain Paul Block*); Joe E. Ross (*Gunther Toody*); and Ruth White (*Mrs. Parker*).

Plot: Muldoon gets furious when the boys in the locker room make one too many jokes about his being a "momma's boy." To counteract their jests, he fibs about a big date at a night club Saturday night, and then realizes his mistake when the officers decide to tail him. As he has no actual date, Muldoon is forced to "pick up" a sweet young girl who happens to be seated at the club with her parents - and she's as much of a "momma's boy" as Muldoon. When the girl's parents observe the police keeping an eye on Muldoon, and notice their table guest possessing a hand gun, they mistake him for a gangster. Too terrified and frightened to call for help, the family spends the evening in fear while he insists on remaining in their company until the police leave. A surprise is in store for everyone when the evening concludes - the sweet young thing falls hard for Muldoon, pleading for a life away from her parents!

Trivia, etc. This episode was originally entitled "Muldoon's Date" in early drafts and plot proposal, before it was changed to "Today I Am a Man." On the morning of January 12, the final scenes needed to be filmed were held back a half hour because the final pages of the script needed to be revised and approved and were delivered to the set a little late.

Production #25 "NO MORE PICKPOCKETS"

Copyright Notice: Eupolis Productions, Inc. © March 11, 1962; LP22550
Rehearsal: Monday, January 15, 1962
Filmed: Tuesday to Friday, January 16 - 19, 1962
NBC Review: January 19, 1962
Initial Telecast: March 11, 1962
Teleplay scripted by Tony Webster and Nat Hiken.
Directed by Al De Caprio.

Cast: Tom Ahearne (*the Inspector*); John C. Becher (*the father*); Rick Colitti (*pickpocket Pete*); Wally Cox (*Benny*); Dana Elcar (*van policeman*); Al Ensor (*Felix*); Rex Everhart (*the door guard*); Duke Farley (*the sergeant*); Hank Garrett (*Officer Ed Nicholson*); Fred Gwynne (*Officer Francis Muldoon*); Jerry Jarrett (*the reporter*); Al Lewis (*Officer Leo Schnauser*); Artie Lewis (*the man*); Jimmy Little (*bullpen guard*); Fred O'Neal (*Officer Wallace*); Paul Reed (*Captain Paul Block*); Joe E. Ross (*Gunther Toody*); Nipsey Russell (*Officer Anderson*); Billy Sands (*the hot dog man*); and Herbert Voland (*lineup cop*).

Plot: Toody and Muldoon are determined to win a citation for performing heroic deeds beyond the call of duty. On their day off, they put on civilian clothes and go to the crowded Yankee Stadium in search of pickpockets. Their captain is dead set against it, especially because he knows Toody will create a problem, but they go anyhow. Toody's pocket is picked by Benny, an expert who has always wanted to be a policeman. Using Toody's badge and identification, he arrests all the pickpockets (his competition) in action at the stadium. He also arrests Toody and ships him with the other pickpockets off to headquarters where he has a hard time identifying himself. Muldoon and the captain have no better luck, for their wallets are also stolen when they go to headquarters to identify Toody, and by the same adept pickpocket.

Trivia, etc. Revisions on the final draft were made the same day rehearsals were done, on January 15, 1962. Wally Cox is billed in opening credits as "Special Guest." Since Gunther Toody's badge was stolen, it is only fitting to reveal to readers and fans of the series that his badge number is 1432. Patrolman Francis Muldoon's badge number is 723. (Special thanks to Terry Salomonson for pointing this out.)

Production #26 "THE BEAST WHO WALKED THE BRONX"

Copyright Notice: Eupolis Productions, Inc. © March 18, 1962; LP22551
Rehearsal: Monday, January 22, 1962
Filmed: Tuesday to Friday, January 23 - 26, 1962
NBC Review: January 23, 1962
Initial Telecast: March 18, 1962
Teleplay scripted by Terry Ryan and Nat Hiken.
Directed by Al DeCaprio.

Cast: Arthur Anderson (*Carter*); Raymond Bramley (*McCoy*); Maurice Brenner (*Kramer*); Heywood Broun (*Simpson*); Phil Carter (*Feldman*); Howard Freeman (*Burkholtz*); Fred Gwynne (*Officer Francis Muldoon*); Jack Healy (*Rodriguez*); Jerry Jarrett (*Edwards*); Bob Kaliban (*Thompson*); David Kerman (*Lt. Graves*); Bruce Kirby (*Officer Kissel*); Al Lewis (*Officer Leo Schnauser*); Paul Reed (*Captain Paul Block*); Joe E. Ross (*Gunther Toody*); and Nipsey Russell (*Officer Anderson*).

Plot: Captain Block's chief insists that the captain take a well-earned vacation from the cares of his precinct - foremost among them the lack of discipline among his men. Replacing the captain is another who is mistaken by the men of the 53rd as a tyrant. In reality, he is a well-mannered, soft-spoken, tender-hearted man. However, Toody and Muldoon spread the erroneous information, and the mild-mannered captain's reputation as being a beast precedes him to the 53rd which suddenly undergoes a change in discipline and appearance. This is as startling to Captain Block as it is to the chief.

Trivia, etc. Because of casting difficulties (actor Phil Carter was available and Duke Farley was not), the character of Reilly was replaced by the character of Feldman throughout the script.

Production #27 "THE COURTSHIP OF SYLVIA SCHNAUSER"

Copyright Notice: Eupolis Productions, Inc. © March 25, 1962; LP22552
NBC Review: January 30, 1962
Initial Telecast: March 25, 1962

Teleplay scripted by Tony Webster.
Directed by Al De Caprio.

Cast: Billie Allen (*the woman*); Fred Gwynne (*Officer Francis Muldoon*); Al Lewis (*Officer Leo Schnauser*); Beatrice Pons (*Lucille Toody*); Charlotte Rae (*Sylvia Schnauser*); Joe E. Ross (*Gunther Toody*); and Nipsey Russell (*Officer Anderson*).

Plot: After attending the colorful wedding of a friend, Sylvia Schnauser wants her husband Leo to marry her all over again. Apparently 15 years before they were married at City Hall on her lunch hour, and since he was in the service, they never had a proper honeymoon. This time she wants to do it right - bridal gown, flowers and champagne. Leo objects, and tries to hold out against the pressure of Sylvia, Toody and Lucille, but finally yields when he discovers that, living alone, "the laundry is piling up." After all the preparations are made and the big day arrives, Leo and Sylvia suddenly discover what it was that made them admire each other. Unable to wait for the marriage ceremony, they rush off to city hall to get married again. Back at the reception party, not wanting to waste any of the food or preparations that went into the big day, Toody and Lucille renew their vows.

Trivia, etc. NBC Broadcast Standards Department suggested that the name of the Bronx Plaza Hotel on page one be replaced with a fictitious one. Nat Hiken chose to ignore the suggestion, and the name "Bronx Plaza Hotel" remained. Originally, Schnauser's speech called for him to say "She's gonna drive me nuts," but the line was changed at the advice of the NBC Broadcast Standards Department to read "She's gonna drive me screwy."

Production #28 "THE AUCTION"
Copyright Notice: Eupolis Productions, Inc. © April 1, 1962; LP22553
NBC Review: February 6, 1962
Initial Telecast: April 1, 1962
Teleplay scripted by Sydney Zelinka, Will Glickman and Nat Hiken, based on a story by Syd and Will.
Directed by Al De Caprio.

Cast: Hank Garrett (*Officer Ed Nicholson*); Fred Gwynne (*Officer Francis Muldoon*); Al Henderson (*Officer O'Hara*); Louise Kirtland (*Mrs. Block*); Al Lewis (*Officer Leo Schnauser*); Paul Lipson (*the man*); Paul Reed (*Captain Paul Block*); and Joe E. Ross (*Gunther Toody*).

Plot: The members of the 53rd Precinct cannot agree on what to get Captain Block for his 25th wedding anniversary. Muldoon and Toody discover that what the captain would like more than anything else in the world is the mate to an antique chair he owns. They find the chair which is up for auction. With Officer Schnauser, they devise a scheme to keep the bids low at the auction. The scheme backfires when the men find themselves paying much more than planned (and purchasing more items than they intended to buy), but the chair brings such joy to the captain that the whole precinct agrees it was worth every dollar.

Production #29 "QUIET! WE'RE THINKING"
Copyright Notice: Eupolis Productions, Inc. © April 8, 1962; LP22554
(Copyrighted under the title "Quiet, We're Thinking")
NBC Review: February 12, 1962
Initial Telecast: April 8, 1962
Teleplay scripted by Terry Ryan.
Directed by Al De Capro.

Cast: Carl Ballantine (*Al*); Frank Campanella (*Lt. Kogan*); Lawrence Fletcher (*the Chief Inspector*); Martha Greenhouse (*Rose*); Fred Gwynne (*Officer Francis Muldoon*); Paul O'Keefe (*Marvin*); Beatrice Pons (*Lucille Toody*); Paul Reed (*Captain Paul Block*); and Joe E. Ross (*Gunther Toody*).

Plot: A series of unsolved robberies puzzle the detectives and patrolmen of the 53rd Precinct. A concerted drive is started to solve these crimes and Toody and Muldoon are given some of the toughest cases of their career to work on. No results are expected, but when the two cops solve the cases, they are commended for possessing that rare quality seldom found in detectives today - a child-like imagination. Truth be told, it is Toody's 11-year-old Boy Scout nephew who had put his vivid imagination to work on the cases and come up with the solutions.

PRE-EMPTION

On April 15, 1962, *Car 54, Where Are You?* was not broadcast. The comedy was pre-empted due to a television special in recognition of Easter Sunday. The special broadcast entitled "He Is Risen" continued the series that began with the award-winning Christmas program, "The Coming of Christ." This special was part of an ongoing series entitled *Project 20*, and was sponsored by United States Steel. The half-hour color special featured art masterpieces of the late Middle Ages, the Renaissance and the Baroque period, depicting the crucifixion, death and resurrection of Jesus Christ.

Production #30 "I LOVE LUCILLE"

Copyright Notice: Eupolis Productions, Inc. © April 22, 1962; LP22555
NBC Review: February 21, 1962
Initial Telecast: April 22, 1962
Teleplay scripted by Tony Webster and Nat Hiken.
Directed by Al DeCaprio.

Cast: William Fort (*patrolman*); Hank Garrett (*Officer Ed Nicholson*); Fred Gwynne (*Officer Francis Muldoon*); Bob Kaliban (*the reporter*); Phil Leeds (*Julius, beauty store owner*); Monica May (*the young blonde*); Beatrice Pons (*Lucille Toody*); Erik Rhodes (*J.J. Jones, the producer*); Florence Robinson (*the secretary*); and Joe E. Ross (*Gunther Toody*).

Plot: Lucille is constantly ignored by her husband, Toody, at public dances, parties and at home. Determined to make him notice her, she puts on attractive makeup, perfume and a slinky dress, and has her hair bleached blonde. Toody becomes so impressed that he goes from one extreme to the other to woo her. It doesn't take long for Lucille to realize that he now notices her "too much." Toody thinks that other men are becoming wildly jealous - to the point where he is convinced that she is planning to run away with his best friend, Muldoon. Unable to stand it anymore, Lucille returns to her natural self and Toody returns to not noticing her.

Trivia, etc. For many years, Beatrice Pons' had been trying to land a role as a glamour girl. This episode almost made up for all the years of past, and future, frustration. Here, Lucille is neglected by Toody, who dances with other women at a policemen's ball. "She becomes jealous of Toody,"

Pons explained to a magazine columnist, commenting about the filming of this episode. "She goes out and has her hair bleached, and wears big fake eyelashes and a black dress with sequins, to lure him back. You don't know how I reveled in this script. I have a bunch of still pictures of me in that glamorous outfit. The pictures are the pride of my life!"

The script originally called for the name of the nightclub as the "Copa Cabana." To prevent possible legal issues, the script supervisor changed the name of the nightclub to the "Casa Cabana."

SUMMER RERUNS

April 29, 1962	"Something Nice for Sol"
May 6, 1962	"Change Your Partner"
May 13, 1962	"Home Sweet Sing Sing"
May 20, 1962	"Gypsy Curse"
May 27, 1962	"Catch Me on the Paar Show"
June 3, 1962	"Put it in the Bank"
June 10, 1962	"Boom, Boom, Boom"
June 17, 1962	"Get Well, Officer Schnauser"

From June 24, 1962 to Sept. 9, 1962, the time slot was used to broadcast *Sir Francis Drake*, a British television series that was brought to the U.S. for syndication. Twenty-six episodes were filmed of *Sir Francis Drake* but only 12 of them were featured in this time slot. Beginning September 16, *Drake* was removed so that *Car 54* could return to the same time slot for the second season.

SEASON TWO

Production #32 "HAIL TO THE CHIEF!"
Copyright Notice: Eupolis Productions, Inc. © September 16, 1962;
LP24126
NBC Review: July 10, 1962
Initial Telecast: September 16, 1962
Teleplay scripted by Tony Webster.
Directed by Nat Hiken.

Cast: Fred Gwynne (*Officer Francis Muldoon*); Jay Jostyn (*Secret Serviceman Hollander*); Walter Klavun (*McQueen*); Al Lewis (*Officer Leo Schnauser*); John McGovern (*Commissoner Brady*); Jeremiah Morris (*the doctor*); Simon Oakland (*Secret Serviceman Cordner*); Paul Reed (*Captain Paul Block*); and Joe E. Ross (*Gunther Toody*).

Extras in the cast: Phil Carter, Gordon B. Clarke, Kenneth Reid, Billy Sands and Mel Stewart.

Plot: When the President of the United States arrives in New York to give an important speech, Toody and Muldoon are selected to drive him from the airport to United Nations Building. A secret service man is assigned to check out Toody and Muldoon, for pre-screening and approval. After riding with them for observation, the secret service man concludes that the best protection the President could have during his visit is for Toody and Muldoon to be kept as far away from him as possible.

Trivia, etc. *Variety* reviewed the season opener as laughs-a-plenty, "but the so-so story on the opener suggests the same format and general plot liner of last season."

The projection effects and stock footage were courtesy of Milt Olshin.

This was one of a handful of episodes to feature Billy Sands in a supporting role. Sands worked with Nat Hiken before when he played the role of Pvt. Dino Paparelli on *The Phil Silvers Show*.

According to Derek Tague, a fan of the television program, it is suspected that this episode never aired in reruns on many television stations, during the 1960s. The news of the assassination of John F. Kennedy shook the emotions of many Americans, and it was feared that this episode might not look favorable in the eyes of those still emotionally affected by that tragic event.

Production #35 "ONE SLEEPY PEOPLE"
Copyright Notice: Eupolis Productions, Inc. © September 23, 1962; LP24127
NBC Review: July 20, 1962
Initial Telecast: September 23, 1962
Teleplay scripted by Terry Ryan.
Directed by Nat Hiken.

Cast: Patricia Cutts (*Pamela*); Edgar Daniels (*Reggie*); Fred Gwynne (*Officer Francis Muldoon*); Hank Garrett (*Officer Ed Nicholson*); Patrick Horgan (*Ashley*); Al Lewis (*Officer Leo Schnauser*); Beatrice Pons (*Lucille Toody*); Dick Powell (*footage on television*); Charlotte Rae (*Sylvia Schnauser*); Paul Reed (*Captain Paul Block*); and Joe E. Ross (*Gunther Toody*).

Plot: The innocent relationship between Francis Muldoon and his partner's wife takes on romantic overtones when he spends a weekend at the Toodys. Muldoon, Toody and Lucille watch an old movie in which a male guest is having an affair with the wife of his unsuspecting host. Suddenly, the similarity of their position with the actors in the movie plunges Muldoon and Lucille into a frantic effort to remain completely above suspicion. But the harder they try, the guiltier their actions appear. Officer Nicholson is caught in the same situation with the wife of his partner, Officer Schnauser. The men compare notes, trace the cause of their difficulty and swear off old movies.

Trivia, etc. Early in the episode, Lucille unzips her husband's house coat in Muldoon's presence and George Norford of the NBC Broadcast Standards Department reminded Arthur Hershkowitz of Eupolis Productions, Inc. that the scene should be carefully filmed to suggest nothing more than the innocence motivating it. And she was required to be duly covered by the coat.

Footage of Dick Powell from one of his television anthologies is used.

In this episode, Nicholson is a bachelor. A mistake in continuity lies here since Nicholson was a married man in a number of previous episodes.

Production #31 "A MAN IS NOT AN OX"

Copyright Notice: Eupolis Productions, Inc. © September 30, 1962; LP24128
Rehearsal: Monday and Tuesday, June 25 and 26, 1962.
Filmed: Wednesday to Friday, June 27 - 29, 1962.
NBC Review: June 25, 1962
Initial Telecast: September 30, 1962
Teleplay scripted by Billy Friedberg and Nat Hiken.
Directed by Nat Hiken.

Cast: Phil Carter (*the desk sergeant*); Mickey Deems (*Officer Charlie Fleischer*); Hank Garrett (*Officer Ed Nicholson*); Fred Gwynne (*Officer Francis Muldoon*); Jack Healy (*the clerk*); Jerry Jarrett (*the driver*); Al Lewis (*Officer Leo Schnauser*); Ruth Masters (*Mrs. Muldoon*); Fred O'Neal (*Officer Wallace*); Pat Pizza (*double for Lucille*); Beatrice Pons (*Lucille Toody*); Paul Reed (*Captain Paul Block*); Joe E. Ross (*Gunther Toody*); Truman Smith (*Dr. Metz*); and Ned Wertimer (*Dr. Meisner*).

Plot: Officers Toody and Muldoon have been together in the same squad car for 10 years. They act so much alike that the captain becomes alarmed, especially after a medical officer examines them and likens them to a famous Sultan and Rajah. These two were oxen-yoked together for ten years. An experiment carried out on them showed if one became ill, the other became ill. Mono-bio-psychosis the theory is called "two bodies, one brain," a ghastly condition to which Toody and Muldoon appear to have fallen victim. The solution seems hopeless when the single Muldoon meets a girl the exact twin of Toody's wife.

Production #34 "SCHNAUSER'S LAST RIDE"

Copyright Notice: Eupolis Productions, Inc. © October 7, 1962; LP24129
NBC Review: July 18, 1962
Initial Telecast: October 7, 1962
Teleplay scripted by Tony Webster.
Directed by Nat Hiken.

Cast: John Becher (*Mr. Connors*); Dort Clark (*crook in suit*); Mickey Deems (*Officer Charlie Fleischer*); Diane Deering (*the woman*); Hank Garrett (*Officer Ed Nicholson*); Fred Gwynne (*Officer Francis Muldoon*); Al Lewis (*Officer Leo Schnauser*); Paul Reed (*Captain Paul Block*); and Joe E. Ross (*Gunther Toody*).

Extras in the cast: Phil Carter, Rex Everhart, Harold Gary, Fred Kareman, Dan Morgan and Melville Ruick.

Plot: The cops of the 53rd Precinct reminisce about the time, ten years earlier, that Officer Schnauser joined them. This had been a result of the disbanding of the Mounted Police. He had come after a 12-year association with Sally, his horse, and found it difficult to accustom himself to a human partner. Toody seems to be the best suited to be Schnauser's partner, until it develops that Schnauser is treating Toody just like he treated Sally. And what is more frightening, Toody is responding the same way a horse would. Now, 10 years later, the precinct and the men still show the influence of Schnauser's love for Sally.

Trivia, etc. The footage shown in the beginning of this episode was the same used for the background of the closing credits for many of the second season episodes. Actor Rex Everhart, who played a brief supporting role in this episode, was nominated for Broadway's 1978 Tony Award as Best Actor (Featured Role - Musical) for *Working*.

Production #33 "TOODY AND MULDOON SING ALONG WITH MITCH"

Copyright Notice: Eupolis Productions, Inc. © October 14, 1962; LP24130
NBC Review: July 6, 1962
Initial Telecast: October 14, 1962
Teleplay scripted by Buddy Arnold and Ben Joelson.
Directed by Nat Hiken.

Cast: Mickey Deems (*Officer Charlie Fleischer*); Fred Gwynne (*Officer Francis Muldoon*); Al Lewis (*Officer Leo Schnauser*); John Miller (*man #1*); Mitch Miller (*as himself*); Fred O'Neal (*Officer Wallace*); Beatrice Pons (*Lucille Toody*); Paul Reed (*Captain Paul Block*); Joe E. Ross (*Gunther Toody*); and Richard Winter (*man #2*).

Plot: "Mitch" of the *Sing Along With Mitch* show, announces that in four weeks he would be presenting "The Municipal Sing Along." Naturally, the 53rd Precinct is very interested inasmuch as they have a singing group called "The 53rd Precinct Whippoorwills." The quartet is composed of Muldoon, Toody, Wallace and Schnauser. They audition for Mitch and are turned down. Mitch, however, tells the Captain to return for another audition with a better bass. The bass happens to be Toody, of course, and because he is so enthusiastic about winning, the rest of the boys hesitate to tell him that he is ruining the quartet. They find a wonderful bass voice in a new man in the Precinct and they secretly practice with him. Toody finds that every male member of his family - after he had his tonsils removed - turns out they have a beautiful voice. Toody arranges for the operation - and then discovers that his relatives got a tenor voice from the operation. Toody doesn't want to disrupt the chances of Muldoon, who is a tenor. At first, Toody refuses to sing or speak. It turns out that Toody's voice didn't change at all from the tonsillectomy, and they go on to audition for Mitch again.

Trivia, etc. This episode originated from the Jan. 29, 1962 issue of *Radio-Television Daily*. The front page headline read "All-American Award Winners" and columnist Charles A. Alicoate reported "a total of 422 radio and TV critics, feature writers and editors serving America's leading newspapers, magazines and fan publications, have voted Mitch Miller and Dinah Shore Television's 'Man of the Year' and 'Woman of the Year.'"

Naturally, this issue of *Radio-Television Daily* would not have come to Nat Hiken's attention if it wasn't for the fact that the same issue announced that *The Bob Newhart Show* emerged as the victor for "Best Comedy Show of the Year" by a very thin margin over *Hazel* and *Car 54, Where Are You?* (Nat Hiken was nominated as best director for a television series, but lost to Marc Daniels for another series)

It was this issue of *Radio-Television Daily* that started the ball rolling for a premise that would ultimately unite the real Mitch Miller (billed as "Special Guest" in the opening credits) with the fictional 53rd Precinct.

George S. Irving, the popular Broadway actor/comedian, makes a brief and unbilled supporting role in this episode. Irving later won a Tony award for Best Featured (i.e., supporting) Actor in a Musical as the foppish dress designer "Madame Lucy" in *Irene* in 1973. Cartoon fans know Irving for supplying the voices for cartoon characters for such series as *Underdog*, *Tennessee Tuxedo* and *Go Go Gophers*.

Production #36 "OCCUPANCY, AUGUST FIRST"

Copyright Notice: Eupolis Productions, Inc. © October 21, 1962; LP24131
NBC Review: July 20, 1962
Initial Telecast: October 21, 1962
Teleplay scripted by Gary Belkin.
Directed by Nat Hiken.

Cast: John Alexander (*the Commissioner*); John Anderson (*Hilton*); Heywood Hale Broun (*man from health department*); Dana Elcar (*construction boss*); Howard Freeman (*Dr. Michaels*); Fred Gwynne (*Officer Francis Muldoon*); Molly Picon (*Mrs. Bronson*); Charles Nelson Reilly (*Harlow*); Paul Reed (*Captain Paul Block*); Joe E. Ross (*Gunther Toody*); and Maurice Shrog (*Ellison*).

Plot: Toody and Muldoon are summoned to save an elderly woman perched on the 14th floor of an unfinished apartment building. After questioning her, they find that she has a lease on the apartment to be built and she has decided to move in on the date the lease stipulates, even when the building is still being constructed. Behind schedule, the building will not be finished for many months but this does not deter the lady. City officials call on health officials, psychiatrists and "trouble-shooters" to intercede, but none are successful—especially when she wins over Toody and Muldoon to her side with her cooking.

Trivia, etc. Molly Picon is announced in the opening screen credits as "Special Guest." Many second season episodes were rewrites and variations of first-season episodes. This is the only exception - instead of a variation-on-a-theme, this is a sequel to production #5, "I Won't Go."

Production #37 "REMEMBER ST. PETERSBURG"
Copyright Notice: Eupolis Productions, Inc. © October 28, 1962; LP24132
NBC Review: July 31, 1962
Initial Telecast: October 28, 1962
Teleplay scripted by Tony Webster.
Directed by Nat Hiken.

Cast: Maurice Brenner (*Charles Brooks*); Fay De Witt (*Madame Sonya*); Fred Gwynne (*Officer Francis Muldoon*); Don Keefer (*Dr. Mitchell, the psychiatrist*); Al Lewis (*Officer Leo Schnauser*); Paul Lipson (*the man*); Mara Lynn (*woman in curlers*); Charlotte Rae (*Sylvia Schnauser*); Paul Reed (*Captain Paul Block*); Joe E. Ross (*Gunther Toody*); and Larry Storch (*Pinky*).

Plot: A trio of con men and one woman operate a fortune-telling shop in order to dupe a nobleman, Count Schnauser-Dosteyevski, into marrying a wealthy Bronx widow. They set up a plan to separate the newly wed countess from a part of her wealth. Their plan goes off track, when (in a case of mistaken identity) they accept Sylvia Schnauser as the wealthy widow and her husband, Officer Schnauser, as the count. Not only do the con men convince them that they are wealthy and titled, but when Officer Toody is sent to investigate the store front operation of the trio, he too is led to believe that he is of royal blood, the long-lost brother of Count Schnauser. On the advice of the police psychiatrist, the other officers go along with the ruse. They do so by dressing as guards, smoking long cigarettes.

Trivia, etc. Larry Storch is credited in opening screen credits as "Special Guest."

Production #39 "THAT'S SHOW BUSINESS"

Copyright Notice: Eupolis Productions, Inc. © November 4, 1962; LP24133
NBC Review: August 10, 1962
Initial Telecast: November 4, 1962
Teleplay scripted by Gary Belkin.
Directed by Nat Hiken.

Cast: Fred Gwynne (*Officer Francis Muldoon*); Ben Hayes (*financial backer*); David Hurst (*Stuart*); House Jameson (*Mr. Fenwick*); Al Lewis (*Officer Leo Schnauser*); Jimmy Little (*McBride*); Ruth Masters (*Mrs. Muldoon*); Paul McGrath (*Mr. Stuart*); Helen Parker (*Peggy Muldoon*); Beatrice Pons (*Lucille Toody*); Paul Reed (*Captain Paul Block*); Joe E. Ross (*Gunther Toody*); John Seymour (*financial backer*); Larry Storch (*Charlie, the drunk*); Joe Sullivan (*financial backer*); and Bernie West (*commissioner's aide*).

Plot: Muldoon's sister Peggy is set to audition for a role in a Broadway play at the producer's apartment. Suspicious of the producer's motives, Toody and Muldoon, garbed in tuxedoes and posing as wealthy "angels," visit the apartment where they are surprised to find other backers. Hearing only about one-tenth of the play, Toody is sold on its merits and, despite Muldoon's warning, raises $2,000 among his fellow officers, the Captain included, to invest in it. All have visions of quick wealth. On closer examination, the theme of the play turns out to be police brutality. The precinct members attempt to show that no such thing exists, and their efforts are met with much amusement. This inspires him to change the play from a drama to a comedy.

Trivia, etc. The producers were reminded by George Norford of the NBC Broadcast Standards Department to keep the names of all the bars depicted in this episode fictitious.

When Gary Belkin sold Nat Hiken this story for a plot proposal in August of 1962, for $350 (check #1098), the original title was "The Angel." It was also known as "Backers' Audition" before the title changed again to "That's Show Business" for the final script.

Production #38 "TOODY, UNDERCOVER"

Copyright Notice: Eupolis Productions, Inc. © November 11, 1962; LP24134
NBC Review: July 20, 1962
Initial Telecast: November 11, 1962
Teleplay scripted by Terry Ryan.
Directed by Nat Hiken.

Cast: Bruce Gordon (*Bigelow*); Fred Gwynne (*Officer Francis Muldoon*); Bernard Hughes (*the Inspector*); Al Lewis (*Officer Leo Schnauser*); George Mathews (*Peru*); Paul Reed (*Captain Paul Block*); and Joe E. Ross (*Gunther Toody*).

Extras in the cast: Sammy Birch, Frankie Gio, Harry Hornick, Jock Livingston, Barney Martin, Al Nessoe, Lou Polan, Brooks Rogers, Jane Rosse, Nick Saunders, Alfred Spindleman, and Harry Stanton.

Plot: Toody, in plainclothes, is mistaken for a hood by some Kansas City mobsters in New York. They take him into their confidence on a big bank job they are planning. When Toody gives the appearance that he is well informed about the movements of the police and their signals and the layout of banks, the crooks defer to him. The bank robbery is more successful than the mobsters dreamed, mainly because Toody, with his miserable memory, has misled the police and has them waiting at the wrong bank. When the kingpins of crime hear of this wizard, they arrange to meet him. Toody claims that he has planned the biggest caper ever - Fort Knox. But to get to that destination, the jumping-off spot is the Federal Penitentiary at Leavenworth, not too far distant from the Fort, where no one would suspect such a caper being planned. The maddest rush to qualify for residence at Leavenworth results and Toody has the mobsters admitting to federal crimes that nobody else could ever pin on them in order to be "in." Toody accommodates them all, providing transportation to jail.

Trivia, etc. Bruce Gordon, best known to television audiences as Frank Nitti on *The Untouchables*, is billed in the opening screen credits as "Special Guest."
    This episode was loosely adapted from the short story, "Convention Pals" by Charles Molyneux Brown; it originally appeared in the January 30, 1937 issue of *Detective Fiction Weekly*. Brown submitted the short story to Nat Hiken of Eupolis Productions, Inc. on Oct. 5, 1962.

The plot of the story: Hunk O'Brien and Angus Christie, two not-overly-bright uniformed cops on the New York force, report to work one morning and are assigned by their captain to plainclothes duty protecting lumbermen attending a convention at a local hotel, from gamblers, chippies and the like. Reporting at the hotel, they are greeted without enthusiasm by the assistant manager and the house dick, both of whom had previous experiences with the pair. The men are presented with free meal tickets and mingle with the lobby crowd. Prowling a corridor later, they encounter a pair of conventioneers who are great practical jokers; they have a drink with them and establish what they refer to as "friendly contacts." Things are quiet while conventioneers are in meetings, but in mid-afternoon the pair get a call to the seventh floor and join the two jokers there, who tell them they've spotted a pair of slickers crashing into a room where there is a friendly craps game going on. The officers are given a description of the suspicious characters. O'Brien and Christie—who always manage to escape from one jam or another—crash the game and put the cuffs on the two protesting players. Suddenly, the door pops open and three armed men barge in to raid the game.

The two cops recognize a much-wanted crook as the leader and in the melee following, manage to subdue the three crooks. The house dick and the assistant manager arrive and identify the first pair the two cops grabbed as the president and vice-president of the Lumbermen's Association. This is an embarrassment to the two cops, who explain that they were tipped off by two members and are told that the pair has a reputation for practical jokes. Just as it looks as though our heroes are in for a stern remonstration from their captain, they learn that they have grabbed a notorious crook and his two accomplices. Luck has once again been on the policemen's side.

Charles M. Brown's previous writing credits included some 100 short stories and novelettes published in pulp mystery and detective magazines from 1934 to 1939; short stories in *Cosmopolitan*, *Colliers*, and *American* from 1939-41; agents in New York at various times, August Lenniger, Lurton Blassingame and Harold Ober Associates. His screen credits included an original story, *Irish Luck*, for Monogram Films in August of 1939.

Brown was familiar with screen comedies, having written three original *Blondie* stories during his twelve weeks at Columbia Pictures from October 1939-February 1940. One of those stories was the basis of the completed film, *Blondie on a Budget*.

While neither the short story nor the author was credited onscreen, Hiken did agree to read the short story Brown submitted to him. After viewing this episode, it remains unclear whether or not this episode was based on or inspired by the short story.

Production #40 "I HATE CAPTAIN BLOCK"

Copyright Notice: Eupolis Productions, Inc. © November 18, 1962; LP24135
NBC Review: August 18, 1962
Initial Telecast: November 18, 1962
Teleplay scripted by Ben Joelson and Buddy Arnold.
Directed by Stanley Prager.

Cast: Patricia Bright (*Mrs. Claire Block*); Heywood Hale Broun (*Thompson, the customer*); Fred Gwynne (*Officer Francis Muldoon*); Holly Irving (*older woman*); James Karen (*customer/bird owner*); Barbara Lang (*Vivian Hanson*); Al Lewis (*Officer Leo Schnauser*); Frank Milano (*customer/bird owner*); Beatrice Pons (*Lucille Toody*); Charlotte Rae (*Sylvia Schnauser*); Paul Reed (*Captain Paul Block*); Joe E. Ross (*Gunther Toody*); Cecil Roy (*voice of the parrot*); Arnold Soboloff (*pet store owner*).

Plot: When Captain Block goes on vacation, he leaves his parrot in Toody's care. Toody is determined to train the bird how to talk, but all he manages to do is teach him the phrase, "I hate Captain Block." After many hilarious machinations to silence the bird, Toody is surprised by Captain Block's unannounced return. To Toody and Muldoon's surprise, the bird now speaks politely . . . until Captain Block teaches the bird to say "I hate Gunther Toody."

Trivia, etc. The original title for this script was "The Captain's Parrot" in the earliest (first) draft of the script.

Production #41 "A STAR IS BORN IN THE BRONX"

Copyright Notice: Eupolis Productions, Inc. © November 25, 1962; LP24136
NBC Review: September 14, 1962
Initial Telecast: November 25, 1962
Teleplay scripted by Terry Ryan.
Directed by Stanley Prager.

Cast: Kenny Delmar (*Colonel Culpepper*); John Gibson (*Babcock*); Fred

Gwynne (*Officer Francis Muldoon*); Lu Leonard (*the shopper*); Al Lewis (*Officer Leo Schnauser*); Beatrice Pons (*Lucille Toody*); Charlotte Rae (*Sylvia Schnauser*); and Joe E. Ross (*Gunther Toody*).

Extras in the cast: David Doyle, Fred Harper, Sammy Smith and Bill Wendell.

Plot: Sylvia Schnauser fears she will not get a desperately desired role in *Tempest of the Tropics*, to be presented by the 53rd Drama Club. She has been frustrated many times before when she was on the brink of being discovered, only to have someone like Dorothy Lamour step in to take the opportunity from her. The owner of a popular cookie company sees her in a film and decides she's just right to appear in the TV commercials. Sylvia thinks this is just a device of a big movie firm to tie her to a contract for a small salary. She makes outrageous demands but they are all met by the advertising firm handling the cookie account that must deliver her or lose the account. She misses her great opportunity again when her demands including filming of *Tempest of the Tropics*, with her in the lead. The owner of the cookie company sees the film becomes disenchanted with Sylvia.

Trivia, etc. Al Lewis recalled in the January 25, 1989 issue of the *New York Daily News* that "Once they added Charlotte Rae - a marvelous, funny actress - as my wife, Sylvia, shows were written for us." His recollection may just have been accurate as there were a few episodes during the second season, like this one, in which Leo Schnauser and Sylvia Schnauser were the central characters, and the scripts had very little to do with Muldoon and Toody as police officers.

The original title for this script was "Sylvia, the Star" in the earliest (first) draft of the script.

Production #42 "PRETZEL MARY"

Copyright Notice: Eupolis Productions, Inc. © December 2, 1962; LP24137
NBC Review: September 21, 1962
Initial Telecast: December 2, 1962
Teleplay scripted by Gary Belkin and Art Baer, based on a story by Art Baer.
Directed by Nat Hiken.

Cast: Sibyl Bowan (*Pretzel Mary*); Ossie Davis (*Officer Omar*); Howard

Freeman (*customer in park*); Hank Garrett (*Officer Ed Nicholson*); Fred Gwynne (*Officer Francis Muldoon*); Teddy Hart (*the junk man*); Al Lewis (*Officer Leo Schnauser*); Paul Reed (*Captain Paul Block*); Joe E. Ross (*Gunther Toody*); and Larry Storch (*Charlie, the drunk*).

Extras in the cast: Bernie Allen, Lou Bernard, Paul Lipson, Janet Paul, Bob Randell, Jane Rose, and Melville Ruick.

Plot: Pretzel Mary, who dresses in rags and presses the public into buying her pretzels, is adamant against buying a $5 sales license. She lives in a hovel with lumpy furniture in which she has stuffed over $1 million dollars in cash that she has made on wise investments. Toody, Muldoon and Schnauser, believing the lady to be poverty-stricken, plan a surprise for her. While she is away, the officers have junkmen move out all the old furniture and outfit the hovel with new pieces. Mary is almost driven mad when she finds her hoard gone. The money is ultimately found, but Mary—having learned her lesson—decides to distribute it all to charity.

Trivia, etc. The original title for this episode was "The Miser." The opening shot was the same used for the closing credits. (The dead giveaway is the flag hanging above the Precinct doors, waving in the wind.)

When Leo complains in the beginning of the episode, he makes references to Charlie's former drinking problem, which would lead to the events depicted in production #53, "Here Comes Charlie."

Production #43 "142 TICKETS ON THE AISLE"

Copyright Notice: Eupolis Productions, Inc. © December 9, 1962; LP24138
NBC Review: September 21, 1962
Initial Telecast: December 9, 1962
Teleplay scripted by Tony Webster.
Directed by Stanley Prager.

Cast: Hank Garrett (*Officer Ed Nicholson*); Betty Garde (*the older woman*); Fred Gwynne (*Officer Francis Muldoon*); Janis Hansen (*the young blonde*); Hilda Haynes (*the black woman*); Al Lewis (*Officer Leo Schnauser*); Beatrice Pons (*Lucille Toody*); Charlotte Rae (*Sylvia Schnauser*); Paul Reed (*Captain Paul Block*); Joe E. Ross (*Gunther Toody*); Eugene Troobnick (*the ticket man*); and Bernie West (*ticket purchaser*).

Extras in the cast: Matt Crowley, Ronald Knight, Parker McCormick, Charles Randall, Stanley Simmonds, Sammy Smith, Ted Thurston, and Michael Vale.

Plot: The entertainment committee of the 53rd Precinct decides on a theater party for their annual social event. As Schnauser, Muldoon and Toody quickly discover, Broadway plays are hot tickets—getting 142 tickets for a single performance without having to wait more than a few months is almost impossible. The only play for which they can get that many tickets for the following week is a flop called *Little Miss Pioneer*. Most of the precinct members do not want to see it, but when a reporter for the city paper observes the officers leaving the theater, the news hits the papers that the so-called "wholesome" entertainment is so lewd that the local police were threatening to shut it down. This starts a run on the box office. By the time the committee finally decides to buy tickets for *Little Miss Pioneer*, they learn that it is sold out for a year.

Trivia, etc. During the meeting in the beginning of this episode, one of the women and one of the officers suggest they all go see *How to Succeed in Business Without Really Trying* on Broadway. Later, another suggestion was made for *A Funny Thing Happened on the Way to the Forum*. This was an in-joke: while a couple of the series' cast members were being filmed during the day for *Car 54*, they were actually playing roles in those Broadway performances in the evening.

The first draft of the script was titled "The Theatre Party." The premise was the same, but the sequence of events was different. In order to convince the committee that the play should be selected, the producer agrees to have the company go to the precinct in costume in police vans to give the precinct a sample of the performance. A reporter and photographer, seeing the cast being loaded into the police vans, misinterpret what is happening and a front-page story appears stating that the show was raided because of a lewd performance. When the script was revised, this sequence was dropped and replaced with a second meeting of the "committee" - this way the producers could avoid filming an additional day to complete this sequence. The revision featured no van, no committee members, and only the reporter (not a photographer) so the cost of hiring actors and equipment was cut for budgetary reasons.

Production #47 "STOP, THIEF!"
Copyright Notice: Eupolis Productions, Inc. © December 16, 1962; LP24139
NBC Review: November 5, 1962
Initial Telecast: December 16, 1962
Teleplay scripted by Tony Webster.
Directed by Stanley Prager.

Cast: Patricia Bright (*Mrs. Claire Block*); Ossie Davis (*Officer Omar*); Hank Garrett (*Officer Ed Nicholson*); Fred Gwynne (*Officer Francis Muldoon*); Jack Healy (*Rodriguez*); Al Lewis (*Officer Leo Schnauser*); Beatrice Pons (*Lucille Toody*); Paul Reed (*Captain Paul Block*); and Joe E. Ross (*Gunther Toody*).

Extras in the cast: Martin Ashe, Roger C. Carmel, Dan Frazer, Alan Manson and Van Palmer.

Plot: A television actor disguised as an inspector arrives at the Precinct by mistake, believing he was supposed to be filmed for a cops-and-robbers series. While waiting for the patrol car to pick him up, Captain Block assists the actor in reading his lines. Muldoon and Toody overhear the men reading their lines, and think (from the dialogue) that the Captain is a kleptomaniac. They think the Captain has stolen the presents he bought for the boys at the precinct - so the men try to replace them. Chaos ensues.

Trivia, etc. The former title for this drama on early drafts of the script was

"Captain Block, Kleptomaniac."

RERUN

December 23, 1962 featured a rebroadcast of "Christmas at the 53rd."

Production #44 "J' ADORE MULDOON"

Copyright Notice: Eupolis Productions, Inc. © December 30, 1962; LP24140
(Copyrighted under the title "Je T'Adore Muldoon")
NBC Review: November 1962
Initial Telecast: December 30, 1962
Teleplay scripted by Ben Joelson.
Directed by Stanley Prager.

Cast: Fred Gwynne (*Officer Francis Muldoon*); Katherine Helmond (*girl who falls for Muldoon*); Jerry Jarrett (*girl who falls for Muldoon*); June Jerome (*Rhoda*); Lynn Karington (*girl who falls for Muldoon*); Lainie Kazan (*girl who falls for Muldoon*); Lisa Loughlin (*Darlene*); Ruth Masters (*Mrs. Muldoon*); Joe E. Ross (*Gunther Toody*); Sheila Smith (*girl who falls for Muldoon*); Jean Stapleton (*girl who falls for Muldoon*); and Inger Stratton (*girl who falls for Muldoon*).

Plot: Muldoon has trouble selecting a queen when he is chosen to be king of the Precinct Brotherhood's Mardi Gras celebration. The officers attempt to build up Muldoon's confidence by making suggestions, and realizing he is the only bachelor in the precinct, Muldoon dons a fake mustache, changes his suit and style, and begins acting like a cross between Francis X. Bushman, Frank Sinatra and David Niven. As "Frankie" Muldoon, he spends the evening wooing all the single young women. His success fails when Captain Block introduces his niece to the revised Muldoon - which fails to get her the spot as queen of the Mardi Gras. In the end, Francis is forced to bring his mother to the party.

Trivia, etc. The former title on early drafts of the script was "The Day Muldoon Had It."

Production #45 "THE WHITE ELEPHANT"

Copyright Notice: Eupolis Productions, Inc. © January 6, 1963; LP24141
NBC Review: October 22, 1962
Initial Telecast: January 6, 1963
Teleplay scripted by Terry Ryan.
Directed by Stanley Prager.

Cast: Dort Clark (*Eddie Fontaine*); Arlene Golonka (*Laverne*); Fred Gwynne (*Officer Francis Muldoon*); Jake LaMotta (*Duke*); Al Lewis (*Officer Leo Schnauser*); Joe Marr (*criminal*); Marie Pinckard (*elderly crook at end of episode*); Paul Reed (*Captain Paul Block*); Joe E. Ross (*Gunther Toody*); Eugene Troobnick (*Barney*); and Wayne Wilson (*elderly crook at end of episode*).

Extras in the cast: Teddy Hart, Janet Paul, Jon Richards and Michael Vale.

Plot: A trio of crooks rent a closed luncheonette next to a bank with assets of $22,000,000. They have all the necessary equipment to break through the kitchen wall of the luncheonette, and into the back of the vault containing the millions - and they hope to have all the time and the privacy to do it. The luncheonette has always been a white elephant, however, and Toody and Muldoon are intent on its success. They pledge their support to that and insist that all the members of the precinct eat there. While Toody and Muldoon become a thorn in the crooks' side, the result is that the luncheonette becomes a success, even adding catering to their services. Courtesy of Toody and Muldoon's interference, the three crooks have been transformed into legitimate businessmen.

Trivia, etc. The title on early drafts of the script was "Out to Lunch."
The actor who plays the role of one of the crooks was Joe Marr, a resident of Brooklyn, New York. Marr had previously served a 10-year sentence in San Quentin for armed robbery. A week after this episode was broadcast, Marr requested in writing that he be given more roles - including that of a police officer. "I would like you to use me as a cop on the show on a regular basis. You see, I have a complete, unconditional pardon for my robbery conviction. People like Elia Kazan, Josh Logan and Jose Quintero are writing letters in my behalf - people I have worked for as an actor."
The idea of having Marr play another role on the series came to a

halt, when, on Jan. 16, 1963, Marr sent Nat Hiken and Billy Friedberg, a ludicrous letter explaining that he was a Catholic-Communist, and proposed that when someone in California recognized him as a police officer, the attention and news would leak to the press. President Kennedy and Nikita Khrushchev would then fight over the ownership of Joe Marr, and after taking a trip to Russia, he would return with two carloads of Stalin buttons. Being hailed as a hero, Marr closed his proposal to Hiken with the statement, "If you put me on *Car 54* on a regular basis, I'll cut you on fifty percent of the profits." Naturally, Hiken and Friedberg decided not to have anything else to do with Joe Marr.

Woody Allen's motion picture, *Small Time Crooks* (2000), features a similar premise and might just be a nod to this classic *Car 54* episode.

Production #46 "BENNY THE BOOKIE'S LAST CHANCE"
Copyright Notice: Eupolis Productions, Inc. © January 13, 1963; LP25010
NBC Review: October 25, 1962
Initial Telecast: January 13, 1963
Written by Art Baer and Gary Belkin.
Directed by Stanley Prager.

Cast: Gene Baylos (*Benny*); Ossie Davis (*Officer Omar*); Fred Gwynne (*Officer Francis Muldoon*); Margaret Hamilton (*the spinster*); Gerald Hiken (*Mr. Katz*); Al Lewis (*Officer Leo Schnauser*); B.S. Pully (*Mrs. Brown*); Paul Reed (*Captain Paul Block*); Florence Robinson (*Mrs. Katz*); and Joe E. Ross (*Gunther Toody*).

Extras in the cast: Robert Ader, Tom Ahearne, Rick Colitti, Lew Herbert, Gilbert Mack and Beatrice Ruth.

Plot: Toody and Muldoon go to the Captain to request that Benny the Bookmaker be paroled. They tell the Captain the neighborhood has signed a petition and has leased a candy store for Benny. When Benny is ensconced in his new job, his old "customers" will not leave him alone, so he falls back into his bookmaking ways. "Mr. Brown," the big boss, finding Benny has invaded his territory, places a bet with Benny - and wins - so Benny owes him $30,000. If he doesn't pay, Mr. Brown threatens to have him "cut up in little bits." Benny tries to get arrested again - and turns in a fire alarm instead. He is hailed as a hero.

Trivia, etc. Previous drafts of this script were entitled "Back to Jail" and "Parole Board." Gene Baylos plays the role of "Benny the Bookie" in this episode, billed during the opening credits as "Special Guest." Baylos played the role of another con, "Backdoor Benny" in episode #3, "How Sweet Sing Sing" and in that episode, he has a scene in which he tries to give a confession to a police officer, but Muldoon and Toody prevent him from returning to prison. Baylos reenacts a scene from a previous episode, in which he remarks, "These are fingerprints? These are *smudges!*" The entire scene is reproduced almost word for word. This was not the only second-season episode to restage a scene or skit from the previous season, which suggests that Nat Hiken was having difficulty in devising new material.

Trivia, etc. While Margaret Hamilton's appearance on this episode was minimal, Eupolis arranged for NEA syndicate to interview Hamilton. The story ran the weekend of the show, in approximately 75 papers.

Production #48 "THE PRESIDENTIAL ITCH"
Copyright Notice: Eupolis Productions, Inc. © January 20, 1963; LP25286
NBC Review: November 23, 1962
Initial Telecast: January 20, 1963
Teleplay scripted by Nat Hiken, Billy Friedberg, and Robert Van Scoyk, from a story by Robert Van Scoyk.
Directed by Stanley Prager.

Cast: Ossie Davis (*Officer Omar*); Hank Garrett (*Officer Ed Nicholson*); Fred Gwynne (*Officer Francis Muldoon*); Al Lewis (*Officer Leo Schnauser*); Jimmy Little (*McBride*); Beatrice Pons (*Lucille Toody*); Paul Reed (*Captain Paul Block*); Joe E. Ross (*Gunther Toody*); and Bernie West (*Mr. Gander*).

Extras in the cast: Bill Adler, Elizabeth Eustis, Bob Kaliban, Paul Melton and Maurice Shrog.

Plot: Toody is selected to run against Muldoon, the incumbent President of the Precinct Club. At first unenthusiastic, Toody succumbs to the presidential itch and launches a vigorous campaign employing the disreputable but remarkably effective tactics of his politically shrewd manager, McBride. Faced with defeat, Muldoon's supporters trick Toody into revealing to all the members that he believes Muldoon to be the only man capable of running the club. This insures Muldoon's re-election.

Trivia, etc. The former title on early drafts of the script was "The Election."

In connection with this episode, Eupolis had exposure on three shows - *Today*, *The Tonight Show* and *The Merv Griffin Show*. The promotion started with an idea suggested by the script. Giant "Toody for President" posters were mailed to columnists, feature writers, TV editors, network program producers and station promotion managers. A few days later, these same people received giant "Muldoon for President" posters. A few of the recipients did not know what the posters were for, but put them up on their office walls.

Next, the newspaper and TV people received a card with Toody and Muldoon buttons attached; also attached was an ersatz political bulletin, describing the election battle and saying the results would be revealed on the January 20 show. All pertinent details of the show were given. The same newspaper and TV people received a bulletin from The Friends of Bronx Culture, explaining that everybody in America could vote by watching, and urging the recipients to help get out the vote. These lists received campaign literature from both Toody and Muldoon headquarters. They received ballots, in a form suitable for reproduction. The last mailing consisted of photos from the episode and a highlight copy.

It could be hard to measure the value of something as intangible as "excitement," but it must have been counted as a plus when columnist Hedda Hopper and UPI's Coast columnist Vernon Scott wore Toody buttons for a week, and the *Los Angeles Times*' Cecil Smith urged his readers to vote for Muldoon.

Posters and ballots were incorporated into local programs broadcast over KOFC-TV in Lake Charles, Louisiana, KUTV in Salt Lake City, Utah, WCIV in Charleston, North Carolina, WFLA-TV in Tampa, Florida, and one television station in Zanesville, Ohio.

Production #49 "TOODY AND MULDOON MEET THE RUSSIANS"

Copyright Notice: Eupolis Productions, Inc. © January 27, 1963; LP25011
NBC Review: November 16, 1962

Initial Telecast: January 27, 1963
Teleplay by Nat Hiken and Billy Friedberg.
Directed by Stanley Prager.

Cast: Heywood Hale Broun (*Julius*); Fred Gwynne (*Officer Francis Muldoon*); Gerald Hiken (*Domsky*); Mara Lynn (*General*); Jules Munshin (*Malonov*); B. S. Pully (*the spy*); and Joe E. Ross (*Gunther Toody*).

Plot: Toody and Muldoon are assigned to accompany two representatives from Russia: Malanov (who is to speak at the U.N.) and a female General. The Russians, believing the New York Police are the most underpaid group in the country, order Toody and Muldoon to show them "the Imperialistic pigs." Toody agrees and takes Malanov to the ball game, where the Russian falls in love with the game—and American hot dogs. Muldoon takes the General to a beauty parlor and dress shop. The General wants to go to a burlesque show because she believes all American women spend all their time in bars and become striptease artistes. She soon learns this is untrue, and gets intoxicated on martinis (much to Muldoon's horror). At a meeting for Generals and their wives, the female officer gives her version of the striptease, removing only her gloves and fur piece in the process. The wives faint. The final scene has Muldoon and Toody seeing the Russian visitors off at the airport. Malanov whispers to Toody to be sure and send him the baseball scores. The General kisses Muldoon goodbye and calls him "pussy cat."

Trivia, etc. The former title on early drafts of the script was "Take Me To Your Leader."

The Columbus, Ohio *Citizen-Journal* reviewed the quality of satire on Communism on this episode as "most expertly handled and effective." The same review closed with: "It was one of the funniest yet on *Car 54* - but carried a philosophical message along with a perfect blend of humor and satire."

To help publicize this episode, it was arranged for McClure's Syndicate to interview Jules Munshin. The story appeared on the weekend of the show, in approximately 60 papers. Opening credits stated Jules Munshin as "Special Guest."

The producer of *Car 54* received a large number of fan letters from viewers. Almost every episode of the series prompted a large handful of letters, and this episode is no exception. Among the fan letters was one from Tinsley W. Rucker, President of the Dixon-Powdermaker Furniture

Company in Jacksonville, Florida, who wrote a letter dated Feb. 1, 1963:

> The other evening I watched the program of *Car 54* regarding the special Russian envoy and the female Russian general's encounter with our two New York Cops. My wife and I both felt that it was one of the finest bits of entertainment we have ever had the opportunity to watch. It was well done and I feel very strongly that you have placed this type of person in proper perspective. If these people coming to this country were handled in the fashion that you have outlined and the information regarding them was handled in the way that your story went, we would probably have a more accurate picture of the leadership of the Russian people.
>
> It was comedy with wonderful underlying philosophy. All of the people responsible for this should receive a big vote of thanks from all of us in the United States. Camay and Gleem, as the sponsors, are also entitled to our thanks for sponsoring such an effective program.

Production #50 "HERE WE GO AGAIN"
Copyright Notice: Eupolis Productions, Inc. © February 3, 1963; LP25012
NBC Review: December 6, 1962
Initial Telecast: February 3, 1963
Teleplay scripted by Gary Belkin and Art Baer.
Directed by Stanley Prager.

Cast: Edward Atienza (*Swifty*); Patricia Bright (*Mrs. Claire Block*); Amelie Darlson (*Trixie*); Fred Gwynne (*Officer Francis Muldoon*); Jake LaMotta (*Muscles*); Al Lewis (*Officer Leo Schnauser*); Judith Lowery (*the old woman*); Conrad Nagel (*as himself*); Beatrice Pons (*Lucille Toody*); Paul Reed (*Captain Paul Block*); and Joe E. Ross (*Gunther Toody*).

Extras in the cast: Cliff Carpenter, Phil Kenneally, Walter Kinsella, and Alan Manson.

Plot: Dawson Cameron Wright of the *Police File* television program, seeks Francis Muldoon's assistance in the preparation of an episode they hope to dramatize - the single-handed capture in 1919 by Captain Patrick Muldoon of the Baby Face Gordon gang as they attempted to escape (dressed in police uniforms) after robbing the Federal Reserve vault of $12 million in gold bullion. The question is - how did Muldoon's father recognize the "policemen" as crooks? Francis learns the answer from his late father's diary - the crooks wore regulation summer uniforms on October 15, the day police change to winter uniforms. When Francis reveals this to Baby Face (now in the "Home for the Aged"), Baby Face and his elderly cohorts attempt to duplicate the crime - this time successfully.

Trivia, etc. A title on an early draft of the script was "Old Bankrobbers Never Die." The first draft was titled "That Old Gang of Mine."

At the end of the episode, a group of men dressed as the Keystone Cops are seen driving down a road in an antique car. Silent-movie music (composed and conducted by John Strauss) is heard on the soundtrack.

The western footage on the television is the signature opening of *Have Gun - Will Travel*, with an actor's voice dubbed over the theme song.

Production #51 "THE STAR BOARDER"

Copyright Notice: Eupolis Productions, Inc. © February 10, 1963; LP25161
NBC Review: December 5, 1962
Initial Telecast: February 10, 1963
Teleplay scripted by Terry Ryan.
Directed by Stanley Prager.

Cast: Tom Bosley (*Peterson*); Ossie Davis (*Omar*); Dana Elcar (*the F.B.I. Agent*); Wallace Engelhard (*Leo's cousin*); Hank Garrett (*Officer Ed Nicholson*); Fred Gwynne (*Officer Francis Muldoon*); Bob Kaliban (*the man*); Al Lewis (*Officer Leo Schnauser*); Brandon Maggart (*store owner*); Beatrice Pons (*Lucille*); Paul Reed (*Captain Paul Block*); Joe E. Ross (*Gunther Toody*); Paula Stewart (*Rhoda*); and Sandi Vincent (*Peterson's woman*).

Plot: To help with finances, the Toodys take in a boarder: The Reverend Peterson. In reality, Peterson is a counterfeiter who only masquerades as a clergyman. Unaware that his landlord is a policeman, Peterson pays his rent with counterfeit bills. Toody, in turn, obliviously uses the phony dollars to pay his own bills. The counterfeit scheme is discovered and the Feds begin to close in on their suspect. The crook is caught while playing the piano at Captain Block's surprise party.

Trivia, etc. Actor Tom Bosley is listed in the opening screen credits as "Special Guest."

Production #52 "THE BIGGEST DAY OF THE YEAR"
Copyright Notice: Eupolis Productions, Inc. © February 17, 1963; LP25162
NBC Review: December 5, 1962
Initial Telecast: February 17, 1963
Teleplay scripted by Lou Solomon and Bob Howard.
Directed by Stanley Prager.

Cast: Patricia Bright (*Mrs. Claire Block*); Hank Garrett (*Officer Ed Nicholson*); Fred Gwynne (*Officer Francis Muldoon*); Al Henderson (*Officer O'Hara*); House Jameson (*the man*); Al Lewis (*Officer Leo Schnauser*); Jimmie Little (*McBride*); Beatrice Pons (*Lucille Toody*); Paul Reed (*Captain Paul Block*); and Joe E. Ross (*Gunther Toody*).

Extras in the cast: Bernard Barrow, John C. Becher, Ed Bryce, Vince Carrol, Phil Carter, Matt Crowley, Nicholas Grimes, Ed Wagner and Charles White.

Plot: Toody is sick and tired of Muldoon remonstrating with him about forgetting important anniversaries. To his credit, Muldoon remembers all the birthdays, all the Bar Mitzvahs, all the christenings. Toody "remembers 'em either too late - or too early . . . or forgets 'em altogether." Naturally, Toody is thrilled to remember that in a few days he and Muldoon will be observing a tenth anniversary together on the police force—a date his conscientious partner has apparently forgotten. He even teases Muldoon about the big day. Muldoon racks his brain trying to remember *what* big day that is. He gets everybody on the force thinking a big thing will happen - but nobody, including Muldoon, will admit he doesn't know what it will be. When the day arrives and Toody hands Muldoon his present, Muldoon is forced to remind him that it's their *ninth* anniversary together, not their tenth.

Trivia, etc. The former title on early drafts of the script was "A Toast to Wednesday" and "What Day Is It?"

The name "Captain Kangaroo" was included in the script in referencing a children's show. On the advice of Alys Reese, editor of the NBC Broadcast Standards Department, the reference was changed.

Stanley Prager, the director, makes a brief appearance as an "extra" in this episode.

Production #53 "HERE COMES CHARLIE"

Copyright Notice: Eupolis Productions, Inc. © February 24, 1963; LP25163
NBC Review: January 10, 1963
Initial Telecast: February 24, 1963
Teleplay scripted by Nat Hiken and Billy Friedberg.
Directed by Stanley Prager.

Cast: Edwin Cooper (*the old man*); Ossie Davis (*Officer Omar*); Mickey Deems (*Officer Charlie Fleischer*); Sally DeMay (*old woman*); Hank Garrett (*Officer Ed Nicholson*); Fred Gwynne (*Officer Francis Muldoon*); Al Lewis (*Officer Leo Schnauser*); Margaret Hamilton (*Miss Pownthleroy*); Paul Reed (*Captain Paul Block*); Joe E. Ross (*Gunther Toody*); and Larry Storch (*Charlie*).

Extras in the cast: Michael Dana, Jim Demarest, Brendan Fay, Henry Lascoe, Joe E. Marks, Terry O'Sullivan and Joe Sweeney.

Plot: Toody and Muldoon have taken an interest in Charlie, a local fellow named Charlie who perpetually gets drunk and promises not to do it again. They have allowed him to "sleep it off" so often in an empty jail cell that the Captain threatens to put a stop to the philanthropic work. The boys line Charlie up for a job at a dry-cleaning house, but Charlie drinks the cleaning fluid (alcohol); in a bakery, but Charlie drinks all the rum for the rum cakes; a home furnishing store, but Charlie drank the furniture polish. Finally they decide a diamond-cutting establishment would be the only place for the hapless Charlie. This appears to be a good fit. But the upright, timid souls who work with him are completely unnerved by Toody and Muldoon's continuous "inspections" (actually a ruse simply to check up on Charlie), and they all take to the bottle. At the end, Charlie's boss innocently tells him where the lighter fluid is kept . . . and Charlie is back in his "furnished cell" at the precinct station.

Trivia, etc. Larry Storch is listed as "Special Guest" on the opening credits. To help publicize this episode, it was arranged for the NEA to interview Larry Storch. The story appeared on the weekend of the show, in approximately 75 papers. "Nat Hiken was a genius," recalled Storch. "I had a wonderful time on *Car 54*. Joe E. Ross was one of my best friends. And the scripts allowed me to be as funny as I could be during the filming."

Seven names of business places were used in this episode. Alys Reese, editor of the NBC Broadcast Standards Department, looked up each of the businesses in the Bronx telephone directory and finding none apparent in the book, approved the script for filming, under the assumption that all the names of the businesses were fictitious.

Production #55 "SEE YOU AT THE BAR MITZVAH"
Copyright Notice: Eupolis Productions, Inc. © March 3, 1963; LP25164
NBC Review: January 16, 1963
Initial Telecast: March 3, 1963
Teleplay scripted by Max Wilk.
Directed by Stanley Prager.

Cast: Claude Gersene (*Joel Potras*); Perry Greene (*small boy*); Fred Gwynne (*Officer Francis Muldoon*); Gerald Hiken (*Katz*); Al Lewis (*Officer Leo Schnauser*); Paul O'Keefe (*the kid*); Lou Polan (*police officer*); B.S. Pully (*Potras*); Paul Reed (*Captain Paul Block*); and Joe E. Ross (*Gunther Toody*).

Extras in the cast: Phil Carter, Joey Faye, Dan Morgan, Arthur Rubin and Reuben Singer.

Plot: Toody and Muldoon coach the PAL basketball game. One of the boys, Joel Potras, is having his Bar Mitzvah. Joel is afraid no one will come because his father is the landlord and has never done anything for his tenants. Toody and Muldoon try to convince the people to attend - but instead, find confirmation of the boy's suspicions. Toody and Muldoon are to take some prisoners to Night Court - so instead they take them to the Bar

Mitzvah. Potras is so touched that he mends his ways.

Trivia, etc. The former title for this drama on early drafts of the script was "A Funny Thing Happened on the Way to Sing Sing."

While Max Wilk receives sole credit for writing the teleplay, this episode is an excellent example of how much work Nat Hiken put into the series. Not only was the idea and original story by Hiken, but after sitting down with Max Wilk and Billy Friedberg for separate script conferences, he commissioned Wilk to write the first and second draft of the script, before Hiken wrote the final draft. Yet Max Wilk was the only person to receive on screen credit for the teleplay.

Behind the camera, Al Lewis was a basketball talent scout, and did a lot of work for the Police Athletic League.

For this episode, the publicity department of Eupolis Productions alerted all of the members of the National Conference of Police Athletic Leagues that this episode started with a dramatization of a PAL group in action. Each community group received a bulletin and photograph of the show. The PAL in New York placed photographs and bulletins in each of its 30 PAL centers.

The producers of Eupolis productions proposed a project to the Ninth Precinct Youth Council, as a commercial tie-in for the *Car 54* program, but the project was vetoed by the office of the Police Commissioner. The Commissioner felt they could not tie in with any effort that had commercial auspices. Interestingly, they were aware of the show's PAL promotion and said, "Off the record, we're glad that we're at least getting help from you by the back door."

Production #54 "I'VE BEEN HERE BEFORE"
Copyright Notice: Eupolis Productions, Inc. © March 10, 1963; LP25165
NBC Review: January 14, 1963
Initial Telecast: March 10, 1963
Teleplay scripted by Terry Ryan.
Directed by Stanley Prager.

Cast: Dort Clark (*lead crook*); Lawrence Fletcher (*the Chief Inspector*); Arlene Golonka (*female crook*); Fred Gwynne (*Officer Francis Muldoon*); Pat Hosley (*television producer*); Jake LaMotta (*Bugsy*); John McGovern (*the Commissioner*);

Beatrice Pons (*Lucille Toody*); Paul Reed (*Captain Paul Block*); and Joe E. Ross (*Gunther Toody*).

Extras in the cast: Al Leberfeld, Terry Little, Jock Livingston and Bill Martel.

Plot: A gang of unsuccessful crooks hits upon the idea of duplicating the robberies that are performed on the *Crime Busters* television program. In doing so, the crooks manage to baffle the entire New York Police force, with one exception. Toody, an avid *Crime Busters* fan, shares some pertinent details with the Inspector, which leads to the gang's capture. Toody is hailed as the best man on Captain Block's troop.

Trivia, etc. The former title on early drafts of the script was "Patrolman Toody, Ex-Detective."

The *Crime Busters* television program is an imitation to the popular radio/television series, *Gang Busters*, which was a distant memory when *Car 54* premiered. The fictional *Crime Busters* opened with the same police whistle, prison alert and marching feet that was *Gang Busters'* signature opener.

Production #56 "JOAN CRAWFORD DIDN'T SAY NO"
Copyright Notice: Eupolis Productions, Inc. © March 17, 1963; LP26801
NBC Review: January 31, 1963
Initial Telecast: March 17, 1963
Teleplay scripted by Gary Belkin, based on a story by Nat Hiken.
Directed by Stanley Prager.

Cast: Rae Allen (*the woman*); Patricia Bright (*Mrs. Claire Block*); Mickey Deems (*Officer Charlie Fleischer*); Lawrence Fletcher (*the Chief Inspector*); Fred Gwynne (*Officer Francis Muldoon*); Jacob Kalich (*Mr. Eizenberg*); Al Lewis (*Officer Leo Schnauser*); Molly Picon (*Mrs. Bronson*); Paul Reed (*Captain Paul Block*); and Joe E. Ross (*Gunther Toody*).

Plot: Through the efforts of the "Wedding Bells Matrimonial Agency" of Tremont Avenue, Meyer Eisenberg, age 72, owner of a delicatessen in the Bronx claims to be engaged to legendary actress Joan Crawford. His daughter lodges a complaint with Captain Block and Muldoon is sent to close down the agency. He fails in his assignment but does become engaged to Anita

Ekberg (though Kim Novak was his first choice). Mrs. Bronson, the agency's owner, is able to withstand all efforts of the police to close her down by the simple expedient of matching each successive police representative with a motion picture star. Ultimately, she is served with a subpoena to appear in Circuit Court to show cause why she should not be prosecuted for fraud. Mrs. Bronson's defense is that she is trying to make the Hollywood stars happy by arranging for them to marry the nice, simple people from the Bronx and share their happiness. This argument plus the revelation that all her clients end up marrying each other causes the case to be dismissed.

Trivia, etc. The former title for this drama on early drafts of the script was "Mrs. Bronson Makes a Match."

Actor Lawrence Fletcher played supporting roles on numerous television programs as far back as 1949. He made appearances in five different episodes of *Car 54*, his first as a bank president and the other four as Chief Inspector (supervisor of Captain Block) and his appearances on *Car 54* marked the last of his acting career. He retired as soon as the filming for the second season of *Car 54* was completed.

Production #57 "LUCILLE IS FORTY"
Copyright Notice: Eupolis Productions, Inc. © March 24, 1963; LP26802
Rehearsal: Monday morning, January 28, 1963
Filmed: Monday to Friday, January 28 - 31 and February 1, 1963
NBC Review: January 25, 1963
Initial Telecast: March 24, 1963
Teleplay scripted by Ben Joelson and Art Baer.
Directed by Stanley Prager.

Cast: Elizabeth Eustis (*Mrs. McBride*); Fred Gwynne (*Officer Francis Muldoon*); Al Lewis (*Officer Leo Schnauser*); Jimmy Little (*McBride*); Beatrice Pons (*Lucille Toody*); Charlotte Rae (*Sylvia Schnauser*); Paul Reed (*Captain Paul Block*); Joe E. Ross (*Gunther Toody*); and Sandu Scott (*Miss Allison*).

Plot: Gunther wants to get a present for Lucille for her 40th birthday. Lucille, in the meantime, is getting worried that her age is starting to catch up to her. After seeing another patrolman's wife in a blonde wig and notices how she looks so much younger, he decides to get her a wig. Unable to decide whether his wife should be a blonde or brunette, Gunther tries every method to make a decision - giving Schnauser and his wife Sylvia misconceptions that Gunther is cheating behind Lucille's back with another woman. After Sylvia warns Lucille, hilarious complications ensue. Gunther finally reveals the motive for his madness.

Trivia, etc. When Ben Joelson wrote the original story idea, he entitled his story "Lucille's Wig." By the time the second draft of the script was completed, the title had changed to "The Lady Killers." When the final script was co-written with Art Baer, the title was changed again to "Lucille is Forty." Baer and Joelson had also collaborated with a story entitled "The Fastest Gun in the East" (plot unknown), which was purchased and an early draft of the script was penned, but was canceled in favor of this episode.

Production #58 "THE LOVES OF SYLVIA SCHNAUSER"
Copyright Notice: Eupolis Productions, Inc. © March 31, 1963; LP25166
Rehearsal: Friday, February 1, 1963
Filmed: Monday to Thursday, February 4 - 7, 1963
NBC Review: February 4, 1963
Initial Telecast: March 31, 1963
Teleplay scripted by Tony Webster and Nat Hiken.
Directed by Stanley Prager.

Cast: Matt Crowley (*Crown*); Joe de Santis (*Billson*); David Doyle (*Daniels*); Hank Garrett (*Officer Ed Nicholson*); Fred Gwynne (*Officer Francis Muldoon*); Al Henderson (*Officer O'Hara*); Bruce Kirby (*Officer Kissel*); Ruth Kobart (*Mrs. Abernathy*); Al Lewis (*Officer Leo Schnauser*); Jimmy Little (*McBride*); Kenneth Mars (*assistant*); Charlotte Rae (*Sylvia Schnauser*); Paul Reed (*Captain Paul Block*); Charles Nelson Reilly (*Bentley Abernathy*); Joe E. Ross (*Gunther Toody*); and Joseph Sweeney (*the old publisher*).

Plot: The Captain is determined to break up a phony publishing outfit which has been operating in several cities, and is now located on the streets of their precinct. Toody suggests that a woman pose as a housewife, visit the publishing outfit (Discovery Publications) and get evidence on them. Sylvia Schnauser volunteers. She goes to the publishing outfit as an undercover agent for the police. The con men convince her she should write a book, "The 51 Loves of Sylvia Schnauser" - it's a cook book. But her husband thinks the "51 Loves" are men, and begins to write a "tell-all" about the precinct. When the patrolmen suspect their privacy will be exposed, many complications result. In the end, all is straightened out.

Trivia, etc. "Mr. Lewis and I hit it off pretty well," Charlotte Rae recalled. "I said, 'Well, if we're going to play husband and wife, we ought to know each other better.' So that weekend he and I got together and ad-libbed stuff for about two hours and at the end I felt we were 'married.'"

The former title on early drafts of the script was "Precinct Place."

Production #59 "THE PUNCHER AND JUDY"
Copyright Notice: Eupolis Productions, Inc. © April 7, 1963; LP26803
Rehearsal: none
Filmed: Thursday to Friday, February 7, 8, 13, 14, and 15, 1963
NBC Review: February 19, 1963
Initial Telecast: April 7, 1963
Teleplay scripted by Nat Hiken.
Directed by Stanley Prager.

Cast: Maurice Brenner (*Julie*); Hank Garrett (*Officer Ed Nicholson*); Rocky Graziano (*Antoinne*); Fred Gwynne (*Officer Francis Muldoon*); Jack Healy (*Rodriguez*); Lincoln Kilpatrick (*Webster*); Bruce Kirby (*Officer Kissel*); Lu Leonard (*Mrs. Dobernack*); Al Lewis (*Officer Leo Schnauser*); Shari Lewis (*Judy*); Jimmy Little (*McBride*); Judith Lowry (*Mrs. Withers*); Paul Reed (*Captain Paul Block*); Sugar Ray Robinson (*Ray*); Joe E. Ross (*Gunther Toody*); and Elaine Swann (*Mrs. Fenstermacher*).

Plot: Judy's hairdresser boy friend, Antoinne, has intentions of becoming a prize fighter. Judy, however, is afraid he will lose his gentleness, and pleads for him to change his career goals. Antoinne is actually quite vicious in the ring, so Toody and Muldoon plot for him to meet the great Sugar Ray Robinson (disguised as a 70-year-old man), hoping that Antoinne will change his mind after being knocked out by an old man. Sugar Ray knocks him out and Antoinne gives up fighting. Days later, Antoinne begins taking out his aggressions on his customers in the saloon, so Toody and Muldoon are stuck having to tell him the truth. The hairdresser goes back into the ring - and Judy comes to accept the fact that his career has promise.

Trivia, etc. When Nat Hiken wrote for *The Martha Rae Show* in 1955 and 1956, he startled the show business world by using boxer Rocky Graziano as the comedienne's foil. He later called on him to be a guest star on *Car 54*. Another famous boxer—Sugar Ray Robinson—was featured in the episode. Robinson was paid $700 plus $300 in expenses. Rocky Graziano was also paid $700, as was returnee Shari Lewis. All three of them were listed on screen during the opening credits as "Guest Stars."

Sports columnist Donald Freeman took notice of this episode, commenting that "Rocky playing a hairdresser has to be the greatest reversal of form since Mickey Mantle won the waltz prize on the *Arthur Murray Dance Party*."

Production #60 "THE CURSE OF THE SNITKINS"
Copyright Notice: Eupolis Productions, Inc. © April 14, 1963; LP26804
Rehearsal: none
Filmed: Monday to Thursday, February 18 - 21, 1963
NBC Review: February 19, 1963
Initial Telecast: April 14, 1963
Teleplay scripted by Art Baer and Ben Joelson, from a story by Hiken, Baer and Joelson.
Directed by Stanley Prager and Nat Hiken.

Cast: Godfrey Cambridge (*Webster*); Phil Carter (*Feldman*); Jack Dodson (*the workman*); Hank Garrett (*Officer Ed Nicholson*); Jack Gilford (*Luther Snitkin*); Fred Gwynne (*Officer Francis Muldoon*); Jack Healy (*Rodriguez*); David Kerman (*the doctor*); Bruce Kirby (*Officer Kissel*); Al Lewis (*Officer Leo Schnauser*); Jimmy Little (*McBride*); Richard Mulligan (*patrolman*); Paul Reed (*Captain Paul Block*); Joe E. Ross (*Gunther Toody*); and Anne Russell (*Alice*).

Plot: Toody and Muldoon meet by chance with Officer Snitkin from the 12th Precinct and convince him that the 53rd Precinct (which is considered "Siberia" by most policemen) is the friendliest place in the world . . . and just the place for him. So he transfers to the 53rd, much to the relief of the 12th because the men think he is a jinx. Predictably, his "jinx" seems to follow him to the 53rd: "disasters" happen to any officer paired up with him. The Precinct's accident list grows longer and longer, and the hospitals fill up. Muldoon thinks if Snitkin could win something, he would no longer feel unlucky and people would stop thinking of him as a jinx. So he contrives to have Snitkin win a turkey at a raffle, but the delighted Snitkin gives his prize to the first fellow who congratulates him and who - you've guessed it - soon finds himself in the hospital with food poisoning. The Captain appoints Snitkin to drive the Governor's car on an official tour because Snitkin's had some experience in such work before (he drove Richard Nixon in the 1960 Presidential campaign). A voodoo dance seems to have driven the evil spirits away from Snitkin because he completes this duty with no accidents, and the Governor has him transferred to the Transportation Bureau. The 53rd breathes a sigh of relief.

Trivia, etc. Originally the title of this script was "Toody Meets the Jonah," but changed sometime between February 13 and 17. Filming began in the afternoon of February 18, just after the completion of the episode "The Puncher and Judy." The final shooting script is dated February 18, 1963.

PRE-EMPTION

Car 54, Where Are You? was not broadcast on April 21, 1963, as it was preempted by the special, *An American Landmark: Lexington and Concord.* This was a half-hour color program, with Fredric March as the narrator.

SUMMER RERUNS

April 28, 1963	"A Man is Not an Ox"
May 5, 1963	"Hail to the Chief!"
May 12, 1963	"One Sleepy People"
May 19, 1963	"Toody, Undercover"
May 26, 1963	"Occupancy August 1st"
June 2, 1963	"Pretzel Mary"
June 9, 1963	"The White Elephant"

June 16, 1963	"The Presidential Itch"
June 23, 1963	"Who's for Swordfish?"
June 30, 1963	"Toody and Muldoon Crack Down"
July 7, 1963	"Today I Am a Man"
July 14, 1963	"Quiet, We're Thinking"
July 21, 1963	"The Beast Who Walked the Bronx"
July 28, 1963	"Boom, Boom, Boom"
August 4, 1963	"Toody and Muldoon Meet the Russians"
August 11, 1963	"Here We Go Again"
August 18, 1963	"Joan Crawford Didn't Say No"
August 25, 1963	"Lucille is Forty"
September 1, 1963	"The Puncher and Judy"
September 8, 1963	"The Curse of the Snitkins"

APPENDIX
UNUSED PLOT SUGGESTIONS AND OUTLINES

Two untitled plotlines by casting director Lou Melamed

Each week Gunther is assigned to Mrs. Kann's Cozy kitchen - a restaurant. His job is to go to the bank with the cash receipts and return with the payroll. Mr. Kann's recently arrived niece is the hostess. She is a very tall girl and Gunther plays Cupid for Muldoon.

At the bank we see a shifty little thief write a threatening letter to the teller. He gets in line, followed directly by Gunther and the girl. Thief gallantly offers to give up his place but Gunther will have no part of it. Thief nervously drops the note. Gunther obligingly picks it up and hands it back. Eventually, he and Muldoon become the unwitting captors.

＠

A police mission from an Oriental country is here to learn about U.S. crime detection and local police control methods. Suki is assigned to Gunther and Muldoon. He is very polite and seems quite puny. Our heroes are over-protective and almost patronizing.

One night he invites the boys to an authentic Oriental restaurant. It is exotic and mysterious with a beautiful dancer entertaining. They enter without their shoes, sit on cushions and start their dinner. A big Oriental starts to manhandle the dancer. Suki excuses himself and proceeds to subdue the big man with a dazzling display of judo.

Plot Suggestion Entitled "To Be or Not to Be" by Jack Altshul and Lew Barasch

This episode deals with efforts by Toodie and Muldoon to reduce juvenile delinquency in their precinct. The Captain is infuriated by incidents of roughhousing and challenges his patrolmen to come up with a project that will keep kids off street corners and out of trouble. He promises he will take them off all other duties and award a commendation to the two-man team that develops the best idea.

Toody hears Muldoon reciting Hamlet's Soliloquy in the patrol car. When Toody inquires about Shakespeare, between them they come up with idea of organizing dramatic society among neighborhood toughs to stage a production of *Hamlet*. The Captain gives them the go-ahead after rejecting several other ideas. (Pistol Team -- "That's all we need, a gang of kids that knows how to shoot." Boning Team -- "We got enough trouble bringing in violators now.")

Toody and Muldoon visit the toughest hangout in town - a poolroom. Toody impresses the mob with his pool-shooting ability and tells them the way he learned was by acting in Shakespeare plays as a young man. "Develops timing," he explains. They go for the idea.

Muldoon directs the first meeting, and assigns parts and chores. Toody is in charge of the wardrobe. The kid who is cast to play Hamlet is a "Leo Gorcey" type [Gorcey was one of the original Dead End Kids]. There is a suggestion to raid a costume store at night; and he knows how to get in if Toody will lay "Chickie." Toody is horrified, but the boy tells him they will bring the costumes back. When they are caught in the act by the owner of the store, who is about to call the police, a toughie tells what they want the costumes for and suggests free credit on the program to the costume-store owner.

The poolroom has been turned into a rehearsal hall and at first the rehearsal is a scene of riot as kids go berserk with cue sticks during the dueling scene. Flash at top of riot to the Captain's office where he has just received into that the notorious local con has broken jail. He gets a phone call about the riot in the poolroom and remembers that the poolroom's owner turned in the con. When the riot squad is called, they race to the scene. The Captain directs gas-masked cops to fire tear gas and calls out on the loudspeaker for the con to surrender. Toody walks out, eyes streaming, hands in the air.

But the show goes on, the mayor and the commissioner are invited, and Toody acts as a prompter. The kid forgets the "To be or not to be" line which has been repeated for comedy effects throughout the episode. Toody's whispers are heard throughout the audience, eliciting unwanted laughter. He finally comes on stage and does the line himself as the curtain falls.

Two Plot Proposals by television viewer Gloria Alwood of Sacramento, California
Idea No. 1

A reporter wants to ride around in a patrol car to get the inside dope for a novel he is writing on police activity. The Captain owes this reporter a favor and cannot refuse, although he puts up a stiff argument against it.

The reporter says he has heard rumors that Car 54 is a hot one. He insists on riding in Car 54 and also insists his identity be kept a secret so the officers will behave normally.

The Captain rolls his eyes in agony and moans, "Normally." He calls Car 54 in and tells them they are to have an observer with them for a few days, but he is not at liberty to tell them who the man is, as it may influence their behavior one way or another.

Toody and Muldoon debate over who the man could be, a spy, an F.B.I. man, etc. When Toody decides it is a personal friend of the Captain, whom the Captain is trying to persuade into joining the force, but the man is probably skeptical about doing so. Toody tells Muldoon if they can convince the man what a swell job the force is, they will be in solid with the Captain.

Muldoon goes along with this idea, but makes Toody promise "not to overdo it." After all, "they don't want men on the force who don't have it 'here.'" (He indicates his heart.)

Toody says, "You're right; we'll just give him the light treatment." Once the reporter is in the car, they begin to show him the "good side of the job."

Toody has pre-arranged for elaborate free meals with king-type treatment (which has all been prearranged with the restaurant owner). Toody's wife and Muldoon's mother flirt outrageously with "the handsome cops in uniform," also pre-arranged. The men take naps in the car (pre-arranged so that their fellow officers can stand guard for the patrol Sergeant or all their important calls).

Car 54 gets an urgent call that a bank robbery has taken place in their district and the culprit is armed and took one shot at the teller, but missed. He got away with $5,000. The reporter gets very excited.

But in a whispered huddle, Toody and Muldoon decide this might show the man the dangerous side of the job and turn him against joining up. They console each other with the fact that the other boys on the force are covering their calls and they always beat them to their calls first anyway.

Toody says, "What's one little bank robber?"

Muldoon says, "Yeah, but don't forget he shot at the teller."

Toody says, "Oh yeah, but he missed ...."

Toody and Muldoon explain to the reporter that this bank owner makes the same complaint once every week and each time he has just misplaced the money. Their job is really easy and to prove it they go to a bar and watch TV wrestling. While in the bar, a meek-looking little man carrying a sack approaches Toody but Toody shoos him away. They go to the pool hall and shoot a few games. Again the meek little man approaches Toody.

The reporter is going crazy, and keeps saying, "Oh, it wouldn't always be like this, it just couldn't." Toody exaggerates and says it is and just to prove it to him they are going to go play golf. The meek little man is still following Toody about.

On the golf course Toody hits a ball and because the little man is still in the way, he hits him on the head with the ball and knocks him out. The sack goes flying away and money and a water squirt gun goes with it. They discover he is the bank robber. The reporter is thrilled, saying he has never seen such clever detection work before. He goes on to say that Toody and Muldoon were so calm and relaxed, so nonchalant, so cunning and all the while they were systematically stalking the killer - a dangerous bank robber - and he rushes off to file his reports.

The bank robber wakes up and says he is sorry. He didn't really want to be a bank robber, and that is why he used a squirt gun. He was trying to give himself up to Toody because he has such an understanding face.

The Captain congratulates Toody and Muldoon for a good job and they go back to their car very happy. They receive another broadcast of a safe cracker. Immediately Toody wants to start making the rounds again of the bar, pool hall and the golf course. Muldoon says no. To paraphrase Abraham Lincoln, you can fool some of the crooks some of the time, but not all the crooks all of the time.

Toody has talked up a blue storm and has actually convinced himself he was tracking the bank robber when a man walks up to the patrol car and asks Toody for a light. Toody has gotten himself so excited he now thinks this man is the safe cracker.

He leaps out of the car to make the arrest, wrestles the surprised man to the sidewalk. Muldoon screams at Toody. But it is too late. Muldoon leans on the steering wheel sobbing . . . "That's the *Mayor*."

Idea No. 2

Schnauser is in the Captain's office saying he just can't do it. The Captain is arguing with him, telling him how brave, fearless, dependable and clever he is; how risky and important this assignment is. That he can't think of anyone else he would entrust with it.

The Captain explains that there is a fiend grabbing women in the park and strangling them; it is too risky to use a policewoman as bait. Schnauser reluctantly agrees to pose as a woman. When he returns in feminine attire, he is greeted with wolf whistles from the others in the precinct. The Captain says, "See, even *they* can't tell the difference and they know who you are. He then assigns him to patrol the park across the street from the bank.

In Car 54, Toody and Muldoon are receiving a call of a holdup man disguised as a woman, seen heading for the park with $10,000 in stolen money. They head for the park.

Meanwhile, Schnauser is getting more than his share of wolf calls. In the bushes lurks the fiend giving Schnauser the eye. Along comes a Frenchman and he sees Schnauser and falls in love with him. He begins spouting romantic verses. Schnauser tries to get away from him and ends up running, the Frenchman hot on his heels.

The bank robber has slipped into the park but not before Toody and Muldoon spot him and get out of their car and give chase.

The Frenchman has seen the bank robber hiding in the bushes and thinks it is the cutie, (Schnauser) he has been chasing. He jumps into the bushes and grabs the bank robber and begins cooing and billing with her (him). The bank robber is so stunned he tries to hold the Frenchman off and then coyly urges the Frenchman to take her out of "this awful place."

The fiend has seen Schnauser hide in the bushes and sneaks up behind him and, thinking he is a woman, begins kissing him and murmuring how beautiful she is.

The Frenchman is leading the bank robber out of the bushes when Muldoon sees them and thinks it is the fiend with a girl victim. He yells and the bank robber sees the cop and takes off running. Meantime, Schnauser has broken away from the fiend in the bushes, still believing it is the crazy

Frenchman.

In the bushes, the fiend and the bank robber run into each other and a fight ensues and they knock each other out - the fiend, believing it is the girl he is after, and the bank robber thinking it is the crazy man who tried to kiss him.

The Frenchman has now rediscovered Schnauser and begins chasing him through the bushes. Toody and Muldoon are closing in and they are all over each other. They discover the money scattered everywhere around the unconscious bank robber and a man and the strangling rope on the unconscious fiend. The officers make their arrests and the Frenchman goes sobbing off as he has lost "the love of his life."

"TOODY BUYS INSURANCE AGAINST HIMSELF" -- Author unknown
(Note: Most likely this was written by a staff writer, or Nat Hiken himself.)

Orders have come up from downtown that the commissioner has detected a certain laxity in the physical appearance of the police, especially with some of the veterans on the force. Captain Block, acting on orders, says that he wants all the men to get back in top physical shape - good enough to pass the police physical over again, if necessary. Toody is petrified, because in addition to being in terrible physical shape - he's also very much overweight.

Now comes Toody's program to get back into condition. Exercises to the man on TV giving it to ladies - fresh air, open windows when he sleeps . . . everything to cause Lucille a pain in the neck . . . above all, he's going on a diet. Lucille interprets this as a strike against her cooking . . . [or perhaps] Toody is getting tired of her. She prepares the dishes he used to love when they were first married, but he doesn't touch a morsel. He's even gone out and bought a scale -- She knows the "real" reason - he bought it because he's not only tired of her cooking, but he's trying to tell her that she's getting fat and sloppy. "Look Lucille," he protests, "You've been fat and sloppy for years so why should I start telling you now?"

Meanwhile, Lucille has gotten a phone call from her cousin Shaggy (Shecky Greene). Shaggy is out of the Navy now, and is selling insurance. She invites him up for dinner. Shaggy is a perfect guest - he'll eat and get out. But Toody and Lucille feel sorry for him. He doesn't know any girls - he can't sell insurance - he can't get adjusted to civilian life. Toody is trying to make Shaggy sell him an insurance policy, but Shaggy won't - he knows Toody can't pass the physical. This only adds fuel to Toody's conditioning program.

With all his efforts - something is backfiring with Toody's health program. He's now eating just enough to stay alive, and yet, he's putting on weight. Lucille can't figure something out either -- every night Shaggy eats like a horse, watches television, then goes to sleep. Toody doesn't eat at all - yet, every morning, the refrigerator is empty - completely empty. Toody accuses Shaggy of eating his food, thinking that Shaggy's generous nature is only a cover-up for his greed. Shaggy is convinced [the missing food is the work of] a burglar . . . After he's eaten enough for them, he'll start stealing the valuables in the house. They should have insurance . . . but now, Toody is convinced that Shaggy is doing this whole thing to sell a policy. "Sure," he tells Muldoon, "he won't come right out and say we need insurance - he steals everything so we gotta buy a policy. I know them high-pressure insurance men."

Toody is worried about his valuables: The cufflinks he bought when he got married because he needed them for the tuxedo; the wrist-watch he won for Lucille in 1950 at the Policeman's Picnic. There's only one thing to do - he's going to plan a trap for the burglar. When Shaggy and Lucille decide to go to sleep, he says he's going to stay up and watch TV. He watches it for a while, gets drowsy, and falls asleep.

Then we see Toody getting up and start sleepwalking. First he gets all the valuables from all over the house, then he starts to hide them in different places -- then he walks over to the refrigerator and eats up everything in it. He finishes, puts all the dishes back into the refrigerator empty - goes to his bedroom, goes to bed - still in his sleepwalking stage.

The next morning, Lucille screams that the refrigerator has been completely raided again -- Toody starts to look for the valuables. They are missing! THE PHANTOM HAS STRUCK! Now, Toody is convinced it is Shaggy. It can't be Lucille - he's known her for all these years, and she wouldn't steal from him now. It *has* to be Shaggy. He confides this to Muldoon, and he has also figured out a trap to snare him in the act . . .

Because Shaggy is Lucille's cousin, Toody can't arrest him, but Muldoon can. That evening, they all eat together - Shaggy, Lucille, Muldoon and Toody. Once again, Toody will not eat. Shaggy, Toody and Muldoon sit down to play a little pinochle, and Toody is "slyly" questioning Shaggy, "Did you sell any policies?"

"No."

"Oh, ever try selling chickens or a ham? I know a guy who's looking for a set of cufflinks like mine. He'd pay a fortune . . . [he] wants a wristwatch, too."

Finally, Shaggy says he's going to sleep. Now Toody sets the big trap.

Francis Muldoon will pretend that he's leaving - he gets up - long goodnights - slams door - then! Toody announces loudly he's very sleepy and is going off to sleep. He and Muldoon hide. Lights go out - the signal is when the refrigerator light goes on, they'll nab him. Muldoon will grab Shaggy and handcuff him. Toody sits down in the chair, falls asleep waiting . . . Then up he goes, starting the sleepwalk again, goes around the room and gets the valuables out from where he hid them, and starts to hide them again.

Then, Toody sneaks over to the refrigerator, open it up, and the light goes on. Muldoon jumps out, snaps the handcuffs. "I got him, Toody!" Toody wakes up and snaps the handcuffs on Muldoon. "I got him, Francis!" Both start screaming, and out runs Lucille and Shaggy.

In the final scene, we see Shaggy telling Toody that he won't release them until they both buy insurance policies from him.

Unused Plot Proposal Entitled: "THE DECOY" -- Author unknown

At the morning roll call the captain introduces a Mr. McDonald of the U.S. Customs Service. Mr. McDonald explains that a big international jewel smuggling ring is in operation, and that they have information they're getting jewels into the country through a phony diplomatic courier whose dispatch case cannot be searched under international law. He says they have been tipped off that there is a shipment of diamonds on the afternoon plane from Paris and he's asked the Captain for two squads to look for suspects at the airport. The captain designates Muldoon and Gunther and O'Hara and Nelson as the two squads. In closing, McDonald urges extreme caution as a false accusation of arrest could touch off a very serious international incident.

In the prowl car on the way to the airport, Gunther talks excitedly about how glorious it would be to catch a gang of international jewel smugglers, get [his] picture in the paper, a promotion, etc. He contrasts it to their usual humdrum life, handing out tickets for trash can violations, getting cats down out of trees, and [supervising] school crossings. Muldoon says he's happy with his life the way it is, no problems, no trouble. Gunther says he has ambition. Muldoon asks how you know a jewel smuggler when you see one. Gunther says don't worry, he's read all about how they operate in mystery stories, and just follow him.

At the airport, McDonald assigns the two squads' stakeout positions, says the plane is due in soon, he'll give them a signal when the passengers come out, and again urges caution.

In the parked car, Muldoon asks for further details on spotting a smuggler. Gunther says the first thing to look out for is the decoy. They always send one along to act suspicious and draw attention away from the one who is actually carrying the jewels. He says since they don't know this, O'Hara and Nelson are likely to be suckered. He looks off and suddenly says, "Hey, there's Mr. McDonald's signal. The passengers are comin' out."

We see a group of people coming along a sidewalk with suitcases, etc. Prominent among them is a very good-looking blonde with a black scarf over her head and wearing dark glasses. She is carrying a small overnight case. She stops and looks about her furtively, then starts to walk toward the camera, still looking uneasily around.

In the car, Muldoon says, "Hey, see her?" Gunther replies "Sure I see her." Muldoon adds, "She's actin' awful suspicious. Why don't we grab her?" Muldoon moves to get out of the car. Gunther restrains him. "Sit still, idiot! That's what she wants us to do." Muldoon says, "Huh?" Gunther impatiently says, "Remember what I told you? She's the decoy." Muldoon replies, "Oh."

Cut to blonde closer to camera. Muldoon says (voice over) "She's comin' our way." Gunther says, "Yeah." The blonde stops. Muldoon says, "She sees us." The blonde looks around desperately, then turns and walks away rapidly.

Cut to Muldoon and Gunther in car looking off. Gunther says, "What an act she's puttin' on." Muldoon says, "She's goin' toward O'Hara and Nelson." Gunther nods gleefully and grins a wide grin. "Yeah!"

Cut to long shot O'Hara and Nelson beside their car taking the overnight case from the blonde. Muldoon (voice over) "They're pickin' her up."

Cut to Gunther and Muldoon in car. Gunther says gleefully, "Poor chumps. They fell right into her trap!" Muldoon says, "But Gunther, what if she's really . . ." Gunther replies, "I told you how they work. She's only the decoy. Now in just a minute . . ." He suddenly grabs Muldoon's arm and points off. "What did I tell ya? There comes our man!"

Long shot of young man hurrying down sidewalk with attaché case toward a waiting car with liveried chauffeur.

Close-up of young man beside car talking to chauffeur. "Hurry. It's full of ice!"

Muldoon and Gunther in car. Gunther says, "You heard that, didn't ya? Ice! Diamonds! That case is full of diamonds!" Muldoon moves to get out. "Let's grab him." Gunther restrains him. "Will you be patient? We'll tail him and pick up the whole gang."

Long shot [of] young man getting into back seat of car and car driving off.

Muldoon and Gunther in moving prowl car. Muldoon says, "What if there's a whole bunch of them? Shouldn't we call for some help?" Gunther says scornfully, "We're police officers, aren't we? Can't we do our jobs? Besides, do you want to share the credit? This is big government stuff. We might even get the Congressional Medal of Honor." He chuckles. "Poor O'Hara and Nelson."

Long shot of car pulling up to curb, young man getting out and hurrying up sidewalk with attaché case.

Muldoon and Gunther in car. Muldoon asks, "Shall we follow him in?"

Gunther says, "No. They'd be expectin' that. We'll sneak in the back and surprise 'em."

Cut to close-up of closed door from the inside. It opens and Muldoon and Gunther, with guns drawn, slowly come in.

(Mysterious bassoon music accompanies the following)

Cut to medium-long shot of large room. Muldoon and Gunther enter from right, walking slowly with guns drawn. Behind them are two men in business suits, also with guns drawn. They all cross and exit left.

Cut to medium-long-shot of another large room. Muldoon and Gunther enter from right, guns drawn. Behind them now are four men in business suits with guns drawn. They all cross as before.

Cut to medium shot of another large room. Repeat the same business except that now there are eight men following them.

Cut to sleek, well-fed looking middle-aged Frenchman seated at desk. Young man enters with attaché case. They converse in French. The Frenchman says, "You brought them?"

The young man says "Yes, sir."

The Frenchman replies, "Good."

Cut to medium shot Muldoon and Gunther at closed door, the eight men behind them.

Cut to closeup of Muldoon and Gunther. Gunther says, "They must be in here."

Muldoon says, "Yeah. I hear voices."

Gunther says, "Let's rush 'em!"

Medium shot. Door bursts open. Muldoon says, "Don't anybody move!"

Gunther says, "Put your hands up."

Man behind Gunther says, "I'd suggest you do the same, Monsieur."

The Frenchman at the desk asks, "What is the meaning of this?"

The man behind Gunther asks if he should lodge a complaint with the Secretary of State. The Frenchman at the desk says no, [but] maybe the gendarmes can explain.

He asks if they know they are on French territory, that this is the official residence of the French delegation to the United Nations. Gunther says, "Yeah. And I'm a monkey's uncle. We know you've got a valise full of diamonds there."

The Frenchman says, "*Diamonds*? I do not understand."

Gunther says, "Oh yes you do. I dare you to open it up." The Frenchman says he was just about to. He opens the attaché case, revealing several small fish packed in ice. He points to the fish. "Poisson."

Gunther says, "Fish!"

Muldoon says, "And that's just ice."

The Frenchman explains that there are fish found only in the Seine, and he asked to have some flown over by their returning courier for bouillabaise, but they can see there are no diamonds. "Now if monsieur cares to explain . . ." Gunther lamely explains that they were looking for smugglers and "ice" means diamonds in underworld talk, so when they heard the young man say "ice" they were naturally suspicious, etc. The Frenchman laughs and says he understands.

Muldoon says, "Then you won't tell the Secretary of State on us?" The Frenchman says of course not, he's willing to forget the whole thing. He invites them to stay for some bouillabaisse. Gunther is about to eagerly accept, but Muldoon says, "We ain't hungry," and they leave.

In the moving prowl car Muldoon berates Gunther for getting them involved in an international incident. "You could have started a war." Muldoon says they'll keep their mouths shut about what happened; just then he remembers that O'Hara and Nelson might have seen them leave. Gunther says "Don't worry about them. That girl they arrested was probably the Queen of Turkey."

Next morning at roll call: The Captain says two of his men have brought great honor to the precinct. He presents Mr. McDonald of U.S. Customs Office, who thanks O'Hara and Nelson for the arrest of the phony courier, a girl, who was smuggling the diamonds. He says it was her first trip, she was inexperienced, broke under questioning and they got the whole gang.

Cut to close-up of Muldoon and Gunther. Muldoon looks at Gunther contemptuously. "Some decoy!" he says sarcastically.

Cut to medium shot of Muldoon, Gunther, O'Hara and Nelson. O'Hara says he can't understand why Muldoon and Gunther didn't make the arrest when the girl walked toward them, that she was acting so nervous anybody could have spotted her. Muldoon, in disgust, says, "Well, you want to know the truth, O'Hara? We . . ."

Gunther breaks in, "Yeah. We didn't want to hog all the credit so we ran her toward you."

Fade on Muldoon looking in disbelief at the pleased Gunther.

Unproduced Plot Outline:
"NO RUNS, NO HITS, ALL ERRORS!" —- Author unknown

Scene 1

We open in the locker room. A number of men in baseball uniforms are sitting around. All of them appear to be quite dejected. Some are mumbling, "It's no use . . . Let's forget about it . . ." The rest just sit and shake their heads sadly. The camera pulls back and we see Toody and Muldoon in baseball uniforms, too. Only Toody is wearing his police hat instead of a regular baseball cap. He pleads with them not to despair. Riley, number 19 says they're just making fools of themselves again playing Firehouse Hook and Ladder #17 in a few weeks -- they're just gonna get the pants beaten off them again. It seems our boys have been squashed the past four years 18-0 . . . 16-0 . . . 19-0 and last year 24-0. Riley says it's too embarrassing — especially after today's workout game. Toody says the workout game wasn't as bad as they think. Muldoon says "Being beaten 15 to 0 by a Little League team . . .?" Toody reminds the team they've already put up the usual $5 per man. If they call the game off, they'll probably forfeit the $45. The boys feel they'd rather lose the money than lose face.

Scene 2

Firehouse Hook and Ladder #17. Toody (against his better judgment) arrives with Muldoon to call off the game. The boys around the firehouse give it to

Toody and Muldoon but good . . . calling them chicken and offering to play blindfolded or with one arm tied behind their backs so the cops might have a better chance. Toody and Muldoon burn. But Muldoon keeps nudging Toody to remind him of their mission as Toody is almost ready to let the game stand. The only way he believes he can get out gracefully is by calling the game childish and that although the firemen may have plenty of time on their hands for kids' games -- the police are much too busy for this sort of thing. They leave with the firemen calling after them that of course this means they've forfeited their $45.

Scene 3

The Stationhouse. As Toody and Muldoon enter, Captain Block is standing with a new patrolman, Mickey Potter, and glumly looking over Potter's records. Block bemoans the fact that he asks for a replacement and what does headquarters send him - a former professional baseball player — instead of a good, experienced cop. When Toody and Muldoon hear Potter's past profession they rush to the locker room and grab the baseball manual to look up Potter. There it is — in black and white — Mickey Potter . . . Boston Red Sox . . . No-hit pitcher and at bat — average 298! Toody starts to jump up and down, kissing Muldoon — Potter's the answer to their prayers. Muldoon reminds Toody that the team decided to forget the game and besides — they've already called it off. Toody says they'll call it on again. They're not going to lose that $45 without a fight.

Potter enters the locker room with Patrolman Kaplan, his new partner. Toody and Muldoon welcome Potter to the precinct and Toody adds "and to the Prowl Car Pirates . . . The precinct baseball team." To Toody's surprise and utter dismay, Potter thanks them for the welcome to the precinct but as for the baseball team -- baseball is behind him now. From here on in he's concentrating on being a good cop! Of course -- if they want some advice . . .

For a minute Toody is thrown for a loop but soon the minute is up and so is Toody. Pulling Muldoon aside he says that Potter just signed on. Muldoon says how does Toody figure that, especially after Potter says he won't play? Toody says that nobody can resist giving advice and once they've taken that step -- the rest is easy. He grabs Kaplan on the way out and whispers something to him. Kaplan begins to refuse but Toody reminds him that he too has $5 invested in the game.

Scene 4

The police dispatcher speaks into the mike. "Cars 52 . . . 56 . . . 58 . . . And 59 . . ."

Scene 5

Cut to interior of a squad car. Two officers suddenly come alive as they hear the dispatcher. "56 . . . 58 and 59 . . . Central Park Area B . . . assist officer . . . Cars 52 . . . 56 . . ." The two cops look at each other and off they go, their siren screaming . . ."

Scene 6

A baseball diamond in Central Park. Toody and Muldoon stand alongside their car. Muldoon is telling Toody he shouldn't have done what he did — when Cars 52, 56, 58 and 59 converge on the spot from all directions, their sirens blasting. The all come to a screeching stop and all the cops hop out of their respective cars, guns drawn and ready for action. When they see Toody and Muldoon just standing there they ask what is up. Toody calmly says, "Practice!" and begins to hand out the uniforms. The cops say they told him the game is off — and besides, they are on duty. Toody says this'll be a very short practice session —- not lasting more than maybe 15 minutes. The cops try to argue but Toody says for them just to do what he says and not ask any questions — just start warming up.

Scene 7

Cut to interior of car 57. Potter with Kaplan driving. They enter the park, just cruising. Kaplan looks at his watch and heads for the baseball field. Potter spots the cars and the guys in the field. Asks what is going on. Kaplan says it's the precinct team — still wasting their time trying to get in shape for the game. Potter comments on how awful they are — they're doing everything wrong. Kaplan pulls the car up and gets out, followed by Potter. Before Potter realizes it, he's giving advice, showing the boys how it should be done and getting into a uniform . . . Toody and Muldoon smile at each other and shake hands.

Scene 8

Firehouse #17. Toody and Muldoon are shaking hands with the firemen — they've called the game back on. Toody, trying to cover up the real reason, says that they thought it over and decided they should take their usual licking like men. One of the firemen says that he doubts if they'll want to make the usual $5 side bet. Muldoon looks at Toody. Toody says it would be just throwing good money after bad but — and winking at Muldoon — they shouldn't break a tradition so — okay . . .

Scene 9

Toody and Muldoon return to the stationhouse with a feeling of victory in their bones. Muldoon is congratulating Toody on the way he got the firemen to increase the side bet of $5 to $7.50 . . . the extra two-fifty being more of a donation to the company fund. The two of them are almost hysterical with laughter on how they put it over on the firemen until they hear the news from Sgt. Abrams — Potter and Kapland have been assigned by Captain Block to the Code Red Sector. Toody and Muldoon panic. They get hold of Block. Can't the good Captain take Potter out of the Code Red Sector? — it's the toughest neighborhood in the area. Potter could get hurt. Couldn't the good Captain let Car 54 and Car 57 exchange assignments? Muldoon grabs hold of Toody. Is he crazy trying to get them into that neighborhood? Toody says they gotta protect their investment. He goes back to Block — reminding Block how rough a neighborhood it is — especially for an inexperienced cop. Block thinks for a moment and then decides — Toody is right — Red Sector is rough for an inexperienced cop — so maybe there should be two cars assigned to that area — Car 57 and Car 54. Muldoon is crushed. Toody has gotten them one of the worst assignments in the precinct. But Toody is happy about it — being in the same sector — he and Muldoon can keep an eye on Potter so he doesn't get hurt.

Scene 10

Code Red Sector. A real rough neighborhood. Establish tough-looking characters, etc. Car 57 is cruising slowly through the street. Unknown to Potter in Car 57, behind them at a distance is Car 54 with Toody and Muldoon keeping him under surveillance . . . sneaking around corners . . . parking behind other cars so as not to be seen. Potter turns to Kaplan . . .

"I keep getting the strangest feeling we're bein' followed . . ." Kaplan of course, brushes it off.

Suddenly the radio comes alive. In Car 54, Toody and Muldoon hear the call come for Cars 54 and 57 . . . A mysterious prowler. Investigate. Toody says they've gotta get there before Potter -- Can't let anything happen to him. Car 54 turns around and off they go.

Scene 11

Interior of alley. Toody and Muldoon sneak in after the prowler. Turns out to be a harmless drunk who got lost in an alley and couldn't find his way out. As they take him out of the alley, he expresses his delight about being arrested . . . Now he can get a bath, a hot meal and a good bed in the city prison. As they emerge from the alley, Car 57 is just pulling up. Muldoon waves Potter off. Everything's under control. Potter shrugs.

Scene 12

Toody and Muldoon get the drunk in the car. Muldoon is about to head for the precinct but Toody says they can't go back there now — they've got to keep an eye on Potter. The drunk demands to be taken back to prison — he's got his rights. Toody tells him either he finds another place to sleep it off or he's gonna ride with them till they get off duty. The drunk is very unhappy and intends to take this up with his local councilman . . .

Scene 13

A call comes in for Car 57 . . . 1032 . . . Investigate disturbing the peace report. With the drunk in the back seat, Toody and Muldoon take off to get there before Potter. Arriving before Car 57, they enter the building amongst flying pots and pans to break up a fight between a husband and wife.

Scene 14

When Potter and Kaplan arrive, Toody and Muldoon are coming out. Again they wave Potter off — Just a little family spat. All taken care of. Potter scratches his head . . . He can't understand how Toody and Muldoon got there so fast and took care of everything.

Scene 15

Back in the car, the drunk keeps insisting on his rights. He wants to be booked. Another call comes in for 57. Burglary in progress. Toody says, "Let's go . . ." he takes them on a short cut to head off Potter again. They drive on sidewalks to bypass cars, through alleys, through garages going in front and out the back, etc. At the store where the burglary is supposedly in progress, Toody tells Muldoon to cover the front — he'll go in the back way. As Muldoon covers the front, Car 57 pulls up. By now Potter is thoroughly confused. The front door opens and Toody comes out with the burglar protesting his innocence — he wasn't robbing the dress shop — he only came back to exchange a dress his wife bought and she didn't want to wait till the morning when the store opened.

Scene 16

Potter says he guesses Toody and Muldoon will have to take the guy in. Toody realizes this would mean the end of their shadowing Potter so he asks Kaplan to do them a favor. Could he and Potter have the guy booked? Kaplan agrees. The drunk appears. Asks if Kaplan could take him in too — he wants to go to bed. As Potter, Kaplan and the two prisoners drive off, Toody comments how that will take care of Potter for the rest of tonight. Muldoon says, "Yeah — but we still got two weeks more to go before the game."

Scene 17

Interior of Car 54. Muldoon and Toody are bushed. It is now the last night before the game. For two weeks they have covered all of Potter's calls to ensure his safety. A call comes in for Car 57. Prowler. Toody and Muldoon take off. The prowler turns out to be no one else but that drunk again. As they emerge from the alley, there's Car 57 pulling up. Kaplan gets out but instead of Potter — Kaplan's partner is now Riley. Toody asks where Potter is. Kaplan shakes his head. He hasn't any idea. When he came on duty tonight, the Captain told him his new partner would be Riley.

Scene 18

At precinct. Toody and Muldoon arrive with drunk. Toody asks Sgt. Abrams the whereabouts of Potter. Abrams too is mystified. All he knows is that Potter has been taken off the roll.

Scene 19

It's the day of the game. Toody and Muldoon, surrounded by the team in uniform are being questioned about Potter. Toody says he hasn't any idea of what could have happened to him. Muldoon swears they took excellent care of him the past two weeks. The umpire yells to "play ball." As the team gloomily takes to the field, Toody sees Potter putting on his uniform top. Toody rushes over with Muldoon. "Where yuh been? How come you're not on the precinct roll?" Potter buttons up his baseball shirt. As we see the name of the team on it, he says, "Well, you see -- I transferred to the fire department -- there wasn't enough action for me on the police force." And out he goes to the pitchers mound in the uniform of Hook and Ladder #17.

Unproduced Plot Outline Submitted by
Beatrice Manti, a Television Viewer

Nov. 6, 1962

Dear Sir:

The following is an outline for a *Car 54* episode that you may be interested in

Schnauser's wife, Sylvia, becomes a patrol woman and is stationed at a school intersection that is in her husband's beat. He is proud of her until she becomes obnoxious - pompously raising her hand at his approaching patrol car, criticizing the uniform he wears by telling him his pants need pressing, his buttons need polishing, etc. He humors her and then pleads for her removal, all in vain.

Finally, Toody and Muldoon decide to help their buddy. Muldoon and Toody hire a midget friend and dressing up as his parents - go to Sylvia's station. The "child" promptly goes up to her and firmly places his metal-tipped shoe on her shin. She smiles weakly. Then he splashes a puddle on her. It is too much. Sylvia resigns.

Next day - Schnauser's car comes to a stop at the school intersection. Guess who is the new patrol woman? Lucille!

Beatrice Manti
36 Marsdale Street
Albany 8, New York

Unproduced Plot Outline:
"HANDS ACROSS THE SEA" — Author unknown

Scene 1

Newsreel of arrival of Scotland Yard contingent, bowler and all, lined up at airport. They are greeted by city officials and some uniformed police officials. Announcer lauds mission as another example of cooperation between the two countries. Short speech by Grover Whelan type . . . "We are as proud of our methods of crime detection as you are of yours - but we can all learn something from one another."

Scene 2

Inspector Jasper Asherton (with bowler, pipe and umbrella) comes out of Captain's office at 53rd precinct. Captain asks if there is anything else. Jasper would like to go out in a prowl car. Captain asks Sgt. Abrams who's available. Everybody is out. Toody and Muldoon troll in from the other room. They are ready to go on duty. Jasper would like to go out with them. Captain desperately tries to make other arrangements. Trapped, he takes the boys aside and warns them against making a spectacle of themselves with a brother officer from overseas.

Scene 3

Cruising in prowl car. Talk about English bobbies not carrying guns. Must have lots of casualties. Jasper demurs. Every human being can be reached in a civilized way - even a thief. Courtesy begets courtesy. When a thief is caught red-handed he knows he's done something naughty. No need for hysterics or melodrama.

If you must resort to violence to subdue a culprit, it's a sure sign that you've failed. Toody and Muldoon exchange looks . . . boy, have they failed.

They pull a speeding car to curb. Driver is a Balkan type with an accent. It's a U.N. car. Driver late for meeting at U.N. Drives off. Jasper says, "U.N. closed tight today for some repair job. But man was it interesting! Albanian, you know. Did you notice the ridge on his left hand? It's from a game of skill called Baksha. You wrap the reins around your hand and try to keep the horse from driving forward. It only exists in the North Albanian Alps. Also, they're very clannish people . . . the ring on his finger. The boys are impressed. They, of course, observed nothing.

They drive on and come upon a collision at intersection. Two drivers arguing. The boys break it up. Drivers exchange license numbers. Jasper is amused. Obviously, the driver of the black sedan is right. Tire marks indicate he did not turn sharply. The angle of the car bears that out. Driver's entire manner suggests meticulous care and responsibility. Other man never looked you in the eye. The boys are really impressed. Jasper shrugs it off. It's attention to detail that solves crimes. Toody says maybe he could help them with a problem. Invites Jasper to dinner.

They drop Jasper off. Toody says to Muldoon, maybe Jasper could help them with the waterfront murder case they've been trying to solve for years. Muldoon demurs but Toody presses on. Muldoon agrees to come for dinner too. Toody calls Lucille. Maybe he suggests the menu to help Jasper feel at home - fish and chips? English muffins? Real tea?

Scene 4

Toody's house at dinner. Lucille gets up to clear dishes from table. Jasper gets up. Then Toody and Muldoon. She comes back in [as] Jasper springs to his feet, followed by others. Lucille excuses herself. Jasper compliments her on dinner. Lucille curtsies.

The boys ask Jasper's help on case. Murder and a quarter of a million dollar diamond robbery. Victim disembarked, cleared customs and went into a waterfront bar with insurance agent, Jonathan Stewart, who met him at boat. Boys' theory is that it's an international crime organization which knew victim as carrying the diamonds, but they can't find the link.

Jasper smiles tolerantly. "International crime syndicate? That's very romantic. It's all right for the cinema." Jasper presents his theory. The last thing in the world the victim carrying a quarter of a million in diamonds would do is go to a waterfront bar - unless, of course, he were taken there by someone he trusted. In this instance, obviously, the victim was led to his doom by his friend and insurance agent, Jonathan Stewart. It's the really clever criminal who cloaks himself with respectability and is above suspicion.

Who were his henchmen? Who fired the murder weapon? This is the painstaking detail I talked about earlier in the day. We must question each of the witnesses. Boys are impressed. How come Jasper is not further along in his career? Double talk about stories and labor parties. Schism is House of Commons about politics in career service. Scandal almost brought down the government.

Scene 5

53rd Precinct. Scotland Yard official and deputy commissioner come out of captain's office. Thanks Captain for his time. Captain mentions that one of his men, Jasper Asherton, has been spending time at the precinct. He's the biggest bungler in the department. They keep him off the streets in London - he does paper work. Brought him along because the men get a lot of chuckles hearing his theories on crime. Captain says he's met his match with Toody and Muldoon.

Scene 6

Waterfront bar. Our boys in derby hats. We see a calendar: JONATHAN STEWART, INSURANCE AGENT. They nudge each other. Bartender has his back to them. Toody clears throat and says, "We're from the police." Bartender whirls around. He's been caught red-handed watering the booze. He tries to cop a plea. The boys are not interested in petty crime. They're out for big game. Michael denies knowledge of murder or the big boss. He reluctantly agrees to cooperate and standby for instructions.

Scene 7

The next stop is the LILY WHITE LAUNDRY, M. Kramer, prop. Toody says, "I'm from the police." Mrs. K says to husband, "I knew it. You had to get involved with a bookmaker. For $10 a week he lets bookie use the phone. Now, we're ruined." Boys again agree to forget bookmaking for cooperation. Kramer, too, will stand by for instructions. (Maybe bookie comes out of phone booth, sees the law and starts to chew slips of horse bets.) We see another JONATHAN STEWART, INSURANCE calendar on wall.

Scene 8

Muldoon and Toody separate to individually line up witnesses. Montage, no dialogue. Quick cuts from one to the other. Greek florist, Chinese restaurant owner, Spinster teacher.

Scene 9

Meeting of masterminds. Muldoon calls Jonathan Stewart. Says he's calling for a friend who's not happy with the split from waterfront job. Will be at Stewart's home at 9 P.M. that night for more loot. They call witnesses and set rendezvous for 8:45 P.M. across the street from Stewart's house.

Scene 10

Nighttime. Witnesses arrive, one by one. Cloak and dagger stuff. They try to look casual, but they are a cluster of people, nervous and ill-at-ease on a deserted street. The plan is for one to ring doorbell of Stewart town house. Toody and Muldoon are on either side of door. One couple rings bell. Cop with drawn gun greets them at door. Whistle blows. Cops from all over surround our group and haul them away.

Scene 11

Police lineup with our abashed group being paraded in front of the spotlight.

Scene 12

53rd Precinct. Captain chewing them out. This case was solved years ago. They could lead Sherlock Holmes astray. He dismisses them. As they move away from the wall we see calendar - JONATHAN STEWART, INSURANCE.

Fan Letter, with plot proposal

Sept. 17, 1962

Dear Mr. Hiken,

I have an idea for a *Car 54* episode which I think would be very successful. You've heard about New York's 'Operation Decoy' in which city police dressed as women, roam around tough areas in the middle of the night to catch crooks?

Yes, Toody and Muldoon as decoys! I think this would be the wackiest show of the season. Please tell me what you think of this idea.

Thank you.

> Yours Truly,
> Marc Laffie, Age 11
> 3405 Kings Hwy.
> Brooklyn 34, N.Y.

P.S. My whole family enjoys *Car 54* very much.

Nat Hiken sent this personal reply:

Oct. 22, 1962

Master Marc Laffie
3405 Kings Highway
Brooklyn 34, N.Y.

Dear Marc:

Thank you very much for your nice letter of September 17, 1962. We have several ideas on "Operation Decoy," but I am not too sure that we are going to do them. Nevertheless, I want to thank you for your interest in our show.

> Cordially Yours.
> Eupolis Productions, Inc.
> Nat Hiken

Plot Suggestion Entitled
"UNACCUSTOMED AS I AM . . . " by Jack Marshall

The Captain tacks a notice on the bulletin board and in a moment is surrounded by his brood. A tight circle of men read the notice. Toody is in the rear row trying to read over, through or around the men shielding his view. The men finish reading, begin to comment in general tones and still Gunther has not read the notice. "Do you mind - do you mind?" he asks, and they allow him to gain entrance through the ranks. Toody reads aloud. The notice states that somebody will be needed to deliver a speech on traffic safety to a local P.T.A. group.

The men discuss the request for a speaker. The Captain's voice cuts the air and says, "Muldoon." Toody turns to Muldoon and comments, "Francis - looks like you're volunteering." Sure enough, Muldoon is tapped for the job.

That morning in the patrol car Toody and Muldoon discuss the problem. Gunther has faith in Francis and tells him so. Muldoon is not that keen about the assignment and suggests to Toody that he do it. Toody says that he would but since the Captain asked Francis - Muldoon tells Toody that he'll talk to the Captain and see if the assignment can be switched to Toody. Gunther is in fine spirits and, as a way of expressing himself, brings the car radio microphone to his mouth and pretends to deliver a speech on traffic safety. Muldoon is impassive but at Headquarters the Dispatcher and a large group of men listen attentively to Gunther's speech.

The Captain will not hear of Toody making a speech. "He has to prove he can speak English before he talks to a P.T.A. Group" - bellows the Captain. A light comes into Muldoon's eyes as the Captain speaks and he devises a plan. Teach Toody to deliver a speech - that's the project. Gunther is all for it.

Richard Spaulding, Speech Consultant, greets Muldoon and Toody. Francis explains the problem Gunther has and Spaulding suggests that a few lessons will be of help. To this minute, Toody has not spoken to this clipped speech consultant. Spaulding hands Toody a single-spaced typed piece of paper and asks him to read. Gunther glances at the paper for a moment - draws himself up to his full height and nervously begins - "How now brown cow" - The rhetoric confuses Toody but the voice shocks Spaulding. Toody continues the basic exercises and is oblivious of what is happening. When Gunther finally looks up and sees Francis administering first aid to Spaulding who is horizontal to the carpet - he has fainted. They revive him and Spaulding looks as if he had a bad dream. The boys leave.

Muldoon now takes charge. He has a plan. Gunther will study by himself - with Muldoon's assistance. A library is the first move and a book on speech therapy. Toody enters the local library himself. We know he is there because every face looks up from their books to see who is squeaking his way to the front desk. Gunther asks the librarian for the section on speech - The librarian wants to know if Toody is joking. Carrying an armful of books, Gunther squeaks to a table and sits down. His two half-concealed tablemates are buried in books. One of the gentlemen, seated next to Gunther, is reading Homer in the original Greek. Gunther looks at him and the book - then turns the book around. Toody just says, "Upside down."

Across the table from Gunther sits a man reading "The Neanderthal and His Relation to You." Gunther looks at the cover which pictures an ape-like creature. Gunther giggles. The man looks up and we see that it is Spaulding the speech consultant. Spaulding sees Toody and once again he is in a bad dream. Spaulding looks at Toody - then the book cover which Toody is staring at - then back to the book cover - wags his head in disbelief - slowly gets up and leaves, mopping his brow.

Gunther starts to pore through the books. He reads half-aloud which prompts the surrounding readers to shush him. Eventually, everyone near Toody moves to another table across the room. As Toody leaves and checks his book out, we see one side of the library crowded and Toody's vacated section - completely empty.

Now - wherever Toody goes - so goes the book. Muldoon is forced to put up with it chapter by chapter.

Gunther has taken to carrying a throat spray and lozenges. Before speaking on the car radio, he sprays his throat and pops a lozenge in his mouth. While talking into the mike he cups his hand to his ear in true announcer style and fashion. All his reports are now preceded with - "How now brown cow - Toody here in *Car 54* - " he giggles and makes his report.

Each day on patrol before he will speak to Muldoon he sings one octave on the scale. "The voice is a musical instrument" he tells Muldoon.

The book also helps Toody to enlarge his vocabulary. As a result Toody becomes slightly "Malapropian," because the vocabulary is there but the grammar ain't. "Sergeant Abrams, my esteemed good friend" - Gunther intones - "would you be kind enough to notice that the daily report bears both Francis Muldoon's and my signatures." Abrams quizzical look does not begin to penetrate Gunther's new-found sense of power.

A parking violator is Gunther's next victim. After listening to a speech on traffic safety, replete with notes, the violator, who at first wanted to dispute the ticket, now wants only to receive the ticket and get out of this idiot's range.

Once again we see Richard Spaulding, the speech consultant, on a couch on a psychiatrist's office. He is full of delusions of a Neanderthal who wants to make a speech. The nurse enters and the doctor excuses himself for a moment. We stay with Spaulding who goes into further shock when he hears Toody's voice again. Gunther and Francis are in the outer office on an investigation concerning a petty theft from the doctor's office. The doctor explains that it was a mistake, that they had the wrong doctor, then returns to his patient who is now quite incoherent.

Toody and Muldoon leave the building after their investigation and see a car double parked. Gunther, the arresting officer, starts to write a ticket. The owner of the car runs over to them to complain, sees Toody and faints on the spot. It is Richard Spaulding, Speech Consultant.

Toody is now making speeches with or without reason or rhyme. The men in the station house avoid him at all costs. The Captain is not aware of what is happening until a complaint reaches him. It is in the form of a petition. The men in the cell block have requested that Gunther not make speeches in front of them. Gunther, of course, has found captive audiences in the prisoners and is taking full advantage of it.

The Captain calls Gunther in and asks him to explain. When he hears what Gunther is doing, he tells him that Muldoon will make the speech. In an impassioned plea, quoting traffic safety rules by number and code and interspersed with Malapropian but impressive English, the Captain is at least a bit impressed. He relents and tells Gunther that he will consider the request and act upon it eventually.

Gunther is buoyed by this news and now works twice as hard. One day it is breath control. The next morning he will be practicing dramatic pauses. Next it is projection and his wife complains that the neighbors are complaining. The neighbors are a city block away. Gunther is really projecting.

Gunther, his wife and Muldoon are seen leaving a movie. They are discussing the show. Laurence Olivier was great, they agree, and the two of them turn to Gunther, who answers with his impression of a clipped Olivier accent.

Next morning at roll call Sergeant Abrams tells the men that the weather report predicts rain and they should take their raincoats. Gunther says,

"The rain in Spain falls mainly on the plain." The men grimace. Gunther is proud.

Toody continues to practice. He sneaks into the high school auditorium late at night, mounts the stage and moves to the lectern. He bows - holds up his hands to halt the imaginary applause and starts his speech. At its conclusion, he bows to a single pair of hands applauding his efforts. This awakens his being. Looking into the wings, he sees a man with a flashlight. It is the night watchman.

Muldoon, in the meantime, comes down with a bad case of laryngitis and the Captain—for lack of anything else to do—gives Gunther permission to make the speech.

Muldoon and Gunther sit down and plan the talk. It is decided that Gunther work from a series of cards. In this way it will be a planned speech. The 20 cards are filled out after one big argument lasting the entire evening. What does one say to begin a speech? That settled, they fill out the cards. Each card has a heading and a few items to talk about. They are pleased.

The P.T.A. Chairman welcomes the audience. He explains to one and all that on this particular evening they are to be favored by two guest speakers. The first speaker will be Patrolman Gunther Toody of the 53rd Precinct - Traffic Safety his subject. The second speaker will be the eminent speech consultant - Richard Spaulding. Gunther hears the name and drops his prompting cards. Spaulding has not as yet arrived and the Chairman decided to call upon Gunther who is now picking up his speech from the floor - all in the wrong order. No time to make repairs, he mounts the platform. Toody's speech has many valid points and these points hold the interest of the audience. What confuses the audience is Gunther's vacillations. Remembering to project, he blasts them out of their seats. When he loses diaphragmatic control, he breathes deeply as if gasping for air. The grammar confuses all because he is both redundant and Malapropian. He is making his point, however, when Spaulding enters the auditorium. Their eyes meet. Spaulding sits down. Gunther finishes his speech as Spaulding mops his brow and takes out smelling salts. As an afterthought, Gunther ad-libs an ending. In way of leaving the platform, he tells one and all that the next speaker will be most enjoyable. Gunther tells the audience that the applause he received should be given to Richard Spaulding because he is the one who really deserves it - after all, Gunther states - I studied under him at one time.

Unused Plot Outline,
"RALLY 'ROUND THE PRECINCT BOYS" by Hank Garrett

Juvenile Delinquency Problem - Police try to get neighborhood kids off the street and back into their clubhouse by getting them interested in different activities.

Kids are rounded up and brought into precinct locker room. Muldoon tries teaching them basketball, O'Hara - mechanics of outboard motors, Nicholson - wrestling or weightlifting, etc.

Toody begs to assist in different activities and is rejected by each instructor. Each, in turn, reminds him that he knows nothing about their particular specialty (or Toody attempts to assist each instructor and fouls up different pieces of equipment, he shamefully admits he knows nothing about said sports).

As kids are being instructed, they show complete lack of interest and reports of vandalism still continue. Citizens demand youngsters be apprehended.

Toody volunteers to go to clubhouse that evening to talk to kids. Captain agrees, following morning, boys show up at station house asking to borrow pieces if equipment.

Shortly, reports of vandalism end. All are puzzled as to how Patrolman Toody was able to accomplish this.

That evening, kids instructing Toody in basketball, boating and weightlifting.

Conclusion - Boys admire Toody because he is the only adult willing to admit that he is not an expert on all subjects.

Unused Plot Outline,
"GOOD NEIGHBOR POLICE, SEE?" by Ron Ronszel
(Submitted Jan. 4, 1961)

Open with television correspondent speaking from the capitol city of San Sausalito in a South American country experiencing the effects of a new revolutionary government. The correspondent feels that the new government hovers on the brink of becoming as dictatorial as the former regime. The present "President" is known for his pro-American leanings and his beliefs in a classic democracy, but some of the strong men in his cabinet do not share his views, namely one Generalissimo Malagato (a bad cat). Film clips show Malagato with some of his strong-arm police pushing the citizens around. The Generalissimo is the head of the new police system and believes in Storm Trooper tactics. The correspondent reports that the Presidente has requested permission for Malagato to come to the U.S. to study police methods and tactics of the New York Police Department, the permission has been granted and Malagato will soon arrive.

We see police officials discussing the impending arrival of Malagato.

In the Bronx Station House, Gunther and Muldoon discuss the benefit play that the Fraternal Order of Police is putting on to raise funds for the P.A.L. Gunther is delighted that he has been cast as a rough, tough, knock 'em about policeman. He grimaces and glares furiously as he interjects lines from the show into his usually mild conversation. Francis comments that he is certainly glad that the play illustrates the fact that there is no place for this type of cop on the modern police force.

Malagato has arrived and is being conducted, along with his sidekicks, on a tour of police headquarters. He makes it clear that he wants to meet a typical police officer with whom he will send his aide to film the police activities on patrol.

Visiting the Bronx Station House, Malagato overhears snatches of Gunther's theatrical conversations and comes face to face with him as he rehearses in the locker room. He has another cop by the lapels and is giving him the lines from the show. This other cop is in civilian clothes and is playing the part of a sneak thief in the benefit. The result of this encounter is that Malagato believes that he has found the policeman who will aid his cause. If he sends films of this ruthless enforcer back to El Presidente, he will then be able to train his police in a similar manner.

Satisfied that his mission concerning the police survey is now accomplished to his own devious satisfaction, Malagato begins a selfish whirlwind tour of New York night spots.

Montage of intercuts showing aide taking movies, Gunther rehearsing his tough cop role on Francis in the squad car and Malagato doing the town. In scenes of Malagato's aide taking movies, subject matter is not shown.

Malagato instructs his aide to send a coded wire to El Presidente that films would soon be on their way and that they should be shown to the police and then they would be trained accordingly.

Insert of film cans being mailed to San Saucilito, mail plane, etc.

Insert films of Malagato enjoying himself, secure in the knowledge that the movies of the cruel American policeman will turn his own men into a group of merciless enforcers.

Malagato bids goodbye to police officials at Idlewild, boards the plane and collapses into a seat with an accrued hangover.

Malagato arrives at San Sausalito and in a series of incidents which the Generalissimo witnesses, he knows something has gone wrong with his plan. The police are polite, helpful and downright solicitous with both foreign and indigenous persons alike. He storms into his headquarters and demands to know what is wrong. He is informed that his instructions were carried out to the letter. He demands to see the films. As they are shown, an illustrative scene for each of the incidents he has witnessed is performed by Gunther: Wiping small boy's nose, applying band aid to skinned knee, apprehending a thief restoring property, loaning the thief $10 and then helping him find a room and a job, etc. At each humanitarian demonstration by the American policeman, Malagato drops lower in his arm chair. Fade out.

Show final scene of benefit play where tough cop is fired from the force and tumultuous applause received by Gunther.

Dissolve to Gunther and Francis watching newscast on television. Same correspondent as in opening scene is marveling at new police tactics and admits he was wrong about Malagato who has apparently instituted these new practices. Film clip of ceremony where a bewildered but newly appreciative Malagato is receiving congratulations from El Presidente and an affectionate demonstration from the happy citizens. Newscast is over.

Gunther switches off set and comments, "That Malagato is really a pretty good cat!"

SELECT BIBLIOGRAPHY

Books

Brooks, Tim and Earle Marsh. *The Complete Directory to Prime Time Network and Cable TV Shows: 1946 - Present*. Ballantine Books, New York, 1995

Cox, Jim. *Radio Speakers*. McFarland & Company, Inc., Publishers, 2007

Dunning, John. *On the Air: The Encyclopedia of Old-Time Radio*. Oxford University Press, 1998

Payton, Gordon, and Martin Grams, Jr. *The CBS Radio Mystery Theater: An Episode Guide and Handbook*. McFarland & Company, Inc., Publishers, 1999.

O'Neil, Thomas. *The Emmys: Star Wars, Showdowns, and the Supreme Test of TV's Best*. Penguin Books, 1992.

Unpublished Materials

- Hundreds of pieces of correspondences involving representatives of NBC, Eupolis Productions and Nat Hiken.

- Press releases and biographical materials from television networks ABC, NBC and CBS.

- Questionnaires to and from the actors and Eupolis Productions.

- Shooting scripts (both early drafts and final drafts)

housed at the special archives department of the library of the University of Wisconsin, located in Madison.

• Telephone calls and e-mails with actors Arthur Anderson, Larry Storch, Derek Tague, Jim Rosen, and publisher Ben Ohmart.

Periodicals

Alabama Journal, The (Montgomery, Ala.), September 14, 1961, article by Jim Doyle

Alabama Journal, The (Montgomery, Ala.), September 18, 1961, "New TV Season Starts"

Allegro, November 1962, "Another Series Signs in A.F.M. Drive"

American, The, September 25, 1961, "BesTView in Town"

Argus-Courier, The (Petaluma, California), September 23, 1961, "Take to the Sky to Cover Ground"

Atlanta Constitution, The, September 25, 1961, "Author Honored by DuPont"

Bergen Record, February 7, 1963, "Dinner Date"

Berkshire Eagle, The (Pittsfield, Mass.), September 19, 1961, "The Lovely Arts"

Boston Record, The, September 19, 1961, "On TV, Radio"

Boston Record, The, September 27, 1961, review

Boston Traveler, The September 18, 1961, "Let's Have More of *Car 54*"

Bristol Herald Courier/Virginia-Tennessean, July 3, 1993, Fred Gwynne obit

Chicago American, The, September 20, 1961, "New *Car 54* Called Boring Nonsense"

Christian Science Monitor, The (Boston, Mass.), September 19, 1961, review

Christian Science Monitor, The, January 12, 1966

Cincinnati Post-Times Star, The, September 16, 1961, "TV Scout"

Cincinnati Post-Times Star, The, September 18, 1961, "Season's New TV Programs Begin Parade"

Citizen News, The (Hollywood, California), September 20, 1961, "Radio-Television"

Columbus Dispatch, The, September 18, 1961, "The View From Here"

Courier, The (Candor, N.Y.), September 21, 1961, "Yes, Car 54, Where Are You?"

Courier Express, The (Buffalo, N.Y.), September 2, 1961, "Radio and Television"

Cue Magazine, October 29, 1955, "Boffolas in the Barracks"

Daily News, Saturday, February 18, 1961, "Dream Street"

Daily News, Thursday, September 7, 1961, "Fasten Your Laugh Belts"

Denver, Colorado Post, September 17, 1961, promotional photo

Des Moines Register, The, September 18, 1961, "On Television"

Detroit News, The, September 18, 1961, "TV Gossip"

Enquirer and News (Battle Creek, Michigan), September 17, 1961, "Today's TV Key"

Enterprise, The (Berwick, P.A.), September 26, 1961, "TV in Review"

Globe-Democrat, The (St. Louis, Missouri), September 19, 1961, review

Hartford Times, The, September 19, 1961, "A Look at Television"

Herald, The (Austin, Minn.), September 15, 1961, "Much of the Same Stuff"

Herald, The (Bradenton, Florida), September 25, 1961, "The Voice of Broadway"

Herald, The (Rutland, VT), September 21, 1961, "Dial Marie for TV . . . Torre,
        That Is"

Hollywood Daily Variety, The, September 19, 1961, review

Hollywood Reporter, The, Thursday, October 17 and 19, 1961, "On the Air"

Houston Post, The, August 26, 1962, "No Ghosts at the 53rd Precinct"

Kansas City Star, The, September 24, 1961, "New Season Gets Off to Rousing Start"

Knickerbocker News, The, September 18, 1961, "Where's 54? Where Laughs Begin"

Life Magazine, September 29, 1961, "Couple of Loony Cops"

Long Island Press, The (Jamaica, New York), October 9, 1962, "Marshal Dillon
        Collars Gunther Toody"

Los Angeles Examiner, The, Tuesday, September 19, 1961, "Same Games With
        New Players on the TV Plate"

Michigan Times-News, The (Mt. Pleasant, Mich.), September 15, 1961, "Television
        Highlights"

Milwaukee Journal, The, September 18, 1961, review

Milwaukee Journal, The, November 12, 1962, "The Best Show in the Bronx"

Milwaukee Journal, The, December 19, 1962, "She'll Be a Decoy on TV"

Newark (NJ) Evening News, August 8, 1961, "Nat Hiken Puts Together Series for Fall"

Newark (NJ) Evening News, August 12, 1962, "Stars of Car 54"

Newark (NJ) Evening News, August 19, 1962, "Hiken Steers *Car 54*"

Newsday, July 21, 1961, "New TV Series Has Cops, No Robbers"

Newsday, July 20, 1987, "Old *Car 54* Answers the Call for Comedy"

News-Sentinel (Fort Wayne, Ind.), September 18, 1961, "TV Scout Reports"

New York Mirror, June 15, 1956, "Only Human"

New York Daily News, The, September 19, 1961, "Dream Street" (two briefs)

New York Daily News, The, September 19, 1961, "What's On?" (two briefs)

New York Herald Tribune, The, July 20, 1960, "The Thrill is Gone" by Nat Hiken

New York Herald Tribune, The, September 18, 1961, "Television in Review"

New York Herald Tribune, The, September 24, 1961, "An Hour With Yesterday's Yaks"

New York Herald Tribune, The, September 29, 1961, "TV-Radio Today"

New York Journal-American, The, February 23, 1961, "Voice of Broadway"

New York Journal-American, The, September 18, 1961, "Around This Town o' Ours"

New York Journal-American, The, September 25, 1961, "Jack O'Brian Says"

New York Mirror, Wednesday, June 21, 1961, "I See By TV" by John Griffin

New York Mirror, Wednesday, August 30, 1961, "I See By TV" by John Griffin

New York Mirror, Wednesday, September 13, 1961, "I See By TV" by John Griffin

New York Mirror, Wednesday, October 1, 1961, "I See By TV"

New York Observer, The, March 7, 2005, brief and illustration

New York Post, The, March 12, 1962, "Car 54, Where Are You?"

New York Times, The, March 26, 1961, "News of TV and Radio"

New York Times, The, September 18, 1961

New York Times, The, February 11, 1962, "Two Cops, Daffy but Far From Keystone"

New York Times, The, August 25, 1963

New York Times, The, April 14, 1996, article about Nat Hiken

Observer-Dispatch, The (Utica, N.Y.), September 23, 1961, "Police Rap TV's *Car 54*"

Pageant, October 1962, Article by Harold Mehling

Parade Magazine, August 14, 1994

Philadelphia Inquirer, The, September 19, 1961, review

Pittsburgh Press, The, Sunday, August 19, 1962

Playbill, October 22, 1960

Playbill, May 12, 1966

Radio-Television Daily, Monday, January 29, 1962, "It's Three in a Row"

Radio-Television Daily, Friday, June 11, 1962, "Car 54's Toody, Muldoon Booked
      for Freedomland"

Radio-Television Daily, Tuesday, August 4, 1964, "NBC Film Sales Increase 15%"

Robesonian, The (Lumberton, N.C.), September 15, 1961

Pioneer Press, The (St. Paul, Minn.), September 17, 1961, "Will the Police Farce Capture Viewers?"

Plain Dealer (Cleveland, Ohio), September 10, 1961, "Channel Checker"

Post-Gazette and Sun Telegraph, The, September 24, 1961, "Many Old Favorites . . ."

Post-Tribune, The (Gary, Ind.), September 15, 1961, "Television Back Talk"

Press and News (Cleveland, Ohio), September 15, 1961, "TV Moguls See No Future"

Press-Telegram, The (Long Beach, California), September 23, 1961, "Looking and Listening"

Progress Bulletin, The (Pomons, California), November 26, 1961, "And So Do Viewers"

Providence Bulletin, The (Providence, R.I.), September 25, 1961, "Crossing the Channels"

Roanoke Times, The (Roanoke, Virginia), September 23, 1961, "*Car 54* Farce Stars Over-Dedicated Officers"

San Francisco Examiner, The, September 19, 1961, brief

Show, October 1961

Show, January 1965

Show Business, Saturday, June 10, 1961, "Police Station With No Crime"

Show Business, Saturday, July 22, 1961, "*Car 54* Shooting at Biograph Studios"

Sponsor, January 13, 1964, "NBC Films Selling *Car 54*"

States and Item (New Orleans, L.A.), September 19, 1961, "Amusements, TV, Radio"

Sunday News, September 10, 1961, "Hollywood on the Hudson"

Sunday News, November 26, 1961, "Help! Murder! Police!"

Sunday News, March 4, 1962, "What My Partner is Really Like"

Sunday Star-Ledger, The, January 28, 1962, "Paul Reed Hits the Jackpot"

Sun Times (Chicago, Ill.), September 20, 1961, "It's the Molloy"

Sun Times (Chicago, Ill.), September 29, 1961, "A Reader Says *Car 54* Got Started"

Tablet, The (Brooklyn, New York), September 16, 1961, "Spotlight on the Dials"

Television Quarterly, 1990 (Volume XXIV, Number III), "Kingmaker of Comedy"

Times and News Leader, The (San Mateo, C.A.), September 19, 1961, "TV Screenings"

Times Dispatch, The (Richmond, Virginia), August 26, 1962, "One-Shot Role Lead to Permanent One"

Times Herald, The (Dallas, Texas), September 19, 1961, "Critically Speaking"

Tribute Democrat, The (Johnstown, P.A.), August 11, 1962, "Stars' Outlooks Vary Good Deal" by Fred Gwynne

TV Guide, March 23, 1958, "Where Are the Laughs Coming From?"

TV Guide, October 21, 1961, "An Offbeat Pair on the Beat"

TV Guide, December 23, 1961, review by Gilbert Seldes

TV Guide, March 9, 1963, "A Volcano Called Schnauzer"

TV Guide, March 19, 1963, "The Bluecoat Blues"

Variety, Wednesday, March 1, 1961, "Hottest Slot in 3-Web Strategy"

Variety, Wednesday, June 28, 1961, "Two Views of the Badge"

Variety, Wednesday, September 13, 1961, "Nothing Exciting Happens Anymore"

Variety, Wednesday, September 20, 1961, review

Variety, Wednesday, December 27, 1961, "The New Nielsens: CBS in the Lead"

Variety, Wednesday, September 19, 1962, review

Variety, Wednesday, August 14, 1963, "Midsummer Night's Screen"

Variety, September 27, 1963, "Desilu Dickers His 'Car' As Well As Hiken's Services"

Video Review, June 1990, page 64, VHS review

Washington Post, The, Friday, February 2, 1962, "Cheese It!"

Washington Star, The, September 19, 1961, "On the Air"

Westside Resident, June 11, 1998, "Grandpa for Governor"

INDEX

About the Author

Martin Grams Jr. has authored or co-authored over a dozen books about radio and television. He wrote a number of magazine articles for *Filmfax, Scarlet Street*, and SPERDVAC's *Radiogram*. He contributed chapters, short stories and appendixes for various books including Ken Mogg's *The Alfred Hitchcock Story* (1999), Bear Manor Media's *It's That Time Again* (all three volumes, 2002-2005), Midnight Marquee's *Vincent Price* (1998), Arthur Anderson's *Let's Pretend* (2004) and Ben Ohmart's Alan Reed biography (2009).

Martin is the recipient of the 1999 Ray Stanich Award, the 2005 Parley E. Baer Award and the 2005 Stone/Waterman Award. His name appears in the acknowledgements of more than 100 books about radio and television. His 2008 book *The Twilight Zone: Unlocking the Door to a Television Classic* won the Rondo Award for "best book of the year." He is presently finishing a book about *Playhouse 90* and a book about *The Green Hornet*, authorized by The Green Hornet, Inc.

Martin is presently a member of the convention staff for the Mid-Atlantic Nostalgia Convention, held annually in Maryland. He presently lives in Delta, Pennsylvania with his wife and three cats.

Other books by Martin Grams Jr.

The History of the Cavalcade of America (1999, Morris Publishing)

The CBS Radio Mystery Theater: An Episode Guide and Handbook (1999, McFarland Publishing)

The Have Gun - Will Travel Companion (2000, OTR Publishing, LLC)

The Alfred Hitchcock Presents Companion (2001, OTR Publishing, LLC)

The Sound of Detection: Ellery Queen's Adventures in Radio (2002, OTR Publishing, LLC)

Information, Please (2003, Bear Manor Media, LLC)

Gang Busters: The Crime Fighters of American Broadcasting (2004, OTR Publishing, LLC)

The Railroad Hour (2006, Bear Manor Media, LLC)

The Radio Adventures of Sam Spade (2007, OTR Publishing, LLC)

I Led Three Lives: The True Story of Herbert A. Philbrick's Television Program (2007, Bear Manor Media, LLC)

The Twilight Zone: Unlocking the Door to a Television Classic (2008, OTR Publishing, LLC)

The TWILIGHT ZONE

Unlocking the Door to A Television Classic

By **Martin Grams, Jr.**

Foreword by
George Clayton Johnson

Winner of the 2008 Rondo Award
for "Best Book of the Year"
Available from Bear Manor Media
(www.bearmanormedia.com)

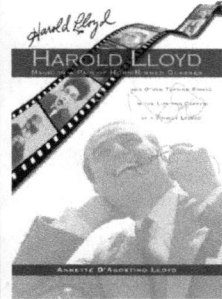
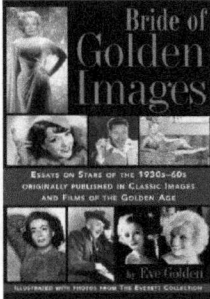